Falling for Therapy

Falling for Therapy

Psychotherapy from a client's point of view

Anna Sands

First published 2000 by
MACMILLAN PRESS LTD
Houndmills, Basingstoke, Hampshire RG21 6XS
and London
Companies and representatives
throughout the world

ISBN 0–333–80430–9

A catalogue record for this book is available
from the British Library.

This book is printed on paper suitable for recycling and
made from fully managed and sustained forest sources.

10   9   8   7   6   5   4   3   2   1
09   08   07   06   05   04   03   02   01   00

Printed in Malaysia

Contents

Acknowledgements

Thanks to all those whose thoughts and comments have helped to provide material for the book. In those cases where I have not sought permission to reproduce what people have said, I hope that those concerned can 'preserve their own freedom not to have themselves identified by anyone else' (Casement, 1985: 226) unless they wish otherwise.

Particular thanks to Frances Arnold at Macmillan, and Colin Feltham, for their encouragement, advice and help; Michael Harris and Vin McNevin, for reading the manuscript and for their support and understanding; Roger Wells, for reading the manuscript and for his comments and criticisms; Windy Dryden, Guy Claxton and James Baxter, for their advice and encouragement.

To Kate, in many ways the co-author of this book, for her warmth, integrity and professionalism; to Maura and Elizabeth, for opening a different door.

To all my family and friends, for their sanity, and for constantly renewing my faith in human nature, especially: Avril, Debbie, Sally and Sue, for reading the manuscript in its infancy and helping me to believe it had value; Vicky, for the thoughts we have shared about being a client in therapy, for reading the manuscript and for her invaluable insights and observations; Mike S. and Chris G., for their kindness; Jean, for all her help; Carole, for her wisdom and care. To my children and step-children, the best teachers of all. To my husband, for sharing it all.

The author and publishers are grateful to the following for permission to reproduce copyright material: The Orion Publishing Group Ltd and David Godwin Associates for Ben Okri, *A Way of Being Free* and the poem *For Ken Saro-wiwa*; Penguin, UK for Laurie Lee, *I Can't Stay Long*; and Hodder & Stoughton for Thomas Moore, *The Re-Enchantment of Everyday Life*.

Introduction

'All psychotherapists are expected to approach their work with the aim of alleviating suffering and promoting the well-being of their clients.'

(Ethical Guidelines of the United Kingdom Council for Psychotherapy, 1995)

If the aim of psychotherapy is to alleviate suffering, then the measure of its validity must be the extent to which it does or does not achieve that goal. But who decides whether suffering has been alleviated, whether the well-being of the client has been promoted, and on what basis are such judgements made? The majority of the literature on therapy is written by therapists so, generally speaking, it is therapists who have the loudest voice when it comes to evaluating the effectiveness of their work. They both offer a service and assess its results. However, the consequences of psychotherapy are also evaluated by those who make use of it – the clients.

Clients can never be entirely objective about their own therapy, but that does not mean that their point of view has no general value. Without it, any scrutiny of therapy will not be a truly balanced one. Therapists too cannot be entirely objective. They are not impartial observers: they are participants in a process which is intense and highly personal, and they have a stake in convincing us that what happens in therapy is good for us.

Although counselling and psychotherapy are often productive and helpful, they can also be counter-productive and detrimental. This book considers, from a client's perspective, the ways in which therapy – in particular, psychoanalytic therapy – might be damaging. It is an attempt to challenge the power of theory and to ask questions about what actually happens in practice.

When I began psychotherapy, I knew little about it, and my first experience ended in a way which left me feeling hurt, shocked and confused. In trying to deal with those feelings, I started to read about therapy; I also worked, over a period of five years, with a second therapist, whose approach was different from that of the first. I talked to friends, to other practitioners and clients, and later to clients who had had negative experiences. I also began to write about how I felt, and that writing became this book.

Because I am a client and not a therapist, the book is not based on a professional knowledge of theory. It is about how it feels to be on the receiving end of therapy. I have not studied the works of Freud or Jung or Klein. What has interested me most in my reading has been what practitioners say about their work and their assumptions, because it is what happens in practice which touches the client. As Ann France points out in *Consuming Therapy*, 'only by saying how the application of theory works in practice can questions about its justification have any relevance' (France, 1988).

It seems to me that 'success' in therapy must be measured in terms of a greater aggregate human well-being, and not in terms of whether theoretical assumptions can be shown to be correct. I think it is important that clients ask questions about therapy and that practitioners encourage them to do so. My reflections about its procedures and practice have been part of an attempt to make sense of two very different experiences of therapy and are, unavoidably, personal. My responses, nevertheless, are unlikely to be unique.

When I first put my thoughts about therapy into writing, there were no personal examples, and I included them reluctantly on the advice of a reader. (The examples given refer only to 'my analyst' where this is stated.) The account that follows hovered and evolved over a period of six years. The decision to develop it into a book for publication took a long time to make and was not an easy one.

The book grew in a somewhat random and sporadic fashion – one of my readers remarked that it reminded him of a spirograph. As a result, the chapter themes are not strictly delineated. I have endeavoured to look at the central theme from a succession of different perspectives which overlap and recur but which, I hope, serve to expand and reinforce each other.

The text was not written with any particular audience in view. If it helps to inform clients and enables them to avoid some of therapy's pitfalls, then it will have served some purpose. For practitioners, much of what I have said will not be new, but I hope it might contain some worthwhile consumer feedback. The debate about therapy is ongoing, and is one which must involve sharing experiences and finding joint solutions for the difficulties it poses.

I am aware that I can only describe what happened to me from my particular point of view, and I hope I have not misrepresented the views and feelings of others. It is not my intention to dismiss the value of therapy which is genuinely therapeutic, but rather to draw attention to what might be counter-productive when one is sitting in the client's chair.

Note

I have used the terms 'therapist', 'practitioner', 'therapy' and 'psychotherapy' to refer to psychotherapy in general. I refer to the first practitioner with whom I worked – who used an analytic approach – as 'my analyst', and the second, Kate – who uses a psycho-spiritual approach – as 'my therapist'.

I have, in most cases, used the pronoun 'he' for the counsellor/analyst/therapist and 'she' for the client/patient/analysand. I have done this primarily for clarity but the choice is not entirely arbitrary. The type of practice which I question seems to me to embody a masculine more than a feminine way of thinking about and dealing with problems. I have argued that, in any type of counselling/psychoanalysis/psychotherapy, just as there needs to be a balance between the standpoint of the practitioner and the needs of each individual client, there also needs to be a balance between what are often seen as the feminine qualities of warmth, feeling, intuition and nourishment and what are often seen as the masculine qualities of form, abstraction, theory and science.

Chapter 1

What's the problem?

My first experience of therapy was about crossed lines. It was about the interplay of conscious and unconscious, and the intricacy of our perceptions of ourselves and others. It was about pride and power, fear and trust, intimacy and love. But most of all, it was about crossed lines.

What takes place in therapy depends on the perceptions of two people and on our perception of another's perception of us. For both client and practitioner, it is about an inclination to latch on to what we believe to be the subtext. I might perceive a hidden agenda which exists only in my mind, and react defensively or inappropriately as a result. I might see an agenda which is actually there but not acknowledged. I might fail to see the therapist's true intention, and respond instead to what seems to me more overtly obvious. I will find it difficult to see when the therapist is projecting his feelings on to me, and I will probably be unable to recognise my own projections. I see agendas where none exist and fail to see those that do exist. I do not always hear clearly.

Are problems more likely to arise in therapy when a propensity on both sides to perceive a hidden agenda is a driving force of the work? Can certain types of therapy increase the frequency of crossed lines? For example, I was talking with a friend a while ago – a nurse who works with the terminally ill. She was telling me about the death of a patient which she had found particularly upsetting. Years ago, I would probably have said something like 'How awful!' But, swayed by my first experience of psychotherapy, I sat and listened, then found myself wondering what was 'underneath' what she was saying. I knew that her parents had both died recently; perhaps she had not yet come to terms with this. Perhaps she 'had a problem'? In fact, she is a skilled and committed

1

carer, the expression of her grief a part of that commitment. Briefly, I had completely missed the point.

What if this conversation had taken place in the course of a session of psychotherapy? The therapist might have encouraged my friend to 'analyse' her response. In doing so, could he have prompted her to question her natural, instinctive sensibility and compassion? The 'analyst' will look under, round, between and behind things in the search for answers to the question 'What does this mean?' But perhaps there is a danger that, in doing so, he may fail to see what is most relevant, or distort and disfigure what he is looking at. Is there a sense in which 'analysis' can pathologise our humanness?

What happens when people are trained to work with others' emotions, when dealing with feelings becomes a profession? And what happens when we engage in a relationship aimed uniquely at helping us to manage our feelings better? In their eagerness to facilitate worthwhile change in areas which are genuinely problematic, do counsellors/analysts/therapists sometimes, unwittingly, risk denying the value and validity of a whole range of emotion and experience? And do they, at times, help to create new problems – problems which stem primarily from the nature of some psychotherapeutic practice?

When misunderstandings arise between therapist and client, they are highly personal, yet they can only be resolved in the context of a professional relationship. Are the two compatible, and are there aspects of therapy which can make its proponents less rather than more sensitive to their clients' needs? What are the contradictions involved in the way psychotherapy is perceived by those who turn to it for help and those for whom it is a career?

Psychotherapy probably throws up as many questions as it answers. My first experience of it ended in a breakdown, causing me to look further not only at my personal struggles, but also at the nature and contradictions of therapy, and at how the two might interact. Was the destructiveness of the encounter due more to the approach and the practitioner, or more to my perception of them? If it was primarily the latter, then why didn't the therapy succeed in identifying the difference between the two? What part do the system and the environment of therapy play, and what part is played by the individual psyches of those who create that environment?

It has been said that psychotherapy does not exist. 'What does exist is people interacting with each other' (Szasz, 1979). What also exists is a way of thinking. It is part of what we buy when we go to therapy. It is a way of thinking to which the client will become particularly susceptible. From the practitioner's point of view, the characteristics of the interaction will, in great measure, be defined by his professional training. The client has no such framework. For her, things are very different.

To professionalise intimacy and trust and make them the basis of a financial transaction where one offers a 'service' and the other is a 'consumer' has an uncomfortable edge to it. And the juxtaposition of the formal nature of the relationship and the private nature of its content lends it an odd kind of polarity. The relationship between a therapist and a client can create a sense of strangeness simply because it *is*, in many ways, a strange one, carrying with it its own idiosyncrasies. It is important that what these idiosyncrasies may give rise to is correctly attributed, and not confused with what the client brings to the therapy room from her life outside it.

For many clients, when we meet our therapist for the first time, we want to appear coherent, pleasant, capable, to represent things accurately, to be brave and honest and good. Yet we are there to talk about our less pleasant traits, the times we do not cope, the emotions that are too painful, the things we cannot face. The difficulty of reconciling these two parallel wishes can set up a peculiarly tense and complex double bind.

Most of us stumble into therapy knowing little about it. Most of us assume it will be beneficial. I did. I did not ask my prospective practitioner whether his particular approach might suit me. Generally speaking, it does not occur to clients to do so; and, if we knew exactly what to ask and what answers we needed, we probably wouldn't be there in any case. Even if the prospective client were to pose such questions, would the practitioner be able to give an objective answer?

When I was given the name of the first practitioner I worked with, I did not give much thought to the difference between psychoanalysis, psychotherapy and counselling. I did make a tentative stab at asking 'my analyst' how he worked, but the answer – inevitably, perhaps – was perfunctory. He said that it was for me to talk about whatever came into my head and that, later, we might talk about our relationship. At the time, that puzzled me. I did not see why it would be necessary to talk about 'our relationship'. I had not gone there to talk about my relationship with him. But, although I was surprised by what he said, I did not ask him what he meant. I had no idea what I was letting myself in for.

In therapy, only one thing is certain: the diversity of the approaches on offer, the complexity of the theories behind them, and the differences in awareness and personality amongst practitioners and clients mean that the outcome of therapy will vary. Which type of therapy and – most important – which therapist we 'buy' may profoundly influence that outcome.

Whatever the approach, doing psychotherapy is unnerving. And, whatever the reason for the client's going to therapy, it is a process that many view with considerable trepidation. Therapists claim to understand this, they are aware that a new client will feel particularly vulnerable. And part of a therapist's training is to undergo analysis himself, so it is an experience which is familiar to him. But someone who has spent time in analysis during his training may not have experienced it in quite the same way as a layperson. The fact that he has been accepted for training as a therapist is, in itself, a tacit endorsement of his mental health.

In contrast, the view that 'those who feel they need psychotherapy tend to be ... the weak, the insecure, the nervous, the lonely, the inadequate, and the depressed, whose desperation is often such that they are willing to do and pay anything for some improvement of their condition' (Foster, 1971) is, even today, not uncommon. This image may have an influence on both the confidence of the client at the outset of therapy and the practitioner's perception of and attitude towards her.

For the counsellor or therapist who has only experienced being an analysand as part of his training, seeking therapy is less likely to be the result of a painful personal crisis or an apprehensive cry for help. It is part of a process of equipping him to do a particular job. Later, it may still be an ongoing adjunct to his professional career, a career with a certain status. When the practitioner is an analysand, he and his analyst are fellow professionals, members of the same group. The context of therapy is therefore different from that of an ordinary client, and one which might, in itself, provide a subtle boost to the therapist's self-esteem.

For many lay clients, on the other hand, to go to a therapist means there is 'something wrong with you'. Going to therapy might seem like a strange thing to do. So the starting line feels very different. Acknowledging that we need help can be beneficial, but acknowledging that we are in a mess, and feeling that we can no longer sort things out for ourselves, can also be frightening. The anxiety and sense of inadequacy that this can create may become a potent part of what follows, both compounding and camouflaging the more specific difficulties which the client arrives with.

I was fearful when I began therapy – afraid of the unknown, afraid of what my analyst would think, afraid of what I might find out about myself. It feels a bit like applying for the job of being oneself, but we're not too sure what the qualifications are. And what will happen if we mess up the interview?

Theories about the unconscious suggest that we are frightened of the 'darker' side of ourselves, but it is worth considering also Nelson Mandela's exultant words:

> Our deepest fear is that we are powerful beyond measure. It is our light, not our darkness, that most frightens us ... There's nothing enlightened about shrinking so that other people won't feel insecure around you.

Will we be able to be truly ourselves? Will we be up to the task? Is this life task – really being who we are – made easier or more difficult when we are analysed? Can psychotherapy sometimes diminish us as a whole person, rather than simply shrink our neuroses?

The practitioner I went to used an approach which, I discovered much later, is termed psychodynamic psychotherapy. I also learnt later that this type of therapy focuses on unconscious conflicts which are said to arise in early childhood and views them as largely accounting for current problematic behaviour. But 'current behaviour' in the therapy room is also affected by the particular nature of that relationship and environment. If therapy is to be of benefit, these factors need to be acknowledged, understood and addressed. Their influence, in all its various hues, and the potential for damage should always be borne in mind. The 'therapeutic' relationship can harm and hurt as well as help and heal.

When I decided to try therapy – in the hope of seeing myself more clearly, and becoming a better wife and mother – it was an entirely new experience. The interaction between me and my analyst turned out to be unlike any other I had known. The uniqueness of this particular relationship can come as something of a shock. I sailed in on a high tide, clever and naive, eager and terrified. Despite my nervousness, the optimist in me said: 'Just get on with it. It'll all be fine.' But in my case it wasn't all fine, and the knock which it gave to my sense of well-being was one which has been hard to bear.

The context of therapy involves particular rules and boundaries, but these are not necessarily apparent or obvious to the client. Therapists vary greatly in terms of what is, for them, appropriate and inappropriate behaviour. They differ in the way in which they begin and end sessions. Some stick strictly to fifty minutes, others do not. Some show their feelings, others avoid doing so. One may welcome physical contact, another may rule it out. Some make reference occasionally to their own lives, others never do. Some answer questions, others circumvent them. The client has to learn the rules of her particular therapist. I learnt them through a process of trial and error and, in that process, felt foolish and inept.

The psychotherapeutic relationship offers both constraints and freedoms. Depending on its nature, it can deform and repress the spontaneity that characterises more naturally contextualised relationships outside. We may then find ourselves squeezing into a pattern of interaction which feels bizarre and unreal.

Is it possible to behave naturally – whatever that may mean – if the therapist's focus is primarily on the potential for there being an unconscious agenda behind what one says and does? Published extracts of conversations between therapists and their clients illustrate how contrived and unnatural they can sometimes be (see Appendix). My personal experience with an analytic practitioner bears this out.

Therapists listen carefully to everything the client says. But do they hear what their clients tell them? For any practitioner, hearing accurately what clients say must be difficult to achieve consistently. Accepting how that person feels is another matter. What happens if a therapist does not accept what the client says, or if he tries to convert it into something else, adding his own connotations to what might be for the client uncomplicated, inconsequential, or without the same significance?

When the client is conveying a piece of information, is there necessarily value in attempting to interpret it? Sometimes we say things simply because we are describing something that has just happened, or is just about to happen. We share it because it is foremost in our minds, and it is foremost in our minds because, at that moment, it is the most immediate event in our lives. For example, in *On Learning from the Patient*, Patrick Casement (1985:114) cites the example of Mrs B who, on arriving at a session late, explains that her car wouldn't start. The client, who is not a native speaker of English, uses the phrase 'There was no light in the battery'. Casement wonders if she is also alluding to his behaviour, to his not being 'more enlightened'.

He may be right, but an equally valid interpretation – and one which I, as a language teacher, would make – might be to refer to the speaker's original language to see if the expression was a literal translation of its mother-tongue equivalent. If she were using it to imply that her therapist was not working well, it would have been a remarkably sophisticated manipulation of language by a non-native speaker since, in English, the word 'light' is not normally linked with electric current in the same way as it is in some other languages.

Are psychotherapists sometimes tempted to try to be too clever? If a practitioner works on the basis that what we say frequently has a hidden meaning, a meaning which is more apparent to the listener than to the speaker, then how does this make the client feel? Of course, there are times when we don't say what we mean or don't mean quite what we say, and there is often more to what we say than meets the eye. But isn't it important to accept what someone says at face value first, before then seeing whether there is anything to be explored further?

A client will respond differently to someone who hears than to someone who only listens and interprets. The convolutions of the interpretations we may be offered in a psychoanalytic context can negate a sense of our own validity and tie us up in knots rather than straighten us out. If the person we are with seems to relate to us only in order to comment on, rather than to acknowledge, what we have said, how does this affect the relationship? To what extent can one feel normal – whatever normal may mean – in such an encounter? To what extent might it provoke anxiety and unease?

The context of therapy has to be one which is fruitful, one which both urges and enables us to learn. We have to relearn how to be and, in the process, acquire a new language to encompass and describe our experience. The therapy room is the training ground. But anxiety can disrupt our ability to learn, to function fully, to think through problems clearly and give ourselves time to experience what we are feeling accurately. It can encourage us to engage in a superficial and transitory way. In language learning, for example, research has shown that total involvement and lack of anxiety are fundamental to successful, fully internalised learning over the long term.

A certain amount of 'facilitative' anxiety is probably essential to motivation in any context where we wish to make progress, but its role needs careful monitoring. The practitioner who doubts his client's motivation perhaps overlooks the courage it has taken her to pick up the phone, make her first appointment and keep it. Of course, not all clients do make progress – whatever 'making progress' may mean. But the very fact of going to a therapist is a recognition on the part of the client of a wish to change in some way. The prospect of change can alarm. So shouldn't the relationship between therapist and client endeavour to minimise the inevitable anxiety that most new analysands will feel?

If we are ill at ease, our focus shifts. The wish to feel accepted and affirmed pushes its way to the fore, so that an unconscious priority may become the attempt to meet a basic need to feel secure. Our need to feel validated may then take precedence over an aspiration to change and develop in more specific ways. What happens if the aims of the therapist and the aims of his client begin to work against each other? The therapist will hope to initiate change in the client. Paradoxically, we find the courage to change when we feel we are accepted as we are.

Chapter 2

Beginnings and endings

The way that our experience of therapy or counselling begins and ends matters a great deal. It matters in terms of the overall experience and in terms of each individual session.

When I first went to 'my analyst', I was surprised by his formality. I mentioned, hesitantly, during our second session that he didn't smile very often, thinking, foolishly, that he would smile. He didn't, and gave no response. At the end of the session he said he thought I 'could do with some therapy' and that he would need to write to my GP to tell him he was seeing me. I was surprised and felt rather embarrassed. I wondered what dire neuroses he had sniffed out during the two sessions we had had, and felt a sense of foreboding. It seemed, in retrospect, to set the tone.

Two years later, I went to a very different kind of practitioner in order to look at the traumatic feelings which my first experience of therapy had left me with. She did smile and, when we spoke about the task ahead of us, she said she saw it as a journey, and that she wanted me to know that it was one she was very much looking forward to making with me. The analogy of a journey was no more familiar to me at the time than the techniques of psychoanalysis, but the phrases 'I want you to know', 'looking forward to' and the word 'with' meant a lot to me. Again, it helped to set the tone.

Whatever the practitioner's approach, doing psychotherapy is, in many respects, an odd sort of venture. Nevertheless, if it is to be beneficial, then it needs to feel normal, to make sense, to be meaningfully linked to the client's everyday life. The beginnings and endings of sessions can influence greatly the way the work is experienced in this respect. For me, it is important that they are not disconcerting or jarring.

From the therapist's point of view, 'the beginning...often provides a clue to the main theme or feelings that are to follow' (Jacobs, 1988:65). I started my sessions in a variety of ways, sometimes going back to what we had spoken about the previous week, sometimes telling my analyst about something that had just happened at home. Once I talked about a programme I had been listening to on the car radio. On another occasion I explained why I had been delayed. Looking back, I think my 'main theme' was a wish to connect.

My analyst's response was often either silence or a comment which led into a consideration of my 'inner reality'. This tended to throw me, since I had not achieved what I was unconsciously trying to achieve – a sense of normality and a sense of connection. Instead, a feeling of optimism at the beginning of the session was transformed into a vague feeling of having failed, as one human being simply wishing to communicate with another human being.

In my experience, good therapy feels not unlike a normal conversation, even though one person does more of the talking. Within this vast and meandering journey, the 'normal conversations' about everyday things which some therapists avoid can have an important role to play. They act as a bridge, as a lubricator, or as a restful stop on our way. If the client's opening comments are met by silence, it can be deeply disturbing. If a therapist only talks to his client in order to discuss one of her problems, the rest of her can begin to feel left out. And if her initial remarks are seen only as material to be analysed, this may be quite inappropriate. Such a reaction can be equally as unsettling as getting no response at all, because it can seem like a fundamental challenge to one's ability to make sense of the world.

In his listening, a therapist will endeavour to find underlying themes in what the client says. But in his wish to do so, could he make connections where there are none in the client's (conscious or unconscious) mind? Imagine, for example, a patient at the dentist's who, on arriving for her appointment, says quite casually, 'I didn't think I'd get here on time. It's so annoying having to wait for buses.' The dentist would probably smile in agreement, since he also might find waiting for buses irritating. But a counsellor or therapist may 'wonder what it meant' (Jacobs, 1988:65).

This incident is described in an account of a session with a counsellor and his client, 'Hannah'. At the end of the session,

Hannah sighs and says, 'It'll have to wait till next week then?', and the counsellor responds with, 'I guess that's like having to wait for buses, pretty annoying.' He explains in his discussion of the case that he sees these comments of Hannah's as possible examples of the frustration she experienced at being pushed around by men. Yet it would be absurd to conclude that those of us who dislike waiting for buses, or having to wait for a week in order to finish saying something which is important to us, feel this way because it indicates an underlying problem.

Hannah, it turns out, has been pushed around by men. But is her opening comment really a reflection of this? And wouldn't it have been more human if the counsellor had acknowledged her annoyance, rather than silently 'making a mental note' as he does in this case (Jacobs, 1988:65)? A counsellor might point out here that it is his job to make connections, but the question remains: in whose mind do they exist? And how does Hannah feel while the counsellor is busy trying to make conceptual connections between what she says, rather than connecting with how she's feeling then and there?

There is another dimension to the way we begin and end therapy – the 'conventional social modes of interaction' (Smith, 1996:30) which many practitioners eschew. When people come to our house, we greet them warmly, hang up their coats, and try to make them feel at home. A therapist 'may well limit his gestures of sociability: a neutral and limited greeting when the patient comes and goes' (Brearley, 1996). In doing so, he may lose an opportunity to put his client at ease, an ease which could make the ensuing session a lot more effective. To some, he may appear cold and unfriendly, giving the client an unnecessary hurdle to climb over before she has even begun.

On this particular point, an analytic therapist said to me: 'Why go to a therapist rather than a friend? What is it you are wanting?' If I want a friend, I go to a friend. What I want from a psychotherapist is an opportunity to take a closer look at what is really going on. Few clients would want a therapist who is chummy or over-familiar, but that does not mean that practitioners have to behave in an unfriendly manner. It is a question of balance.

A former student told me of the time when, anorexic and using heroin, she finally plucked up the courage to go to the college counsellor. He sat in silence and stared at her. She spoke haltingly, then waited. Silence. Her confidence, at an already perilously low ebb, took another nose-dive. She stood up and left.

It is not uncommon for practitioners to make a point of remaining silent when their clients arrive: 'I...said nothing when they first came in, not even to introduce myself. I waited for them to start' (Jacobs, 1988:30). To be greeted by silence is, in itself, unnerving. If the practitioner says nothing and does not introduce himself, it immediately lends an air of oddness to the encounter. It can also make it more difficult for the client to know how to address him.

In my case, I did not want to use my analyst's surname as it would have seemed too formal. At the same time I felt he might think I was being overfamiliar if I used his first name at the outset. It was a subject that neither of us got around to broaching. With the exception of one occasion, he did not use my name at all. So, in the end, I never used his. This impersonality, within a highly personal setting, was an additional contribution to the contradictory nature of the relationship.

A friend described to me how her psychoanalyst routinely greeted her arrival with a stony silence, her eyes to the floor. She (the practitioner) then spent a great deal of time asking the client why she found this discomforting. The response the client gave – that greeting someone in such a manner simply feels 'inhuman and anti-social' – did not satisfy her analyst. Yet this does not seem to be an unreasonable answer. A likely reason why someone would find this unpleasant is that it feels distant and strange; the analyst's behaviour bears little resemblance to the way human beings usually treat each other.

The psychoanalyst in the above example wanted to know why my friend 'needed' to end the sessions pleasantly and say thank you. This may indeed be related to other, relevant issues, but it does not change the fact that basic courtesy is rarely out of place, whatever the context. And, if the practitioner's manner or style causes the client to leave the therapy, then an opportunity for her to explore, for example, a possible need for reassurance is lost in any case. The therapist's manner not only serves no useful purpose, it is actually counter-productive.

A therapist might point out here that the practitioner's avoidance of imposing courtesies is liberating for many clients. He might also argue that the client does not have to conform to the therapist's manner or style. But, if our initial friendliness evokes no response, it can tend eventually to feel gauche or extraneous. It seems as if an important part of my way of being has no place.

It could also be argued that for the therapist to question an instinctive rejection of something which represents bad manners is an insult to the intelligence and sensibility of the client and, ultimately, to that of the practitioner. The client is not only expected to go along with ungracious behaviour; she is also invited to doubt her motives for disliking it. Might psychotherapists who behave in this way unconsciously expect the client to encompass their reality, and the reality of their particular school, rather than the other way around?

The friend in the above example had been to several therapists and was more used to their ways than I had been. The explanation for her feelings was not accepted by the analyst, but at least she said what she felt. She found the silent beginnings and sudden endings difficult, but her request for some kind of reminder when it was getting towards the end of the session was refused. She soon after decided to terminate the therapy. But not all clients will feel able to challenge the therapist in this way or to leave because of a resulting impasse.

In many therapies, it seems, one has to forgo previously held notions regarding the shape and texture of courteous discourse. We may wonder why such principles no longer seem to apply, but we may not choose to discuss them. I found the way my analyst greeted me cool, but I did not question it. To do so would have seemed inappropriate, too personal, ill-mannered. After all, it was his room, his personal style and his way of working. It was only when I later did therapy with someone who was more open and natural that I fully realised how much my analyst's behaviour had affected me. Don't the majority of clients need to feel welcome, and to be welcomed, if they are to feel entirely at ease?

In therapy we stretch our psychic muscles and sometimes the work is very hard, so we may need time to warm up and cool down. The client cannot switch herself on and off like a machine. Some may need more time than others to settle into the work, and some of us may need a hand with the brakes. I come into and out of the therapy room with my head full of many things: work, Safeways – and 'safe' ways, collecting children from school, supper, phone calls, and how much petrol there is in the car because there's a meeting to go to in the evening. My inner reality and outer reality have to live alongside each other. There need to be links and managed transition.

In psychoanalytic therapy in particular, the practitioner is likely to keep to a precise fifty-minute hour, regardless of what the client is saying or how she is feeling. It is usually the therapist, and not the client, who chooses the length of the sessions. If a practitioner sticks unrelentingly to the traditional fifty minutes, this will at times entail finishing sessions brusquely or abruptly.

My analyst, for example, occasionally cut me off in the middle of a sentence. I particularly remember the time when, with some difficulty, I summoned up the courage to try to share with him a poem I had written about how I felt in his room. I was trying to overcome my awkwardness and put together the first few lines in my head when he said, 'I'm afraid it's time to finish'. It is hard to believe that someone is really interested in or concerned about how one feels in the face of such a response.

When the client leaves the therapy session, there is no button she can press. What if I start to cry after forty-nine minutes? Knowing that the session will finish exactly on time might discourage the client from venturing into areas she finds deeply upsetting. This will be particularly painful if, as children, we felt discouraged from discussing problems with our parents because they did not give us enough time to express and explain what we were experiencing. Children, of course, have the right to ask for extra time; an adult who is simply one of the day's clients will probably feel she does not.

I found it difficult to package what I wanted to say into a neat fifty-minute parcel. Regardless of how I felt, my analyst kept strictly to my allotted time. There will be occasions when the client leaves feeling particularly unsettled or drained. But, in the context of a formal appointment, and particularly if one knows that the therapist usually has another client to see in a few moments, it seems foolish to object to a hurried ending, so we may not always express our discomfort in this respect.

The client may have to leave a session at a time when she is feeling seriously disorientated, or highly emotional, even in tears. Might this not undo or even override progress which has been made during the session? It is certainly not something the majority of clients would choose; it is imposed on them. This problem could be overcome to a large extent by the practitioner reminding the client when it is getting towards the end of the session, and by allowing enough time between sessions to ensure that there is some flexibility when necessary.

In research on learning, it has been found that, for many students, strict deadlines can be disruptive and traumatic, causing considerable anxiety and impairing general performance. In therapy we may go deep and we are deeply affected mentally, emotionally and physically. So a sudden ending to a session can, in itself, be a stressful experience. It catapults the client back into life on the other side of the therapist's door. She has little time to adjust. She takes the heightened feelings with her and somehow has to blend them into the edges of her day-to-day routines and demands.

In my second experience of therapy, I was greeted warmly and naturally. At the end of sessions in which I felt particularly disorientated or upset, Kate would always check how I was before I left. Our sessions ended gracefully and with a sense of things being rounded off, at least until the next time. The exact time at which they finished was not written in tablets of stone. I found this enormously helpful, and it relieved the pressure of feeling that I had to somehow switch off as soon as the appointed time came. It was a pressure which felt, at times, considerable when I worked with a psychoanalyst. With Kate, we later agreed to have sessions of an hour and a half, which suited me far better. I felt that my way of being and my needs were taken into account and part of a responsibly negotiated agreement.

The practitioner who is so rigid that he never deviates from the norm, whatever the circumstances, may not be serving his clients well. It should be possible to strike a sensible balance between flexibility and consistency in terms of appointments. In theory, the client is responsible for deciding how to start and what to talk about, but in reality she is interacting with another person, so this decision will inevitably be contingent to some extent on how the therapist behaves. The absence of a common *modus operandi* may result in the client having little sense of ownership of the sessions.

It goes without saying that starting sessions on time is a sign of courtesy and efficiency, and of respect and concern for the client – even though some clients may not offer the practitioner the same consideration. When this is not possible, it is reasonable for the client to expect that the session begins with an apology from the therapist. If he prefers to keep to a rule of silence, it can feel curt and hurtful.

On one occasion, I remember, my session with Kate started late because the client before me overstayed his time. When he came out of the room, he was obviously distressed. My initial irritation gave way to a feeling of reassurance – because I realised that, in a crisis, my therapist would, if necessary, do the same for me. She asked if I would mind giving her a few more moments, which I willingly did. It was an isolated incident but, in its way, an important one which served to enhance, rather than detract from, my view of her as a truly conscientious professional. It also brought sharply into focus the complexities that practitioners must face in making decisions about what it means to be professionally conscientious. At the time I was not feeling particularly needy but, if I had, I might not have been quite so magnanimous.

In theory, breaks and terminations provide a way of looking at loss. In practice, when breaks come at a time which is particularly difficult for the client, they can cause considerable anguish. In some cases, the distress caused by frequent or prolonged absences on the part of the therapist can outweigh any gains which are made (see, for example, Ann France, 1988). As France points out, if a psychotherapist does not take roughly the same sort of holidays that one would expect from a full-time practitioner, he should perhaps warn prospective clients of this before the work begins.

My first experience of therapy ended so badly that it never really ended, and the pain it caused went on. This made me particularly concerned about how to finish therapy the second time around even though, in practice, my therapist's absence was never a cause of distress. For me, the solution was to meet at increasingly infrequent intervals, and this was an arrangement she was happy to go along with. There was very little absolutism in our relationship, so I never felt under pressure in this respect. I feel that her door is still open.

In practice, sensitively handled beginnings and endings can enable the client to feel seen and valued, as well as helping to keep the work on the right track. If they are well attended to, they are, in themselves, therapeutic. They become a model for successful encounters; and they can help to oil the wheels of therapy and keep it running reasonably smoothly. They might also help to model and guide the client's matching and bridging of her inner and outer realities, so that she remains true to herself. I make sense of the therapy through my life outside it and I make sense of my life through the work of therapy.

In the therapy room, all our usual props fall away. Doing psychotherapy behind a closed door, shut off from the outside world, sometimes feels like sitting in a space capsule, embarking on a journey into unknown territory. It can be a frightening feeling. So it is here, more than anywhere else, that we need to feel earthed. For me, warm greetings and carefully managed farewells are an integral part of this earthing.

Chapter 3

Theory – and practice

Theories are not always right. Even when they are, there is frequently a discrepancy between espoused theory and theory in practice, which may result in mixed messages being conveyed to clients. In her *Report on Effective Psychotherapy*, Roberta Russell found that the 'active ingredients' in the therapy process were 'quite different from what any of the individual schools of thought had postulated'. Her findings confirmed the view that it is primarily the empathy and intention between the therapist and client that is healing (Russell, 1992:7).

What is the therapist's intention? Whilst there are many practitioners who wish to offer, and do offer, a nourishing and redemptive breathing space, are there others whose wish to serve gets overtaken by an eagerness to reveal to the client the extent of her dysfunction? Whatever the therapist's true motivation, it is the client's perception of his intention which will, initially at least, most affect how she feels.

A textbook description of the psychoanalytic approach highlights the premise that Freudian analysts should never reproach their patients, but never praise or reassure them either. In theory, this creates 'an atmosphere of safety' (Schafer, 1983, cited in Smith, 1990:29). In practice, it may not be the case. Not being praised or reassured often makes me feel insecure. So, although the aim of the therapist is to make the client feel safe whilst she is with him, he may actually do the opposite. But there can be no assumption that the resultant anxiety will be expressed or dealt with.

In theory, a psychoanalyst 'serves the function of providing a template by which the patient can more readily find in him whatever she is liable to find in others' (Brearley, 1996). Remaining unknown and anonymous is the stock-in-trade of many practitioners, who claim that not to do so would muddy the waters. But, from the client's point of view, this can make it more difficult to deal with problems, rather than making it easier. For a human being to assume the theoretical role of blank screen can give the whole procedure an air of inauthenticity. Isn't it also a dangerously flawed assumption on which to base the work?

No therapist is clean as a whistle when it comes to the trappings of psychic accumulation; no human being is a blank sheet. So a model of working based on the notion of the practitioner as a mirror is surely both unrealistic and risky. The therapist will not always be able to 'keep out of the client's way' (Smith, 1996:30), as he is supposed to do in theory. Once we are with another person, the picture changes. 'When you're with another person you're out of yourself because the other person is flowing into you and you are flowing into them' (Hillman and Ventura, 1993:41).

'Free association', for instance, is likely to be different when we are with someone else than when we are alone. If, for example, I make notes when I am alone and then read them to my therapist when I go to the next session, the notes represent my thoughts and feelings at a time when they were not being influenced by the presence of someone else. But if I 'free associate' in the company of a professional psychotherapist at a preordained time during a fifty-minute session for which I am paying, it may be a very different matter.

Most therapists will be well aware that, in practice, they can never be a blank screen. But doesn't the methodology of a psychoanalytic approach expect that they will behave in this way? For example, a description of psychoanalytic practice maintains that the therapist's neutrality provides a 'sufficiently uncontaminated field of enquiry' (Brearley, 1996). Might this, in practice, demand that in some ways he behave rather like a machine, and that the client treats him like one? If it does, then this, in itself, is likely to colour what then transpires.

In practice, the 'field of enquiry' will inevitably be 'contaminated' by the therapist's outlook on life, his temperament, personality and presence, and by the way he behaves towards each individual client. It will be shaped by his training, a training which will have changed the way he sees and hears the people who become his clients. The therapist's reality – the lens through which he looks at his 'patients' – will not be without an effect. Could it even help to create what his training has told him to look for?

Therapeutic 'neutrality' has been described as the capacity to be open, without preconceptions (Orbach, 1998b). At the same time, a professional training will equip the practitioner with particular ways of conceptualising the client's difficulties. He cannot be free of the theoretical assumptions on which he works. One might question, therefore, how open he will be.

Neutrality also means that the therapist will think about feelings rather than act on them. But this may not always be possible. Sometimes a therapist might say the 'right' thing, but his feelings do not accord with his words. The client then receives confusing signals, which may have the effect of entangling rather than teasing out the difficulties that need to be dealt with.

The rule of abstinence demands that the practitioner holds back, both verbally and physically. But this, along with the relative neutrality of the therapist, will surely be expedient only if it is liberating. There are aspects of this stance which, if taken too far, can thwart rather than enhance progress. The client needs to interact with a real person and not a system, a person who is genuinely caring and interested. For the therapist, endeavouring to remain unobtrusive and objective, and at the same time provide genuine support, involves a skilful and sensitive awareness of the client's needs. It is a precarious balance, a balance which can sometimes backfire.

If the therapist is expected to think about his feelings rather than allow them expression, might this principle then spill over into his stance towards his client's behaviour? For instance, he might encourage the client only to interpret and analyse, to think about her feelings rather than experience them. Could this, in practice, actually stifle her emotions and, in the long run, increase their hold? Being told by a therapist that it is important to feel rather than simply describe one's feelings can put the client under considerable pressure, and it is a far cry from actually being asked how one is feeling.

I remember an occasion when I arrived at a session with my second therapist, Kate, feeling worried about what to choose to talk about. I kept a notebook of thoughts, questions and dreams and quite often I did not know where to begin. Kate acknowledged my anxiety and then suggested I put my notebook on one side for a moment, try to concentrate on my bodily sensations and describe how I was feeling. I found what followed very informative. I remember a similar occasion with my analyst and, in that instance, when I expressed my confusion, he asked me if it mattered if I got things in the right order. It did, but I couldn't say clearly why, and I felt even more boxed in and apprehensive.

An important element in the theory of psychotherapy is that clients are encouraged to be completely candid, to say whatever comes into their mind. In practice, of course, we frequently don't say whatever comes into our head. For example, clients may not be entirely frank about the negative aspects of how they experience their therapy and their therapists. We may be equally reticent about divulging strong feelings of attraction or attachment. One of the reasons for this might simply be that too much frankness can seem indiscreet or inappropriate in the context of a professional relationship. So a client's most immediate considerations in this respect may be very different from those which occur to a psychotherapist.

In practice, the nature of the client's difficulties in her everyday life may not always be the same as those which arise in the context of therapy. The therapeutic relationship is one between a professional and a client who, generally speaking, have never met each other before and do not see each other outside that context. In many cases, it is relatively formal. At the same time, it is unusually intimate. To me, the two seemed at times to be impossibly incompatible.

It is also a relationship for which the therapist receives and the client pays a fee, and this can be both an advantage and a hindrance. The money helps to create a healthy kind of distance, acts as a kind of buffer zone. It is a reminder that two people have entered into a contract, that there is work to be done. It may also cause the client to question whether the therapist really cares about her. Do we buy a therapy package, or is there a heartfelt commitment which transcends the financial transaction?

Viewed in the context of a formalised encounter with a paid professional, the question of what is or isn't appropriate is both pertinent and particular. The therapist has the right, and professional duty, not to comply with a client's behaviour which is disrespectful or intrusive. But doesn't he also have to be genuinely present? 'In any thoroughgoing analysis, the whole personality of both patient and doctor is called into play...the doctor's whole being is challenged' (Jung, 1935). In meeting that challenge, just how honest is the therapist prepared to be, and how honest does he actually want his clients to be?

In psychoanalysis, the client's fantasies about the practitioner are considered to be an important part of the work. But the line between brash intrusiveness and legitimate psychological exploration is not always easy to draw. For example, if one day a client notices her therapist's car parked in a back street far from his family home, and if she fantasises as to whether he might be having an affair with a woman on the other side of town, does she explore this fantasy with him the next time she goes to therapy? Or does she refrain from mentioning it, feeling that to do so would be intrusive and, despite the context, disregarding his right to keep his private life separate from his work?

Where do the client's boundaries lie? I have found that, in the very particular context of therapy, it is difficult sometimes to determine how much of one's view of, and curiosity about, the practitioner it is appropriate to express. How far do we go when it comes to that most fundamental aspect of the 'analytic attitude' – 'a devotion to the pursuit of truth' (Dorpat, 1979)? The client is expected to free associate, that is, 'letting thoughts emerge into your mind without censoring them in any way' (Smith, 1996:31). Yet she might also wish to strike a balance between openness and discretion. Therapy is all about boundaries. The therapist has the advantage of having been trained in this respect. But no one tells the client the rules of the psychotherapy 'game'.

If the therapist is to serve as a template, to what extent should he provide a kind of fodder for the work of therapy? There seems little humanity in such a situation. In any case, many clients will feel unable to treat their therapists in this way. For example, for someone who, as a child, was abused by a father who was a heavy smoker, a therapist's halitosis might be a particularly significant factor in her feelings about him. Yet this is hardly something which most of us would feel comfortable expressing. So an important element in the relationship may never be discussed.

Expressing negative feelings about the therapeutic relationship is a crucial part of the work, but this may not come easily. And, in any case, no one expects things to be exactly as we might wish them to be. So, if the practitioner does not help to put the therapy relationship on the agenda, the client may feel that it is not an appropriate area for discussion.

For the client, social conventions will come into play and form part of the framework in which she operates. For example, a friend described a conversation she had with a counsellor when she telephoned to apologise for missing her second appointment. This particular friend is a busy, slightly scatty person and she had genuinely mistaken the date, but she also had doubts about whether she could work with that particular practitioner. The counsellor – who trains other counsellors – told my friend why, in her view, she had avoided keeping the appointment and why she needed to address the issues which, in the counsellor's opinion, her not attending suggested. My friend was too polite to tell her that her doubts about returning were not because of the challenge of the work, but because she did not like the counsellor very much. If this possibility occurred to the practitioner, then wouldn't her appraisal of the prospective client's position have been more honest if she had said so?

Some clients may be slower to reject what does not feel right, not necessarily because they are unable to get up and leave, but because they are sufficiently easy-going to be willing to continue trying. How many of us have chewed our way through a badly cooked meal in a restaurant, beamed at the waitress when she asked if everything was all right, then gone home and wondered why we did not say anything?

In theory, of course, this should not happen in therapy. In theory, we go back the following week and talk about our new insights. But in practice, we may not. In any case, time is limited and the agenda may have taken a different route by then. So, in practice, we may actually neglect to address a great deal that is relevant. It takes a long time to realise, express and explore the many thoughts and feelings which arise during or after a therapy session.

Psychotherapy will work through many levels of emotion and experience. We may forget sometimes that what we want, in the end, is to feel good about ourselves and our relationships. We concentrate on the most immediate, and therefore more super-ficial, layers. This can leave one with a nagging sense of 'Yes, but . . .'. It isn't the whole story, there is something more, a deeper motivation, a more fundamental truth. In my experience, if the therapist makes clear from the start that he acknowledges and holds for the client the concept of her wholeness, then it is less likely that she will get stuck in the layers, trapped in a web of 'Yes, but...'s.

According to the theory, we give vent to the pain of our repressed inner child when we go to therapy. In practice, I wanted to behave like a courteous, sensible and dignified adult, and to be treated like one. However confused or misplaced such a wish might be in the theoretical context of psychotherapy, an attachment to human dignity and intelligence can, in my view, never be invalid.

A therapist commented to me that this attitude could result in my 'foreclosing on making myself available to be helped'. He cited a client who had not responded despite his expressions of help and support. Maybe she did not respond overtly because she was not used to being offered support, because she was taken aback by its unfamiliarity. I remember a time when my analyst said to me, 'You must have been very hurt', and I said 'Pardon?' because I was surprised; he had seen my hurt in a situation in which I had expressed primarily anger.

The point about being open to what is offered is an important one, but the therapist may misinterpret the client's response in this respect. I know I was helped a great deal by my second therapist and that, for all the tears and anger and shame, I never lost sight of my 'dignified adult' in her room. I believe it was in great measure due to the way she behaved towards me on such occasions.

Can there be a sound basis for the work of therapy if the client and the practitioner have different ground rules, if there is no shared implicit agreement about the way we interact? Such principles are, of course, hard to define, and often equally hard to agree on. Nevertheless, if a therapist appears to call into question what are, in essence, common mores about communication, and elemental principles about honesty, responsibility and consideration, then there are no starting blocks.

A lack of recognition of the validity – as opposed to the problematic nature – of wanting the basic 'givens' in a relationship skews our overall perspective, suggesting there is a pathological aspect in what is essentially an ethical view of the way we behave. Therapy tries to avoid judgements about what is right and wrong, so questions which are essentially moral or philo-sophical can get mixed up with those which are psychological. Does this mean that, in some practice, our conscience and the spiritual element in our nature are then neglected?

When the rules of therapy are in some way incongruous, at odds with what we are trying to achieve, then isn't this, in itself, a problem? What happens if the guidelines which govern the relationship between practitioner and client take precedence over the ground rules about decent human behaviour? If they aren't one and the same, which rules does the client respect? Which reality does she suspend? When an exchange between practitioner and client – despite its inevitable asymmetry – does not mirror essential aspects of what a constructive relationship is, how does this affect us? Do the problems which arise in psychotherapy come only from the client's past, or might they also be caused by the confused nature of the relationship?

Generally speaking, we expect a courteous, caring and consid-erate response from those we engage to help us. An analyst is trained to sustain an unrelenting analytic abstinence, yet at the same time to expect that the relationship between therapist and client 'becomes and remains the central focus' (Smith, 1996:33). To the client, however, these two positions may feel both unreal-istically extreme and irresolvably contradictory.

In theory, the client will benefit from her relationship with her therapist. In theory, the therapist knows what he is doing and will act in the best interests of the client. In practice, she is at the mercy of his view of what is good for her, his skills and his strength of character. She needs to bear this in mind but, in practice, it is not always easy. She has to remember – and perhaps to be reminded – that the therapist is also fallible. She has to balance a readiness to accept that he may be right when he draws attention to uncomfortable truths against an awareness that he will some-times be wrong. But the odds are unevenly stacked in this respect.

She has sought out his services because, in theory, he is an expert. She is paying for his expertise. The client is unlikely to have read the textbooks which point out that, in practice, 'even successful treatments may include therapist errors of considerable magnitude' (Smith, 1996:35). It may not have occurred to her that 'therapists are all too easily seduced into abusing the therapy relationship' and that 'when this occurs, the relationship is no longer therapeutic' (Aveline, 1996:376). Going into any kind of potentially healing relationship is, inevitably, an act of faith, based on the hope that it will be therapeutic.

We go to a therapist because we need a different perspective, a new pair of eyes. But, if the therapist is the expert, does that mean that he knows more than I do about why I am the way I am? If so, what do I have to offer in this context? If the therapist thinks he knows more than I do about why I am the way I am, how does this affect his attitude towards me? And how will he view my interpretations if they differ from his? In practice, the client, unsure of herself in the hitherto unknown environment of therapy, can find herself thinking that the therapist knows her better than she does, disempowering herself without realising. The practitioner, in his desire to be a good analyst, can fuel this insecurity.

In practice, I can unearth my true feelings only if I am confident that the therapist has faith in me, that he is on my side, that he in turn recognises my expertise. But, precisely because he is a trained and qualified 'expert' in human behaviour, there can be an exaggerated fear that one will be seen as a failure – a fear which will then need to be identified and assuaged. In theory, fears about inadequacy and failure will be worked through and resolved, but this may not happen in practice. In my experience, analytic therapy can actually reinforce this fear.

It is a grave mistake to assume that all practitioners will have faith in their clients. One of the greatest problems which I came up against was that my analyst did not seem to trust me, and I am not the only client who has had this experience. It took me years to understand the implications of this, and the extent to which it undermines one's ability to trust oneself. It is hard to do good work with someone who does not feel that one is worthy of their trust, or to feel safe with someone who seems more concerned with diagnosis than acceptance. My feeling of not being trusted did not arise in my second experience of therapy, which felt quite different.

So what happens when theories don't work in practice? If a fundamental supposition about feeling safe is misplaced, if underlying principles about objectivity do not have validity, if what arises in therapy is wrongly attributed, then can the 'thera-peutic' relationship be therapeutic? Or does therapy then become fraudulent? The ways in which this can happen will often be subtle and complex. They might be obscured, rather than revealed, by an immodest faith on the part of the practitioner in his ability to maintain a position of neutrality, by an undiscerning adherence to the principle of abstinence, by an overzealous emphasis on the notion of transference. The fraudulence waiting in the wings can enter and exit unobserved, messing up the real script without either of the protagonists noticing.

It has been claimed by opponents of therapy that, in practice, the psychotherapeutic relationship can never be good for the client. It is always negative and destructive, in part, it is argued, because it will always be an unequal one. It is interesting that this tends to be seen in terms of the client being 'less equal'. One could also argue that the therapist is 'less equal' because I, the client, am paying him. He is, therefore, in a sense, my servant. One could say that the customer is always right. But that would be equally one-sided.

Many therapists assume that there is an imbalance of power between therapist and client. It is, in many ways, a strange claim to make. The client might be, intrinsically, a stronger or more powerful person than the therapist. The therapist's power may lie primarily in the fact that he knows more than the client about psychotherapy, and in the situation which evolves from this. The negative influence of that power is unleashed by the client when she falls into the trap of being overawed by 'professional expertise'. For the client, the trick in therapy is to be able to take advantage of its possibilities without being intimidated by it.

When I worked with Kate, I did not feel unequal or less powerful. Two people can meet as equals in a relationship which is asymmetrical, if they meet first and foremost as two people, and if the bottom line really is truth. It is not inevitable that there is a sense of inequality in therapeutic work, provided that difference and inequality are not confused. It depends on how the therapist relates to the client, as well as on how the client relates to the therapist.

There is a strong case for maintaining that the psychotherapy relationship should be, in itself, a 'corrective emotional experience' (Alexander and French, 1946; cited in Dryden, 1997:6). For this to happen, the therapist will avoid engaging in behaviour which denigrates both himself and his client. If human dignity is placed at the centre of the stage, then the 'container' of therapy will be constructed with humility and grace, using universal principles about sound, ethical behaviour.

It is perhaps unavoidable that the therapist will be seen, to some degree, as an expert, as an authority figure, and that we are therefore more likely to accept than to reject the things he says. But this does not have to be detrimental. It can be to the advantage of the client. When a therapist says 'Perhaps you ...' or 'You seem to...', with reference to something which is problematic, it can begin to feel as if I am a lost cause. But if I then hear 'We often tend to...' or even 'I'm the same...', the fear subsides. I feel that my problem is not insurmountable because it is a problem that I share to some degree with everyone else.

This realisation does not induce complacency, or stop me from being aware and wanting to change. On the contrary, it means that I can do so more effectively, in an atmosphere free of guilt. I am acknowledged as having a rightful place in the world, reintegrated into the human race. It is as if the authority the therapist represents is saying: 'It's OK. You're allowed to be you.' If my problems are played back to me as an indelible consequence of my particular and defective upbringing, as evidence of what is wrong with me, I feel pathologised. There is a sense of disconnection from the world around me. The abstinence of the therapist may feed this feeling of chilly isolation.

In practice, the therapist has to behave like a real human being, not a professional interpreter. If he does, key issues of power and control will not necessarily work against the client. But these things have to be talked about and their manifestations seen and owned appropriately by both parties. Their potential for damage lies in their implicitness. Once something is on the table for discussion, it is less threatening. But in practice, as I learnt to my cost, the way in which the work is structured can prevent this from happening.

Chapter 4

Who calls the tune?

We go to therapy in order to talk about what we have already experienced. But, if the practitioner adopts a passive, 'blank screen' approach, we are subsequently confronted by a new situation. Therapy then becomes, in part, a process of learning how to deal with an environment which is – for the client – singular and unknown. It could be argued that, if the situation seems contradictory and artificial, then this becomes, in itself, an additional source of disturbance.

A therapist once said to me that psychotherapy was a bit like a microcosm of real life; but the context of therapy is also very different from everyday life, so my behaviour and my boundaries will not necessarily be the same there. And the emotions that are most strongly felt may be ones which do not consciously arise in our everyday relationships. In therapy, we look at what is hidden, so what turns up may be the opposite of what seems to typify our life outside it.

Therapy is unusual in being a close encounter which we go into with the aim that it should not last. Another of its characteristics is its exclusivity. Although he endeavours to see the whole person, the practitioner only experiences, first-hand, what the client is like when she is alone with him in the therapy room. So how well can he know her? And, for the client, what does it mean to put one's trust in someone who makes a point of not revealing what kind of person he is?

In the field of medicine, one hears sometimes the comment, 'He's a wonderful consultant. He's just got rather an unfortunate manner.' Because the practitioner is knowledgeable and technically skilled, he is considered to be 'good', even though his patients feel anxious, insecure and unable to seek the information and support they need. Might this also apply to some psychotherapists?

Do those practitioners who abandon 'naturalistic attitudes' (Smith, 1990:29) tell their clients why they do so? In the absence of any explanation, it can feel frustrating, disorientating, even hurtful. However, the client will probably go along with it. After all, she is no longer in the conventional world, she is in the world of therapy. In therapy, 'what procedures the therapist propounds, the patient is predisposed to accept' (Aveline, 1996:377), particularly if she is unsure because the situation is new to her.

In theory, the seeming austerity of the therapeutic context is offset by the fact that it is 'designed to create a situation in which clients can authentically be themselves' (Smith, 1996:30). In my case, with my analyst I felt it did the opposite. I ended up behaving in a way which seemed alien to me. In my second experience of therapy, I learnt to confirm and appreciate intuitively – rather than intellectually – what was authentic, through being with someone who was open and authentic, and who was fully herself.

When I met my analyst, he was a total stranger – but I wrongly assumed that, as time went by, this would change. I knew he was well qualified and highly experienced. Later, I would look at his clothes, his glasses, his diary, his pen, the way he sat and spoke, his facial expressions, his eyes, the pictures and furniture in his room, and wonder what they told me about him. But I had no concrete idea of the kind of person he was, his perception of and values about human behaviour in general, or how he saw me in particular. He offered little in the way of clues.

Client and practitioner will become known to each other primarily through what they do and do not say, so a therapist's mode of communication can be what therapy stands or falls by. Anthony Clare once joked about how, during his training, he was told that if a patient asked a question, the psychiatrist's response should be to ask why she asked it. To be on the receiving end of such a procedure – even in modified form – is not so funny. Such an approach to interpersonal communication may be more likely to engender bewilderment or exasperation than a feeling of safety. If the client discovers that the hitherto normal activity of asking questions and getting a response is suddenly no longer legitimate, it can seem embarrassingly silly or be deeply disconcerting.

In the field of experiential learning, much is made of the importance of 'dialogue' or 'conversation'. It is seen as a central means of reality construction and transformation. It is a 'vehicle of reality maintenance' and, at the same time, a means for identity-building. It is an 'existential necessity'. Without it 'we are less able to engage in the transformation of our reality and more likely to get caught up in the imperative of the status quo' (Wildemeersch, 1989:60ff.). So how does the form of the dialogue of therapy influence what takes place? What is its effect?

In certain types of therapy, normal dialogue is discouraged. For example, in some psychoanalytic practice, the practitioner 'rarely asks questions, or directly answers the patient's' (Brearley, 1996). From the client's point of view – and the therapist's also, perhaps – it is reassuring to know that one's privacy will be respected, that one will not be questioned in an intrusive way. Inappropriate questions may block or divert what one is trying to make sense of. But questions can help us to see things more clearly, they encourage reflection, and are invaluable signposts.

Questions can be a clear sign for the client that her problem has been recognised, is valid and worthy of consideration. They then become a source of strength. The art of a good, insightful therapist is to find the question that opens a door. It may often be a question to which the client has no immediate answer, and that factor has to be accommodated. By the same token, things a therapist says that might seem of little use at the time can suddenly, or gradually, make sense several weeks, months or even years later.

My analyst did ask me questions, but I was often unsure whether they were opinions, genuine questions or rhetorical questions, and their ambiguity in this respect confused me. When I could not answer, I felt under pressure. This was sometimes because it was something too wide or too fundamental to take on board in the space of the few seconds that usually elapse between a question and answer, or simply because I did not know.

There were many questions I should have asked my analyst. At the time I did not feel able to – maybe a leftover from the past, maybe because I felt he would not welcome questions, also because I felt that I was not there to ask him questions. Perhaps I had been influenced by an image of the stereotypical analyst who never answers questions, so that I started with assumptions which may or may not have been true in my case.

By all accounts, psychotherapists, like politicians, are often adept at side-stepping the questions their clients ask, and my analyst was not averse to doing so occasionally. The elusiveness inherent in rarely giving direct answers can be disarming rather than helpful, but such elusiveness does more than simply make us feel uncomfortable. It may actually prevent therapeutic work from taking place.

Understanding our perception of reality is what therapy is all about. Asking questions and getting clear answers is an essential part of our personal reality-testing, so an absence of natural dialogue can interfere with our propensity to elucidate and redefine our sense of ourselves through talking. The essential role of dialogue is further hampered if the style of the therapist seems so much based on a prescription that it lacks naturalness and spontaneity. The interaction itself then becomes artificial, lending an air of incongruity to the work.

Studies of how talk is used in different contexts and in different societies show that 'people do not think through the problems of everyday life in the same way that trained scientists go about solving a problem' (Wardhaugh, 1986:245). We 'make use of a commonsense knowledge, which is different in kind from scientific knowledge, and ... employ principles of practical reasoning' (ibid.:285). The practitioner may not be a trained scientist, but much psychotherapy is based on the application of Freud's work, 'the science of the human mind', and therapy is sometimes described as a combination of art and science. So how does this affect the interchange between a layperson and a trained therapist? Do their different approaches clash with or complement each other?

Studies of talk also show that, generally speaking, when we interact we do not 'insist on the literal interpretations of remarks, question another's assumptions, attack perceived wisdom, require logical proofs in all reasoning' (Wardhaugh, 1986:285). Such conventions may play a major role in the way the client interacts with the practitioner. How much are these habits rooted in our emotional and psychological make-up, and how much are they influenced by the linguistic behaviour we have grown up with? The two are undoubtedly connected, but which comes first and what is their relative impact?

In everyday life, 'there is an unwritten agreement to deal with the world in certain ways; consequently, we put ourselves in serious peril of misunderstanding if we violate that agreement' (ibid.). In our ordinary dialogues with each other, 'many things do not occur...because they would violate the unconscious agreement that holds between speakers and listeners that only certain kinds of things will happen in a normal conversation' (ibid.).

Of course, therapists may not feel constrained by such 'agreements', believing they no longer apply because the concept of normal conversation is irrelevant in the context of therapy. But, although her view of what might happen in therapy can change as time goes on, the client does not necessarily perceive the interaction in the same way as the practitioner. We may often violate unconscious agreements about discourse with, for example, our partners or children, but we tend not to in less close relationships.

In therapy, as in all interactions, patterns of communication can become set, making it difficult to break out of that pattern when the need arises. My analyst's style was relatively formal, and our relationship was ironically more formal than my relationship with, for example, our GP, our homeopath, or the man who does our pensions. I sometimes felt he did not speak to me as if I was a normal human being. What he said and the way he said it at times evoked in me feelings of inadequacy, confusion and distance. The confusion could have been put to good use, if it had been successfully worked through, but in my case it was not.

I found that my sense of being able to connect and converse with another person was gradually eroded. In theory, a psychotherapist gives his client the freedom to say whatever she wishes, but does he allow her to communicate? My analyst looked grave and not infrequently responded to what I said to him with a solemn silence. My sentences would hang momentarily in mid-air and then slink away feeling more and more unsure of themselves. My questions – already haunted by insecurity – gave up and sulked in a corner, feeling awkward and unwelcome.

According to the theory, the therapist's silence assists the client's free association. The therapist is silent in order to make room for the client, and as a means of indicating respect or support. But the client will not always be aware of his reasons and may not necessarily perceive it in this way. In our everyday exchanges, when we tell someone something and they remain silent, there could be a whole range of other explanations too: perhaps our interlocutor is uninterested, or bored, or upset, or doesn't understand what we have said, or feels embarrassed or shocked or angry, or simply doesn't know what to say. So silence may sometimes make us feel awkward, we worry in case we have said the wrong thing or caused the other person to feel uncomfortable. Silence can also be used as a weapon, an instrument of power, keeping the other person hanging on a thread.

Usually, we pick up clues from our interlocutor's facial expression or body language. But many therapists consider that 'the ability to be poker-faced is a considerable asset' (Jacobs, 1988:26). The practitioner will cultivate a neutral stance. So it is difficult for the client to gauge what is happening through habitual clues, and she may wonder what the silence indicates. She may want to engage in dialogue rather than to free associate. Perhaps she ends up monologising simply to fill the silence, and not necessarily because, for her, such monologue serves a useful purpose. In theory, looking at what the silence signifies can be a means of making the unconscious conscious, but it does not always work out that way.

In her account of 'consuming therapy', the late Ann France describes how painful and traumatic she found the silences of her analyst. She did not find silence difficult in other situations, but she would leave sessions early because she could not bear the silence. She describes an occasion when she left with a feeling of 'total numbness and unreality' which caused her existing depression to worsen considerably. It 'was not a healing crisis. It remained in my memory as a trauma which could prove fatal if it recurred' (France, 1988:182). Ann France suffered from serious depression. I do not, but my analyst's silence made me feel nervous and confused, because I had no idea what it signified and because it felt very different from the warm, companionable silence of someone to whom one feels close.

In my experience, a psychoanalytic approach can weaken our sense of connection with the world and our faith in the validity of all our judgements and perceptions. For example, if the therapist seems tired or stressed on a particular occasion, this may prompt the client to express concern. If this is met by a response of the sort 'I wonder why it is that the way I'm feeling is important to you?', then it can imply several things – that the client has overstepped some invisible boundary, that it is not appropriate for her to treat the practitioner like a fellow human and enquire about his well-being, or that the real issue lies elsewhere. It can suggest that the client's powers of perception are faulty or that she does not know how to behave appropriately. Her faith in herself is subtly undermined and her feelings about the here and now are belittled, dismissed, it seems, as debris from the past.

The therapist's comment above could suggest a path of enquiry that is worth pursuing but, on its own, it reduces the client to a clinical phenomenon. That she is observant, sensitive and caring is neither acknowledged nor appreciated. Worse, her concern is immediately interpreted as indicating that she has a problem. This type of response removes the therapist from the arena of humanness. The client feels a chasm open up between them. Her concern does not appear to have touched him. She is merely the object of his professional curiosity. This is psychotherapy at its most dehumanising.

Psychotherapists are trained to look at and deal with problems. Can this, in itself, sometimes affect their objectivity? Does it mean that everything has the potential to be seen as a problem, allowing a kind of patronising, humourless meanness to creep in? For example, a client who makes 'little lists' may be seen as having a particular need for control. Don't therapists ever need to write things down in order to remember them? The client who engages in small talk may not necessarily be trying to avoid 'big talk'. For me, it was a way of easing the transition, at the beginning and end of sessions, between therapy and the rest of the day. And I tried to use it – unsuccessfully – as a means of drawing out my analyst, of getting to know him a little, of making him into a real person instead of a blank screen.

When I first went to therapy, I was surprised when my analyst suggested that something which had not felt like a problem was, in fact, a problem. My resistance to this view of things stemmed partly from my inability to see, at that time, the subtler implications and causes of my behaviour. But it was also to do with a wish to trust, to keep a perspective on life which is essentially positive. Such a perspective surely deserves to be honoured and nurtured. If it is undermined, then our capacity to cope with our everyday difficulties can be undermined also.

'Our day-to-day life, especially in the future...very much depends on hope' (Dalai Lama, 1995:45). In therapy, a positive outlook should be one of the tools of the work, a useful asset, an affirmation of human hopefulness. Negative experiences in the past need to be looked at from every point of view. They do not only have negative consequences; they are also teachers: 'Our life histories are not liabilities to be exorcised but are the very precondition of knowing' (Pinar). For me, a good therapist will convey a sense of optimism, an enthusiasm for life. He will have the curiosity, tenacity and sense of involvement of the detective rather than the coolly detached, academic interest of the scholar.

It is liberating when we are able to let go of problematic patterns of behaviour. At the same time, these patterns may, in some measure, have a certain validity. It is disempowering and hurtful if parts of ourselves seem to be reduced to the level of a developmental malfunction. There is a sterility and a heartlessness in this approach which leaves one with a feeling of invalidation. For example, does a wish to get on well with the therapist stem from some deeply rooted insecurity, or is it simply a natural, healthy desire to be on good terms with a fellow human being? It may be both. If it is, then acknowledging and respecting the healthy aspect of such a wish can clear the way for looking at times when it might be the cause of difficulties.

In a description of psychodynamic counselling, the writer describes an incident when his imaginary client, 'Karl', gives him the gift of a book (Jacobs, 1988:75). The counsellor puts the book on the table by Karl's side and asks him what it is that the book says about him which he is unable to say himself – thus ignoring what his client has just done. Such behaviour is, in my view, not only rude and insensitive; in any other context, it would seem extremely strange. However, seen from a therapist's perspective, it is not necessarily unacceptable.

In the above example, the book does, indeed, have relevance but, from a client's point of view, it would probably feel more acceptable if the practitioner drew attention to that later and, initially, showed appreciation. If that is what the writer intended, it is a pity he did not say so, since his text is read by trainee counsellors, who may be tempted to emulate what many would see as an absence of tact. Karl's gift was, in part at least, an attempt to apologise for his lateness and missed appointments. In dismissing a gift, a counsellor may hope to show that the client does not need to appease him, but he also shows a lack of respect for the client's wish to give. I found the experience of having a gift returned deeply hurtful.

In another example, Karl says during their first session: 'I've heard a lot about you.' The practitioner sees this as 'an attempt at familiarity ... which was also perhaps a piece of flattery' (Jacobs, 1988:24). And when his client tells him he has heard he is 'good', he also interprets this as an attempt to flatter, though he later wonders if it was a moral quality to which Karl alluded.

To the layperson, the explanation which springs to mind is that Karl needs reassurance that the counsellor is competent, just as we would want to know if a doctor, dentist, builder or solicitor was competent before we put our trust in them. And is it surprising that the client wishes to feel familiar with his counsellor – it may be a little premature, but is his behaviour necessarily impertinent or inappropriate? Does a practitioner's reaction to the client sometimes smack of the narcissism and grandiosity which is often cited by therapists as being characteristic of their patients?

Behaving abnormally seems to be an odd way of trying to help someone towards a greater normality. Therapists who act in what is, for the client, an unnatural, and often disconcerting, manner risk making their encounters destabilising experiences for those they hope to help. The wish for a supportive, natural and open relationship where the client is treated as an equal can be pathologised in therapy. Instead of using it as the basis for creating a healthy framework where real progress can be made, a psychotherapist may attempt to analyse it. He treats it as something to be 'processed'. It is not surprising if the client begins to flounder.

In learning how to spot the point at which our ways of coping tip into a recipe for conflict, we should not leave out their positive aspects. At what point is a 'defence' destructively defensive, and not a successful and appropriate adaptation? Much will depend on who is at the receiving end of our behaviour. What is repression and what is leaving things behind? What is denial and what is courage? There may be many areas in the client's life in which she functions well, and in which she does not need to change. So 'if it ain't broke, don't fix it'. Perhaps some clients as well as therapists need reminding of this saying.

In order to 'own our shadow', we need to have faith that there is light there as well as darkness. There has to be building as well as dismantling. Good therapy will not only consider the past and make us less attached to our habitual adaptations; it will be lateral as well as vertical. It expands us, shows us that there is strength in our weaknesses, and that there are often two sides to what we consider as our strengths. It enlarges our understanding of human-beingness, enabling us to feel less threatened by our inadequacies, less dependent on our abilities, and therefore more complete.

If our experience has not taught us to see difficulties as containable, then the therapist needs to emphasise this broader perspective for us, so that the client feels a sense of containment. Putting problems into perspective, and realigning them within a wider parameter, makes them seem smaller and more manageable and gives us breathing space. In many instances, however, 'the therapist's silence is broken only infrequently, usually to share with clients their ideas about the client's inner struggles' (Smith, 1996:30). If this is the case, then isn't there a danger that the client will begin to feel that, in the therapist's eyes, her problems pervade everything she feels, thinks and says? And if it goes on for long enough, might she start to believe this herself? If her precious, and sometimes painfully acquired, life skills are not also included in the picture, it can seem as if they no longer have a rightful place there.

Isn't there a risk, then, that such an approach has the effect of stripping the client of her normality? If her 'inner struggles' are seen primarily as the result of neurotic maladjustment, rather than part of the instinctive human drive to seek balance, then to what extent will she able to experience herself as normal? If our perception of and way of dealing with reality seem constantly to be called into question, this undermines our faith in our own sanity. And if our ways of interacting with the world seem suddenly no longer valid, then our sense of being able to manage in the world can begin to dissolve.

Chapter 5

The power of language

The way we think influences the language we use. The language we use in turn influences the way we think, feel and behave and the way that others perceive and respond to us. Language is pivotal in therapy, both at the level of naming our experience of the world in discerning, precise terms and at the level of how we interact with each other. It will shape the way in which our past experiences are remembered and reconstrued, as well as the evolution of the therapy relationship.

Therapy is contingent on our modes of expression – through words, mood, appearance, feeling, gesture and movement. We reveal ourselves through the way in which we communicate, both verbally and bodily. Many therapists consider that any kind of physical contact with the client is unadvisable. Some Freudian analysts even sit outside the client's field of vision. So therapy depends greatly on the ability to use words with accuracy, sensitivity and delicacy, and on the signals which we give each other when we do or do not speak. When two people interact, those interactions are played out in a variety of registers. For the client, it is the tone and style as well as the accuracy of the therapist's contributions which can make the difference between helping and hurting.

The pattern of a psychoanalyst's interventions may be very different from what the layperson is used to: for example, they do not follow the conventions which cover 'turn-taking' (see Wardhaugh, 1986:289) in normal speech. If they occur out of the blue, at times which do not correspond to the cues of familiar discourse, then the client can feel taken aback by them. Her ensuing response could be influenced by that feeling of surprise. When we are startled, we respond without reflection. The client's immediate, impulsive reaction might well have significance, but it should not necessarily be assumed that it is the same as a properly considered one.

What the practitioner says can be heard in different ways. For example, I remember my analyst referring at one point to his 'chucking me out' at the end of sessions, but I did not take advantage of the opportunity to discuss how I felt about this. His description seemed to me exaggerated and unnecessarily dramatic, out of keeping with what actually took place. Disconcerted, I could not find a fitting response. It took me a while to work out why I felt confused and, at the time, I said nothing. A practitioner may not realise that his client's confusion is semantic. Often we are unaware of the effect of the words we use.

For me, psychoanalytic therapy served to create feelings of discomfort partly because the pattern of communication was unfamiliar in its sparsity. Unease can then be aggravated by comments which have no sense for the client, by the starkness of an interpretation or by an absence of any expression of feeling. The fact that my analyst was not, in theory, judgemental did not, on its own, mean that I felt comfortable with him. The principles of neutrality and abstinence can make the practitioner's responses seem inauthentic or uncaring, and therefore distort the true intent of the relationship. There can be a thin line between objectivity and what appears to be aloofness or indifference.

Language can obfuscate or mystify; it can have the effect of disowning responsibility and of dehumanising. An analytic researcher who studied the transcripts of a series of therapy sessions suggests that impersonal, detached statements 'effectively eliminated the patient in a manner which seems quite inappropriate to a dyadic situation' (Dahl, cited in Malcolm, 1980:87). Dahl refers to the possibility of therapy then becoming 'psychological murder by syntax'.

In his discussion of the difficulties involved in working with psychotic patients, the psychologist Don Bannister talks about how much we are influenced by communication and how 'if we can't talk to someone, we become very disturbed by them' (Bannister in Dryden, 1997:177). If we reverse the roles for a moment, we might ask if it is possible for this to happen to the client in therapy. When therapists do not talk to their clients in a way that seems genuine, what is its effect? Might the client become disturbed?

The more dry and formal a therapist is, the more the client may feel alienated from the process of communication. If the practitioner clicks into therapy-speak, the exchange starts to feel discordant. It is difficult then to continue with what one wants to talk about. Telling a practitioner that one finds his language inaccessible, or pretentious and insincere, may not feel like a viable option. One may then feel obliged to choose between engaging in a conversation which seems phoney, asking the therapist to rephrase what he has said, or saying nothing at all.

I have experienced this feeling of falseness with a friend who has recently done a counselling course. It is tragic. We are in the middle of a feisty, vigorous and sensitive talk about our feelings and relationships, and suddenly the counselling-tape switches itself on. It saddens me because, in that moment of change-over, I know we have lost what makes our dialogue fruitful, because I have momentarily lost the real person behind the sentence. The counsellor/person I am talking to is lost too, having retreated into a theory about how we think and behave rather than staying with what feels real.

Bannister finds himself struggling because he feels that his patients 'pretend' to talk to him. From the client's point of view, this is how it can seem in certain styles of psychotherapy, if one feels one is getting a series of prescribed formulas from one's interlocutor rather than an informed and accurate response which is also heartfelt. The relationship then feels like a pretence, a betrayal of the trust one has placed in the therapist and a denial of what one is trying to achieve.

Bannister describes the situation in which a patient 'is apparently communicating, explaining, offering you something in the way of talk and yet what you get is something that is not communication, something simply baffling or frightening' (Dryden, 1997:178). He says that he feels as if the psychotic 'has broken part of the contract we had between us. I think there is an unwritten contract between people, an agreement to try to explain their feelings and desires to each other and to try to do that to the best of their ability. The psychotic has secretly torn up that contract'. When my analyst was elusive, or used esoteric language, or said things which did not seem right, and when he appeared unready to accept what I said to him, that is what I felt he had done. A psychotherapist's behaviour can be baffling or frightening for the client too.

According to Andrew Marshall, president of the Men's Counselling Association: 'Counselling is a female language. It's what women do naturally over the kitchen table without even being aware of it. Men don't have the language.' Regardless of their gender, do therapists always have the appropriate language? There are no diplomas in emotional literacy. In addition, male and female modes of thinking and expression differ, so this might create problems in understanding in some therapy relationships, despite a thorough training.

Is there sufficient emphasis on the relevance and power of words in training courses? For example, are concepts from linguistics such as communicative competence used to full advantage? Or might training inadvertently encourage the use of set phrases and formulations which confound the client, or make the encounter seem unreal or even ridiculous? The exchange then belongs more to the therapist than it does to the client.

In any context, it is necessary to consider 'speech acts' not only in terms of the words they contain but also in terms of what linguists call their 'illocutionary force' (see, for example, Searle, 1969; Austin, 1962). The same utterance might be a suggestion, a statement of fact, a request for information, a warning, a piece of advice, an invitation, giving permission, an order, an apology, or a reprimand. In therapy, the way in which we hear what is said will be particularly affected by the setting and by how we feel, so a suggestion, for example, may not be heard as such.

When a therapist offers a point of view, does he always make it clear that he is simply venturing an opinion by using phrases such as 'I may be wrong, but...' or 'This is only my view, but...'? Does he ensure that the client has understood what he has said? And does he take the trouble to check out the accuracy of his understanding? How many practitioners say things like: 'What do you think?', 'Am I getting it right?', 'Is that what you mean?' If a therapist does not do this, he increases the risk both of getting things wrong and of giving the impression that he thinks he is always right.

Does a psychotherapy training sometimes make practitioners less rather than better able to communicate with their clients? Can it get in the way of effective communication, and suppress the spontaneity and individuality which are essential elements of creative interchange? For example, humour is, for many of us, an important part of the way we interact. In most exchanges, I feel able to move easily between seriousness, irony and jest, and to be correctly understood at a variety of levels. But, in the context of psychotherapy, comments which are made tongue in cheek may well be taken seriously, sometimes resulting in serious misunderstandings.

My analyst's seeming unwillingness to share my occasional laughter was, for me, a major obstacle in our relationship. It served to reinforce a deep – and, at the time, unconscious – fear in me that he did not wish truly to share anything of me, because it was not worth sharing. And it prevented me from expressing myself in a way which was, from my point of view, natural and free.

It has been said that the client often wants the therapist to be like a friend. What I wanted was for my analyst to communicate with me in a way which felt straightforward and comfortable, not so very different from the sort of dialogue that I, and probably he, has when discussing life's vicissitudes with friends round the kitchen table. Of course, we go to therapy because it offers something other than friendly conversation. But the language it uses has to link and clarify rather than divide and confound. Therapy has been called the 'talking cure'. But, if the talk is counterproductive, creating apprehension and getting in the way of understanding, then the therapy session, in itself, becomes a destabilising experience.

Naming experience well is what helps to make us sane, and this is a key area of expertise in a therapist's job. Discrimination is part of his art, and discrimination entails an ability to conceptualise finely and to land smoothly on what is the most apt word. Therapy needs to distinguish clearly between opinion and hypothesis, desire and intention, motivation and consequence, need and convenience, between a suggestion, a request and a statement of fact, between fantasised wishes and actual expectation, and to elucidate these correctly. If it is to be constructive, it needs to place them all in a context of healthiness.

Therapy cannot feel healthy if the therapist fails to employ a language of health. Does he sometimes do exactly the opposite? Isn't it primarily the vocabulary of psychological disturbance which informs the concepts framing the work of much psychotherapy?

In his wish to use skilfully the tools his training has given him, is the psychoanalytic practitioner sometimes too ready to look for explanations in terms of complexes, neurosis, disorder, defence, avoidance, denial, repression, projection?

These terms, of course, simply describe what goes on in our psyche, and they will probably not be employed directly with a client in any case. Used intelligently, such concepts will often provide useful insights and open doors. Undiluted, without balance, or in the hands of an unskilled practitioner, they might be a source of consternation rather than offering inspiration. And there may be other ways of looking at things which are actually more illuminating.

Our modes of behaviour exist on a continuum. So, in looking at how we might modify our responses, which end of the continuum do we begin from? Do we work from the basis that we are more or less insane, rather than more or less sane? Are practitioners inadvertently encouraged to stick unhelpful and unfitting labels on their clients, pathologising rather than improving their self-image? And how might these concepts affect the way the client thinks the therapist perceives her?

Much of the language and many of the ideas of therapy have become part of our common culture, so clients will probably be familiar with some of them. Words such as 'denial', 'fixation', 'regression', 'repression' have – in everyday language – a negative connotation, creating the feeling that we are doing something 'bad'. For example, 'to deny' implies deceit, it has the meaning of 'to refuse to admit' (*Chambers 20th-Century Dictionary*). 'Disown' means 'to refuse to own or acknowledge as belonging to oneself'. The words, and the inherent element of refusal, feel very different from the concept that 'I have not realised . . .', 'I am unaware of . . .', or even 'I do not choose to dwell on this because to do so does not seem productive or helpful'.

So the concepts of psychoanalysis – indirectly, as well as through our uninformed and crude, everyday encounters with them – might have an adverse affect on the client's self-perception. This may happen regardless of what the therapist actually says to her. Can they, in themselves, steer us towards a notion that we are naturally unhealthy rather than naturally healthy?

The labels which we risk pinning on ourselves when we engage in psychotherapy are not only those which describe how we may, or may not, behave. They also describe the hat I wear when I am sitting in the therapy room. I may be a client – someone who, the dictionary tells us, is 'a vassal, dependant or hanger-on, a customer, one who employs a professional adviser'. Or I may be a 'patient', 'a person under medical or surgical treatment'. So does this mean I am 'being treated' because I am 'sick'? In therapy, one does not experience the same sort of detachment from one's sense of self as one has when discussing a damaged knee cartilage. When I go to a professional psychoanalyst, do I then become an 'analysand' – and what does that mean?

The labels which are pinned on to the practitioner are rarely neutral. They may affect our expectations and sometimes lead us in the wrong direction. For example, counselling is defined in the dictionary as meaning 'giving advice', something which, in reality, counsellors don't usually do. An analyst 'separates things into their component parts' and 'traces things to their source' – something which the client should be doing as well; so perhaps a better name for the client might be 'co-analyst'? A therapist is someone with 'curative power' – but how many fit that description?

When a practitioner is known as 'a Jungian' or 'a Freudian', this might sound rather impressive to a layperson. If we are not very careful, we might assume, even unconsciously, that the person so named must be some kind of blueprint, imbued with large quantities of insight and skill, and then we forget that the reality may not be at all like that. And how does such vocabulary influence the practitioner's view of himself?

Any kind of encounter is a cooperative venture in which

> speakers and listeners tend to accept each other for what they claim to be ... I will judge your words against the 'face' you are presenting ...
> We will be involved in what Goffman (1955) has called 'face-work', the work of presenting faces to each other, protecting our own face, and protecting the other's face. (Wardhaugh, 1986:284)

Studies show that we are strongly influenced by the labels we use, so it is incorrect to claim that the client is free to choose whether or not she is influenced by such terms.

The associations which accompany much of the language of therapy might help to create a covert, unspoken skew to what we feel when we walk into the therapy room. Perhaps these associations sometimes linger in a practitioner's psyche. Regardless of what he actually says, does the therapist see the client as someone who is suffering or as someone who is sick? And what emotions do each of these terms evoke in him?

The terminology which a professional acquires might render him less humane, less generous, precisely because he is talking to a client/patient. Taking on the jargon might carry with it a danger that normal human-beingness is ring-fenced – classed, seen and treated as illness or, conversely, that illness is seen impatiently – as something which the client/patient has brought on herself.

Robert Johnson (1991:2) argues that, in endeavouring to understand our emotional lives, we are hampered by the fact that the English language is 'bankrupt' in this respect. In addition, can the vocabulary of psychoanalysis be restrictive and depressing? What about exuberance, passion, hope, the inspiration of the spirit, the power of the imagination, the strength of the will, the potential of the human heart? Where is their language? Therapy should be about soul-making. The process of soul-making reaches into music, art, dance, poetry, the spiritual and philosophical as well as the psychological. It invites us to further our acquaintance with magic and mystery, to explore the metaphorical richness of fantasy.

If they are to be used to bring about healing, the language and concepts of psychotherapy need as a backdrop a balanced view of human nature. It is a positive perspective, more than anything, which the therapist needs to hold. John Welwood, in his book *Awakening the Heart*, says the therapist must

> stay attuned to the client's inherent intelligence and positive life directions . . . When a therapist can maintain a larger awareness of the client's inherent goodness and well-being . . . this provides a model for how a client can begin to trust himself. (Welwood, 1985:xii)

A therapist's thinking and his lexical repertoire should include ways of representing such a model. If he does trust in 'the client's inherent goodness', then this needs to be manifest, because it will help to build the feeling of being held which is so vital. At the same time, though, the language of therapy should avoid setting up false expectations by appearing to make promises that cannot be kept.

Person-centred therapy is said to offer the client the experience of being given unconditional regard. But one can never get around the fact that, whatever is on offer in therapy, it comes with a price tag. The regard is given in return for a fee. From the client's point of view, it is difficult sometimes to get away from the reality that the 'unconditional positive regard' is something we have bought. So it seems a less authentic bargain than one with someone who says, for example, 'I will give you unconditional regard if you are nice to me, or if you do what I want' – even though these are extortionate arrangements. The regard depends on my ability to pay money – something which, for most people, is limited and temporary – rather than on an inner resource: my ability to give something of myself.

In any case, 'unconditional' acceptance will extend only as far as the therapist can extend himself. The work will be limited by the character, motivation and potential of both the client and the practitioner. So there is nothing unconditional about it. For a therapist to believe, or to imply, that this is what he is able to provide is, at best, misleading and, at worst, arrogant and foolish. The promise of this type of therapy is a myth. But does the client have to believe in the myth in order for the myth to touch her? And how can a myth be measured and packaged and sold?

The psychodynamic approach 'takes into account the impossibility of the counsellor ever being able to become the type of good and loving parent whom the client might have wished for' (Jacobs, 1988:14). In this respect, he is perhaps more honest than his colleague practising a person-centred approach. I did feel, in my second experience of therapy, that I was given consistent positive regard, and that I benefited as a result. But 'unconditional' means 'absolute, unlimited', which is unlikely to be the case.

Therapists sometimes describe the process they offer as one of 'containment'. But what and how much might be contained? The container will hold only what the therapist wishes and is able to hold. The practitioner's limitations need to be recognised if the therapy is to be truthful, though the therapist's own vulnerabilities may then serve to reinforce the client's past feelings of being uncontainable. Sometimes those problems the client most needs to talk about might be the very things the therapist cannot deal with successfully himself. The concept of a container is a deceptive and dangerous misnomer.

Another phrase which arises in descriptions of therapy is 'a safe place'. To say that therapy offers a safe place where 'healing can occur' is assuming a great deal. Healing may not occur, and in whose mind lies the concept of safety? A relationship with a therapist is, by its very nature, an intimate one, and intimate relationships often do not feel safe because they expose us to the risk of being deeply hurt. The harder we try to get things right, the more painful it is when they seem to go wrong. If the client does not feel safe in a place where she thinks she is supposed to feel safe, this can compound her anxiety. And what happens if the therapist doesn't feel safe? Psychotherapy is a hazardous journey to an unknown destination in which we are each dependent on our travelling companion.

The client may be encouraged to believe that, for the time that she is in it, the consulting room is 'her space'. But it is actually the therapist's, and he has an agenda too which will inevitably impinge upon the client's. 'The arena in which individual therapy takes place is constructed essentially by the therapist' (Aveline, 1996:377). Doesn't the practitioner expect his clients to proceed according to his rules?

The language of therapy is about a finely struck balance between newness and familiarity. Contrived, self-conscious exchanges sound silly and are an insult to the intelligence of the unfortunate client who is caught up in them. They do little to help us understand and learn. The practitioner must be prepared and able to evolve a mode of communication which is shared and which has mutual validity. Only if he is, will the interaction then represent the uniqueness of that particular client/practitioner relationship and give it a truth of its own. Only if he is, will the space then belong to both of them.

Chapter 6

Blind alleys

When I first went to therapy, I was not familiar with the notion of 'interpretation'. I think at the time I took it for granted that psychoanalytic theories were correct, so had more faith in what my analyst said than in my own intuition. In reality, making connections at a genuine, experiential level between our childhood attributions and the feelings and behaviour they may still evoke is often difficult. It can be equally difficult to be sure about the relevance of the conflicting drives and desires of infancy to which the psychoanalyst may allude. After all, 'an interpretative response is aimed ... at elucidating unconscious feelings or ideas, of which the client is unaware' (Jacobs, 1988:35).

When adults talk about thoughts, feelings, experiences, they usually do so using the language and cognition of adults. When we discuss our early lives, we base our exchanges on adult interpretations and observations of children and on our adult memories of childhood. Many of the feelings described by psychologists are, if their theories are right, experienced at a time when the infant has no language with which to describe those feelings. We cannot be sure if experts on child development have made the right interpretations, and maybe we never will know.

It is not always possible to express our memories and feelings through language alone, or to use words with the subtlety and precision needed to describe experience exactly. (The poet seems to get nearest to the mark.) What we say in therapy will never be more than our best shot at the truth at that particular moment, especially if we are talking about something in the past. We may think, with hindsight, 'That wasn't exactly what I meant'. The intensity and strict timekeeping of therapy might make this more likely. Nevertheless, our words may set up a particular train of thought in a practitioner's mind.

As adults, we can never entirely reinhabit the country of childhood, so we often have only imprecise data to refer back to. Our recollections and reconstructions will not necessarily be based on fact and will be, at best, uneven. And, in therapy, we are being closely observed by the therapist, which has an influence of its own. It is as if we are in the studio, rather than out on location, and the camera is constantly running.

For all these reasons, interpretations and theories which try to link our present to our past can rarely be more than tentative. Yet many practitioners see them as a cornerstone of their work. For the client, trying to remember and interpret how we felt in the past can sometimes be like a game of Chinese whispers.

When my analyst linked particular emotions to specific events in the past, I often had difficulty in making such connections, because I was unable to remember clearly how I had felt at the time. I could not say one way or the other. For example, on one occasion, when I was talking about my mother, he suggested that perhaps I had resented the birth of my younger sister. I may have, but I had no memory of this and do not consciously feel jealous of her; my sisters and I have always been close. Looking back, I don't think the incident I was describing was to do with jealousy or envy, but was about something entirely different.

Because I could not remember 'correctly' what had made me feel a certain way, I felt at times under considerable pressure. It began to seem a bit like *Mastermind*, and I was rarely sure of the answer. Sometimes my analyst was right but the connections did not link up in a way that, at that stage, allowed me to make sense of them.

When I met with my analyst for the first time, he asked me what I remembered about my childhood. My answer was and still is: the sea. I remember the awe and exuberance and delight of an eight-year-old girl alone on the beach early one summer morning with the tide way out and only the seagulls for company, the rush of the wind, salt taste in my mouth, a strong body and an open mind, bare feet running on vast hard soft wet sand, the warmth of the sun, the wide horizon, and the magic and gleam and splosh and pull of the sea. That is what I most value and cherish and remember. But my analyst did not seem interested, and we never spoke about it again.

Whose truths do we investigate during therapy? The client's, or that of the therapist, or of the particular school of thought which the therapist follows? Who decides what is and isn't a problem? Interpretations regarding both the past and the present should be experimental and open to discussion. Yet many clients fail to realise this, and to challenge their therapist's suggestions when they feel they are inappropriate.

Psychodynamic work is 'not...an exercise in brain-washing (although there are some similarities to desensitisation and reeducation in behaviour therapy)'. Nevertheless, it 'lays stress on the constant repetition of an interpretation...As long as an interpretation appears to make sense to a client, it is essential to go on repeating it' (Jacobs, 1988:105). But who actually decides what 'makes sense'?

My analyst sometimes used innuendo and allusion, said things which, to me, seemed ambiguous and open to interpretation. Looking back, I wonder why I didn't simply ask him what he meant, or why he had said what he said. But I didn't ask, because it seemed somehow impolite to do so, and because I did not want to appear stupid. Instead, I dithered or I said I didn't know.

Of course, no therapist would deny the precariousness of offering interpretations, or that he may sometimes get things wrong. But what if, when he does get things wrong, the client – keen to listen to what the therapist is suggesting, to make progress, and not to be defensive – unwittingly adds to the momentum, causing them to collude in embarking on the wrong track? Confusion and counter-confusion follow.

When a client disagrees with her therapist, she may not neces-sarily say so. When I felt my analyst was wrong, I didn't know whether he really was wrong or whether he could see something that I could not see. So I left it to simmer, added it to the pot. Now, of course, I wonder why I never said 'No, I don't think that's right'. Instead, I found myself thinking, lemming-like, 'So is that what I think/want/feel...why I do such and such? Now I know.'

With my second therapist, things felt very different. There seemed to be more elasticity, more place for reflection and for focusing on how I felt. What she said usually made sense to me and disagreements – if they arose – were never a problem. My experience of working with two very different practitioners has suggested to me that, when what a therapist says is right, it feels right. And it registers in a particular way, even if it is not necessarily very pleasant.

What happens if we get stuck when something does not ring true, but we cannot see a way forward to truth? A psychoanalyst, in particular, is often skilled at deflecting attention away from himself and back on to the client. The client may then remain in the 'stuckness' rather than requesting or achieving clarification. I felt that it must be my denseness, my lack of clarity about myself and the world, that was the problem. It was, but not in the way that it felt at the time.

My most immediate problem was a lack of awareness, not necessarily of the particular things which we discussed, but of more fundamental, underlying issues: my unwillingness to challenge my analyst, a reticence in admitting that I didn't understand what he meant, and an indiscriminate willingness to follow just about any route that was suggested to me. It was these common denominators characterising our interaction which were to prove so crippling.

When a client is struggling, her therapist may not see that the problem is, in fact, her struggle to realise and to suggest that it is him who is being obscure, or that he might be wrong. In psycho-analytically orientated therapy, it is often assumed that the therapist is more likely to be right than the client. And the more confident and articulate the therapist appears to be, the more the client will feel predisposed to thinking that that must be the case.

In practice, does the practitioner actually draw attention to his possible errors? To what extent does he look at how his misjudge-ment has 'been disowned'? Does he 'track it by its signs' in his own 'moments of anxiety, hesitation, blandness, false cheerfulness' (Brearley, 1996, in his discussion of the way the analyst looks at the analysand's behaviour)? Or do some hope that their mistakes will be forgotten, absorbed by the density of the rest of the work?

What happens if the work of therapy is distorted by an assumption on the part of a practitioner that the client will misperceive the therapist's true nature? In reality, perhaps the client perceives only too well, and it is the therapist who does not like what he hears. What happens if a practitioner is unwilling to acknowledge his own feelings, and so works on the basis that it is probably all in the client's imagination? Does he then fail to appreciate the ways in which his personality and behaviour affect those with whom he works?

If a client thinks that her therapist is envious, or ashamed or angry, this is likely to be seen by the therapist as the client's projection – it is actually the client who feels these things, but she projects them on to the therapist to avoid the discomfort they engender. Projection is, of course, very different from the process of recognising and accepting feelings in ourselves and also re-cognising and accepting them in other people. In the latter case, we talk about them with the acceptance and understanding of insight, rather than with the denial or guilt which may accompany projection.

When a therapist thinks that the client feels envious or ashamed or angry, this is, in theory, not projection, but accurate thera-peutic insight. It may well be, but what happens if the therapist's insight comes only from outside – from lectures and textbooks – rather than from inside, through real awareness? It may be that the practitioner's understanding is not a part of his felt experience, but remains at a more superficial, verbal level.

Trainee therapists and counsellors learn about themselves, and their fellow human beings, both at a personal, experiential level and at a theoretical one. It is unlikely that many practitioners will have a felt sense of every area of feeling and behaviour which is covered in the theory. If the therapist is not comfortable with the problem that is being dealt with, how will this affect the client? If he experiences feelings of discord or conflict when it is discussed, what might he then project? Who is more discomforted by notions of anger, jealousy, sexuality – infantile or adult – the therapist or the client?

For instance, a New York analyst describes how difficult she used to find it to talk about orgasm (see Malcolm, 1980:82). If this is so, it is unlikely that the client will not pick up the therapist's feelings of unease. It may be that the client does not usually feel uncomfortable discussing sexual matters, or that what would otherwise be no more than a slight awkwardness is increased because of the practitioner's apprehension. The client may also feel uneasy because she is aware that the therapist is uneasy about feeling uneasy, and trying hard not to be. Yet a sense of inhibition or emotional charge in the therapy room might be attributed solely to the client, regardless of who it really belongs to and who is experiencing the greater strain.

If a therapist's insights are merely words, and not accompanied by a genuine embrace of what is being talked about, does any tension or judgement still hanging round its edges in his own mind get transferred on to the client? Might the client's resistance then be a resistance to the emotional baggage which is attached, unconsciously, to what the therapist is saying – and, more specifically, to the practitioner's efforts to attribute his discomfort to the client, rather than take responsibility for it himself?

Holding on to one's own truth can be a struggle in psychotherapy. For example, a practitioner thinking in terms of projection may, when I talk about another person's behaviour or emotions, suggest, 'Perhaps it's you who feels...'. He cannot be entirely wrong, since we all contain aspects of everything that makes us human. But perhaps, in this particular case, it is the behaviour of the other person which is more relevant. The therapist's suggestion can appear to infer that the responsibility of the other is somehow waived, or that one's response to his or her behaviour is invalid, or that his or her influence is immaterial. For the client who frequently feels that things are her fault, such an approach can make her feel there is no way out of her difficulties.

Because we are not always conscious of what drives us, any interpretation or explanation is, potentially, valid. Because we are so complex, it is impossible to say 'I have never said, felt, done that'. So what the therapist says may well be true to a degree, but less influential overall than he implies. Therapy may then overemphasise difficulties, giving them a significance which is disproportionate to the overall picture. We forget about the 'Yes, but...'s.

As we become attuned to psychoanalytic mode, do we turn a deaf ear to what logic, common sense and gut feeling tell us? This must, we begin to think, tell me something about my inner reality. Did I feel this way about my mother? Am I being defensive? Am I denying, repressing, projecting? And, if I have spent my life denying vital truths, does this mean there is a sort of underlying deviousness in much of what I do? The spiral begins. If it isn't denial, it's resistance and if it isn't resistance then it's rationalisation.

If I disagree with what my therapist says, he can infer that I am denying it, that it is something I am unable or unwilling to look at. If this angers me, my anger can be taken as a further indication of my need to deny. I am being defensive, so what the therapist says must be true:

> The traditional attitude is categorical, as the chapter on 'Interpretation and its application' in Fromm-Reichmann's *The Principles of Intensive Psychotherapy* shows: 'If a patient gets upset or angry about an interpretation, this is usually indicative of its being correct ... otherwise the patient would not react so strongly to the interpretation.' (France, 1988:169)

This concept is well-known. So I may try not to get angry, in case my anger is misinterpreted. If the therapist constantly puts the ball back into the client's court, he can create a vicious circle which leaves her feeling that she has nowhere to go.

Once again, the centrality of the practitioner's attitude and mode of communication cannot be ignored. His comments might appear to promote a negative, somewhat tortured, gloss on life. For example, when a problem arose with my employers, my objection to what they had done was interpreted by my analyst as illustrating that perhaps I got pleasure from 'making trouble'. In reality, I have a dread of being a nuisance, but I did not have the presence of mind to say so, or to point out that my principle motive was a wish to be treated fairly and honestly. I once told my analyst that I thought he made the work of therapy sound extremely grim. 'It is grim,' he said. This sort of attitude will hardly inspire the client with hope.

A resistance to notions which feel inaccurate should be encouraged rather than disparaged. Some of the interpretations which analytic practitioners offer can be insulting or absurd to the client. For example, a client describes how her analyst, 'Sybil', attributed her love of dancing when she was a child 'to hermaphroditic yearnings, satisfied by the wearing of unisex leotards' (France, 1988:168). This interpretation might say more about the analyst than it does about the client, suggesting a rather stiff, repressed person who has never experienced the sheer joy of dance. If Sybil had been a good dancer, she probably would not have responded in this way, complicating and distorting something which is a basic source of pleasure and self-expression.

The client, like me, 'did not like to contradict my otherwise much respected therapist', even though she had never actually worn a leotard. France points out how such assertions defy logical discussion. Yet the client is expected to take this kind of thing seriously. Ann France finds many examples of 'force-feeding' of interpretative clichés and inappropriate stereotypes both in the literature and in her dialogue with other analysands.

Discussions about what may or may not be an unconscious feeling or conflict can go on for ever and become a cul-de-sac. Clients may well run away from what we find distressing, but we do not always behave in this way, and it is a gross distortion to suggest that a client gets angry because she has heard the truth. She may get angry because she feels that her point of view, her problem, has not been heard, rather than because an alternative view has been suggested. And, if a therapist is wedded to the questionable – and inherently disrespectful – sort of logic expressed in Fromm-Reichmann (above), his client can feel trapped by the notion that any objection proves that the therapist's suggestion is correct. Her objection might be to the fact that her feelings – even though she may have misperceived – have been so peremptorily dismissed.

When practitioners reflect on difficulties regarding their interpretations, do they tend to focus on the client's resistance rather than on ways of working through misunderstandings together? In one case history, the analyst says 'when I make an interpretation he does not like, he immediately becomes defensive and mulish' (Casement, 1996:99). Does a client behave like this because the therapist is right and the client does not like what she hears, or could there be other reasons? For example, it might feel as if the therapist is experimenting with an interpretation, but attaches more significance to the way the client reacts rather than to what she actually says in response. This is reminiscent of Skinner and rats, and few clients want to be the object of an experiment.

It is important to be clear about exactly what it is that a client 'resists' or dislikes, and to work through the feelings that block cooperation between the therapist and the client. In any context, we respond both to the content of what is said – and whether or not it rings true – and also to the person who says it. On the receiving end of therapy, our natural propensity for reading a range of meanings or significance into what we hear will be heightened by the intensity of the atmosphere. The way we feel about the practitioner and his behaviour and attitudes, and the detail of a particular interpretation, are two separate things. Does the client dislike the therapist's tone? Might she need time to absorb and reflect on what has been said? Is she angry because the practitioner has told her rather than helping her to discover something for herself?

If one feels one is being assessed rather than heard, it is hard to identify and draw attention to the feeling of not being heard, and to its consequences. One is trying to do two things – to take on board the new and possibly helpful suggestion, whilst at the same time grappling with a feeling of 'Yes, but did you hear what I said and do you accept that, even though I might have misunderstood, that is how I have been feeling until you pointed out that there is another way of looking at it?' And, if we feel we are being 'examined', it is difficult to have the confidence to reject what we sense is erroneous, or to have the presence of mind to point out the strain of feeling one is under a microscope.

Alternatively, an apparent dogmatism on the part of the practitioner in making interpretations may inadvertently fuel any tendency on the client's part towards thinking that the therapist will 'sort the client out'. He may actually discourage her from believing in herself and in her potential to become her own therapist. The client is 'socialized to act as a patient' (Goldfried, 1985:65). For some clients, the label 'patient', in the context of therapy, is hardly encouraging, and does the opposite of fostering self-confidence.

I took everything my analyst said seriously, and many of his comments were very astute. However, looking back, I do now feel confident in saying that some of them were irrelevant, far-fetched or illogical. But at the time I was seduced. I had fallen for therapy and, as a result, my truth and my common sense too often took a back seat. Instead of rejecting ideas that felt out of place, I tried to find meaning in them.

A therapist can easily cultivate insecurity and acquiescence. For example, there is a world of difference between a genuine question – one which seeks to discover unknown information – and a question which hopes to elicit what the questioner thinks he already knows. In language teaching, questions designed to elicit a predetermined response are known as 'display questions'. They are a pretence, simply a means of extracting the required piece of language. They are now discouraged, because they hide their true significance – as questions – and are felt to be patronising to the learner.

In therapy, an opinion dressed up as a convoluted question leaves the client in a kind of linguistic limbo-land. We can disagree with an unambiguously phrased opinion – provided we have the confidence to do so. We can endeavour to find answers to an authentic question. But a ventured supposition put in a round-about way because, in theory, it sounds less authoritarian, is neither one thing nor the other. It can make it more difficult for the client to disagree – because it has been presented as a 'maybe', and maybes always contain the potential to be seen as the truth.

With friends and family, we feel justified in making the asser-tion that 'That's just your opinion'. With a therapist, it is difficult for the client to remember that, in the end, that is also the case. We pay for therapy because – rightly or wrongly – we expect to hear there what is true, and not what is untrue. But my reluctance to disagree with my analyst was not just because I saw him as an expert, a figure of authority, or because of my need for his approval; it also came from a desire to see myself clearly, to consider every possibility, look at every angle.

When I went into therapy, I was open to suggestion. I tried to leave behind old ways of seeing things and to investigate new perspectives. So is the client sometimes a blank wall for the ther-apist's projections? When a psychotherapist offers his view, is it sometimes he who is making a 'Freudian slip'? Therapists make their clients the object of their negative projections, as well as the other way around.

Despite a theoretical commitment to neutrality, are some practitioners so geared up to the notion of interpreting that they actually forget to listen to what is being said? The therapist might also forget that what the client most needs at the time may not be an interpretation, but an acceptance and understanding of her present feelings. And does he genuinely believe that he may, quite often, be wrong?

Therapists who counter disagreements with further attempts to justify their own theories show scant respect for the person they are talking to. They also risk making therapy into a self-fulfilling prophesy. Lewis Carroll (in *The Hunting of the Snark*) said 'What I tell you three times is true'. Therapists can be very insistent and, if disagreement is taken to be proof that they are right, there is little the client can do. If the client's rejection of what the practitioner says is interpreted as resistance, as evidence of further problems, and if this happens often enough, she may be brainwashed into accepting the 'expert's' view of things instead of developing one which is truly her own. There is a fine line sometimes between reexamining our own beliefs and simply replacing them with someone else's.

Apparent defensiveness, then, might be an attempt to refute what is not valid. In reality, it may be the therapist who is being defensive – of his own ideas and self-image – and who, in failing to recognise that this is the case, projects it on to the client. Does the practitioner really allow the client equal rights in deciding what her problems might be about, and does he acknowledge this clearly? If a client does not feel confident in her therapist in this respect, then the practitioner may well meet resistance.

Mistakes may go unchallenged because we do not always simply agree or disagree with what other people tell us. We sometimes absorb rather than react to what comes from those around us, and the extent to which this might happen in therapy must be fully considered. Some clients might be especially absorbent, and highly sensitive to the defences, projections, complexities and vulnerabilities of other people. In the concentrated air of the therapy room, and in a context where the client allows herself to be naked and open, such sensitivity can be heightened.

When a therapist gets things wrong, which he is bound to do at times, does the agenda switch, and become the practitioner's agenda rather than the client's? It has been said that dream interpretations usually reflect the training and personal convictions of the therapist, so it is reasonable to suggest that this might be true of other types of interpretation.

Maybe the client does not fit the practitioner's particular perspective or theory. Maybe Freud, Jung and Klein were sometimes wrong. Or what if they were all right? If each of them shone a light on one particular aspect of our nature, then none of them painted a complete picture. And perhaps none of it is as important to the client as it was to the person who first thought of it. What if the therapist ends up being the one who cannot see the wood for the trees?

Ironically, the greater one's desire for honesty, the more entangled one can get. An intuitive awareness of our true feelings may, inadvertently, be stifled by the practitioner, who instead rekindles feelings of rejection or insecurity. When he infers that the client may be talking about 'something else', this can reproduce the queasy childhood feeling of not being believed, causing us to question what we instinctively feel to be true. An insistence on the notion of an underlying problem can become a habit in psychoanalysis – a habit which is catching. It can set up, in the analysand, a downward spiral of self-doubt, giving a certain credence to Jeffrey Masson's view that 'blaming the victim . . . is the hallmark of psychotherapy' (Masson, 1992:46).

With a practitioner who does not reassure and who frequently remains silent, the client can become her own judge and jury, making herself the victim of what has been called the 'persecuting ideal'. 'The analyser becomes the censor . . . [and] must examine every thought' (Krishnamurti, 1978:33). Everything is then called into question. Everything starts to feel problematic. We latch on to the negative, poke holes in legitimate strategies for living, using a stick of predetermined psychodynamic formulations. We become mesmerised by conjecture and hypotheses about what things mean, disappear up blind alleys and lose sight of the target – our wish to make life less stressful and more comprehensible.

One of the things we need to learn in therapy is what to say when we talk to ourselves; we practise a revised internal dialogue. It is important that the dialogue which is set in train enables us to emerge from, rather than become immersed in, the detail of our conflicts. This entails staying in tune with both our ordinariness and our extraordinariness.

Does the seriousness of therapy cause some of its practitioners to lose a sense of perspective? Does expertise then actuate an absence of neutrality, a loss in the capacity for what has been called 'beginner's mind'? Should professionals heed Mark Twain's words: 'The researches of many eminent authorities have already thrown much darkness on the subject and, if it continues, we will soon know nothing at all about it'?

In my experience, there may be a gap of years between discussing something from the past with a therapist and actually realising what its true significance was. We often need to revisit our experiences many times over. On each visit, the territory looks slightly different. If we try to unravel things too quickly, or see them too narrowly, the threads get knotted and we miss what is most important.

The therapist must listen to each client with openness because, although action A may have result B in person C, in person D the outcome might be entirely different. Human beings do not arrive in the world as a *tabula rasa*, a clean slate. But are differences in nature and temperament always sufficiently considered in therapy, since they may be fundamental to the way we deal with life?

We can never be sure how our past has influenced us, or be able to weigh accurately the myriad factors which shape our lives. What about the terror I felt when I read *The Devil Rides Out*, the woman I once met on a train who said she believed in angels, what about Monteverdi, and the sound of the humpback whale?

There is a danger that 'in seeking to recreate the patient's internal and fantasized world of childhood, the [therapist] is perhaps too eager to divorce patients from their social and cultural background' (Cooper, 1996:65). We are affected not only by our families but by the values and conventions of the society we live in, by our peers, our teachers, the type of school we go to, where we live, the extent to which we are exposed – or not – to the nourishing and healing effect of culture and of the natural world.

There may be one single, traumatic event in the past which has had far-reaching repercussions. We often find that profound changes take place in us when we become parents, and children have a powerful impact on their parents' emotions and awareness. There are so many things which brush against us in life.

How many therapy rooms end up as unhelpful pigeon-holes? Isn't it the client, not the therapist, who needs – initially – to be seen as a blank screen? Her individuality should be the driving force of the work. Does the practitioner sometimes forget that each client is unique, and that discovering and appreciating her particular way of being has to be both the starting point and constant theme of the work? Some people might need more rather than fewer defences. We all have different personalities and different needs, and we all have different thicknesses of skin.

The capacity for both experiencing and perceiving pain is a variable which is crucial. In *Women Who Run with the Wolves*, Clarissa Pinkola Estés (1992:494) points out how 'the one with the least "receivers" so to speak will consciously feel the least effect of abuse. The child with the most sensors will consciously feel it all, and perhaps strongly sense the wounds of others as well.' The client who feels most hurt by misunderstandings may also sense the wounds of the therapist and be strongly influenced by them.

If the therapist is not in touch with what is happening, the threads do not loosen and fall into place. The hurt, frustration and confusion of the client may then belong more in the present than in the past. As Estés says:

> it should not be misconstrued that when an adult feels or expresses anger that this is a sure sign of unfinished business in childhood. There is much need and place for rightful and clear anger, especially when previous calls to consciousness . . . have gone unheard. (ibid.)

Therapy is a 'call to consciousness', a call to be heard clearly.

It is only when we have been heard clearly that we can be clear about the times when we are not. I realised this most distinctly after working with my second therapist, Kate. In her, I found someone who genuinely appreciated and respected me and who was not afraid to say so. She accepted and understood what I said and took responsibility for her part in the relationship. Her reflections were plausible, sensitive and refreshing. Blind alleys were rare and, when they appeared, they often turned into highways.

When a therapist is reluctant to take on board things which do not suit him or do not fit his particular framework, it is hampering and demoralising for the client. More than that, it means that, in the end, her truth is spurned and lost. This can lead to mental and emotional chaos rather than resolution.

Children's greatest anger and despair frequently come when they are faced with what they see as dishonesty, hypocrisy or injustice. In adulthood and in childhood, untruths may engender deeply felt passion, a passion which is often commensurate with the degree of certainty in the other person. It has been suggested that 'one of the roots of mental illness is invariably an interlocking system of lies we have been told and lies we have told ourselves' (Peck, 1978:60). Might this sometimes apply to an interlocking system of ill-construed pronouncements in therapy, as well as in our everyday lives?

In therapy, one is in a highly suggestible state. Therapists are in a uniquely powerful position when it comes to putting ideas into other people's heads. And the fewer the therapist's words, the greater might be their weight. If a practitioner does not realise and own his mistakes, the client can be left with them hanging around her neck.

A seemingly insurmountable problem facing an analysand is that, once someone suggests that something is unconscious, anything, in theory, is possible. This gives the therapist tremendous power. Whilst we need to acknowledge that life involves living with uncertainty, this is not the same as presenting a client with a series of uncertainties in the hope – and often the expectation – that she will verify what the therapist has said.

Because the client is frequently unclear herself, it is inevitable that she will not always be heard clearly. But how many therapists seek clarity using the wrong criteria? When something becomes a routine, and a way of earning a living, it is perhaps inevitable that a practitioner – like his clients – can be lulled into a false sense of safety by falling back on what feels familiar, on what his training told him. He may then forget that 'the depth of our ignorance and the absence of objective means for investigating psychotherapeutic theories warrants a cautious and sceptical attitude towards all forms of psychotherapy' (Smith, 1996:38). Not all therapists are blessed with such reassuring dubiety.

A vital part of the therapist's work is an ability to cope with not knowing. He will also need to negotiate ways out of the blind alleys in the labyrinth of the therapy room. But can a psychodynamic model encourage him to press on rather than to backtrack and try an alternative route?

Chapter 7

Transference – cure or catch-22?

Schools of therapy differ in the way that they see and treat transference. Generally speaking, the term 'transference' refers to feelings and behaviour which we 'transfer' from the past. Psychoanalysts define it as 'a hypothetical process in which present-day figures are unconsciously used as surrogates for unconscious images of significant persons from the client's past' (Smith, 1996:33). We all relate to present-day figures in ways which relate back to the past so, in that sense, transference is not hypothetical, it is simply a very real part of the way we behave.

In psychotherapy, transference feelings are perceived as being in some way misplaced, 'that set of ways of perceiving and responding to the world which is developed in childhood and which is ... inappropriately transferred into the adult environment' (Peck, 1978:48). Its 'inappropriateness' is precisely what singles it out for attention. How we distinguish between transference and simple human-beingness is unclear. And who decides what is or isn't appropriate?

According to psychoanalytic theory, 'it is the transference that makes the cure; the client transfers the unresolved past onto the therapist and the therapeutic relationship is there to sort it out' (Zeal, 1992:49). But what if it doesn't 'sort it out'? The two don't necessarily follow. In theory, 'transference becomes the stage upon which the long forgotten dramas of childhood are repeated and reintegrated' (Smith, 1996:33). Old wounds becomes less painful and have less influence. But theory does not always work out in practice. Sometimes these dramas are repeated and reinforced rather than reintegrated.

In theory, 'the so-called resolution of the transference takes place through the client coming to understand (partly intellect-ually, partly experientially) what transference is' (Jacobs, 1988:100). In practice, the 'resolution' of 'the transference' may not take place at all, and it will probably never be complete. It can be a lengthy, complicated and precarious process, dependent as much on the skill and awareness of the therapist as on the commitment of the client. Unsuccessful therapy can leave the client distraught and disturbed, with a nagging sense of failure and unfinished business.

In order for the client to slay the transference dragon, she needs to work in a context which does not undermine her. The procedures of some psychotherapy practice can be seriously undermining. A way of working which deliberately activates 'transference issues' – at the expense of considering the client's wider reality and the quality of the client/therapist relationship – can actually mitigate against those issues being properly worked through. If the client is not given the help and support she needs, and if at the same time the negative aspects of the past are overemphasised, then the practitioner can make it doubly hard for her to free herself from their effect.

Psychodynamic therapy, in particular, can reproduce a great deal of the original pain of childhood, negative feelings which arise from the gap between what we want and what we get. That is, apparently, one of its aims. The practitioner 'forces the client to relive negative experiences which go on influencing the present' (Jacobs, 1988:14). But it will only be therapeutic if we rediscover this pain in a context which is endurable, and which then enables us to change our habits and make more constructive choices.

The client needs to believe that what is happening is, ulti-mately, for her benefit. She needs to feel free to criticise the system of working so that she can work through the childhood dis-appointments it reflects, but she has to maintain her faith in that system in order to emerge from it in a more healthy state than when she began. She needs both to trust the therapist and to have the confidence to shoot him down occasionally. But, if she feels dependent on him, how willing will she be to risk alienating him by questioning the validity of what he says and does? Most of us fear rejection – unless and until we are shown in practice that fear is unfounded.

Do clients always feel able to challenge their therapist, or to tell him what they really feel about him – thereby creating the conditions for their own healing? And do therapists always feel able to accept and respond to this challenge? Inevitably, the answer will be: no, not always. The client may never receive the subtle push needed to get her over the most difficult humps, so it is dangerously naive to assume that the transference will be resolved.

What happens if neither the therapist nor the client has the confidence to deal effectively with challenge? Part of a therapist's job is to enable the client to manage challenge better, whilst also making it clear that he is on her side. His own openness to challenge will help to create an atmosphere where disagreement or protest is not seen as a problem.

The therapeutic alliance – if it really is an alliance – will follow the same principles as those for any good working relationship. It will be one in which each person feels able to ask challenging questions without being regarded as confrontational. Forging such an alliance is the first step in successful therapy, but if strong transference feelings are aroused, this may be less likely to come about. I was not, as far as I can remember, invited by my analyst to question what he said or to suggest he may be wrong, though in my second experience of therapy, this was the case.

In therapy, the client is often coaxed into reexperiencing her childhood feelings. As a child, I was not encouraged to question my 'elders and betters'. Powerfully significant figures in a young person's life – parents, teachers, the family doctor – do not always take kindly to being challenged, and the child may be punished for doing so.

Isn't psychodynamic technique hazardous, because it gets its priorities wrong? It makes 'deliberate use of the transference over and above the actual relationship between counsellor and client' (Jacobs, 1988:15). Yet the client is expected to engage with the therapist at a most intimate level, to draw on her capacity for trust, openness and commitment. The work that is being done involves our most delicate and difficult feelings, and the emotional agony of the sense of shame which so often accompanies them.

I never felt at ease with my analyst. I felt that, in so many ways, he didn't really know me, and he never allowed me to get to know him. He was very good at being a blank screen. I assumed, nevertheless, that he was sincere and well-meaning and, for all our difficulties, I still believe that he was. A therapy virgin, I did not know what it was like to be in a relationship with a psychotherapist. We never observe anyone else in that situation, so we have no precedent. But I had considerable experience of what it feels like to be in relationships with other people, so I mistakenly expected it to be similar in some ways.

This, of course, is one of the basic tenets of analysis – that we transfer or put into the empty space of the therapeutic relationship what we bring from our past experience. But, whatever one's previous experience, one is held by the inescapable fact that the practitioner one is working with is, before and after everything else, a real person. Most of us, therefore, expect him to behave in a way which feels real, and are unprepared for the peculiarities of engaging in psychoanalytic therapy.

When I started therapy, I very much wanted to 'get it right'. I assumed I would get on well with my analyst, since that was how it was with other people most of the time, and since he, in any case, was an expert in human behaviour. I think I must have taken it for granted that, in relating to my analyst, there would be no major problems – precisely because he was an analyst. I saw therapy as a means of improving things in my life outside it, not as a process of misperceiving reality within the therapeutic relationship and then putting the misconceptions to good use.

We learn from our mistakes when we are aware of what they are. But 'in states of transference, patients *unconsciously* treat their therapists as a surrogate for a significant figure from the past' (Smith, 1990:32, my italics). So, despite our good intentions, we may fail to engage in the egalitarian exchange needed in order to sort things out – just as it was when we were children. We may fail to realise that it is entirely appropriate to question a therapist's interpretations, to expect open and honest dialogue, and that it might be what is being offered that is inadequate and misplaced, rather than our own feelings.

When I tried to tell my analyst how his manner and way of working made me feel, he said that perhaps I 'needed to hate him and say negative things about him', thereby completely changing the subject. Perhaps he was hoping I would point out that hating and saying negative things don't necessarily go hand in hand but, in fact, I was wondering why he had put them together. I didn't know what to say because I didn't hate him, but I didn't know if that was what he meant. Did he really think that I hated him, and that this was what I needed to experience, or did he mean that it would be helpful for me if I allowed myself to hate him? My uncertainty pushed me back into a place of doubt and wariness.

Transference feelings are powerful, but often undefined and out of focus, nudging us from behind without declaring their true colours. Sometimes it is their validity – rather than their inappropriateness – which needs to be recognised in therapy. Part of the pain of childhood may derive from the experience of being confronted by an unwillingness to answer questions, an absence of lively creative discussion, a lack of spontaneity, enthusiasm and responsiveness. We may find the practitioner's way of working hard for exactly the same reason. But working on oneself is bound to be difficult. I felt it was my responsibility to learn to deal with my analyst's particular approach, since it was the psychotherapy contract I had undertaken to fulfil.

If our parents did not engage fully with us as children, our subsequent disappointment and frustration may be part of the transference we bring to therapy. But, instead of making us aware of it in a way which is helpful, some practitioners simply give us more of the same. The stance of the enigmatic, and apparently indifferent, analyst can turn therapy into a replay. But the implicit message from the practitioner is that this kind of thing is good for us, it is what makes therapy therapeutic.

There is a difference between a healthy detachment which allows the therapist some measure of objectivity and the kind of detachment which gives the impression there is no real sense of concern and no common ground between practitioner and client. For the client, the therapist's stance can create too great a sense of distance, and thus be counter-productive. At the same time, it may be one of the things that the therapist needs to retain as part of his working model. I felt there was little point in trying to discuss it. I simply tried to live with it.

Transference then kicks in with a vengeance, but the therapist's abstinence forces it to stay on hold. We attempt to get to the top of the slide by climbing up the slide instead of the steps, and then wonder why we keep slipping back down again. It is inevitable that most clients will assume that the therapist knows more than they do about good therapeutic practice, so they go on giving him the benefit of the doubt. It may feel odd but one hopes it will eventually bear fruit.

So the frustration and hurt inherent in the transference that the client arrives with can simply become more ingrained. When transference issues are centralised by the therapist, this can intensify their grip and cause them to rebound nastily. If the relationship between psychotherapist and analysand repeats old patterns of relating but does not work through them then, rather than being constructive, it ties the client's hands behind her back.

Transference is complicated because not all of its manifestations are unconscious. An intuitive sense of self often nudges us into an undefined sort of realisation that what we are experiencing is not apt. In some instances, the client is only too well aware that certain feelings are out of place. So we may then feel less, rather than more, inclined to discuss them. We endeavour not to express or act on them. The transference is no less powerful, but it is held back by the dam of our wish to behave like a mature adult. Children, of course, often yearn to be grown-up, so is that wish, in part, another kind of transference?

In any relationship, the realisation that certain feelings and perceptions are misplaced or inaccurate can be a source of optimism and liberation. But their inappropriateness can also cause us to feel awkward, uncomfortable or even afraid – because it means that we have misunderstood, got things wrong. For many children, getting things wrong brings irritation, anger, blame, ridicule, rejection, punishment or dire threat.

Our survival depends on getting things right, on knowing how to act, on an ability to figure things out. As a child, we may have been put in situations which felt beyond us and suffered from anxiety as a result. Worry about coping and about successful outcomes will then run deep.

Might the context of therapy, in itself, create a feeling of pathology? In our day-to-day lives, unconscious aspects of ourselves are enmeshed and buried. In therapy, on the other hand, they begin to poke their disembodied heads above the parapet. The feelings can then take on a vicarious quality, because they are no longer embedded in their original, natural context. As a result they can seem incongruous, unnatural or abnormal.

The client may also experience things which have more to do with our deeper nature than with our specific history, and which are unfamiliar, uncanny and unsettling. So, if the therapist tries to tack such feelings on to her childhood memories, this multiplies a sense of incongruity. We may end up getting stuck in a kind of halfway house where the feelings are no longer unconscious but where we are still not sufficiently detached from them to look at, understand, and then be less controlled by them.

Within the context of our closest relationships, it is normal to feel intensely, to shout and cry, to crave and complain. When it happened in a formal relationship with a paid professional, I felt extremely silly. It seemed contradictory, not in keeping with present reality. When I was feeling particularly strange, I was abusive and intrusive and, as a result, felt demeaned and foolish. And it is difficult sometimes to describe the hugeness of one's feelings sitting in a small room with a very ordinary man who is about to tell you it is time to finish.

Dealing with the transference can feel impossibly anomalous. If the client is aware that her emotions or behaviour are inappropriate, and if the therapist actually suggests that they are, then this may be accompanied not by an understanding of what transference is, but rather by an acute sense of shame. For example, when we spoke about a telephone conversation in which I had shouted and sworn at my analyst, he reminded me that I had been 'belligerent'. I had been, I was painfully aware of it, and his reminder made me want to crawl out of the room through a crack in the floorboards. Neither of us mentioned the fact that I had also felt extremely confused and frightened at the time.

Shame is a powerful incentive not to make the same mistakes again, and it drives us deeper inside ourselves. If we feel we are behaving 'badly', then therapy can, inadvertently, feel shameful. Like hermit crabs, we dart back into our shell. Our naivety and clumsiness, and our own judgements, trip us up. One is left staring down the barrel of a gun. I felt as if my nose was being rubbed in my mistakes, and more than once left the therapy room with my eyes to the floor.

In theory, the therapist helps the client to recognise the 'as if' quality of the transference, but this does not always happen in practice; it did not happen in my case. The practitioner who remains silent in the hope of his client moving further into understanding should not forget that silence can leave us feeling naked, isolated and alone, in an excruciating place of guilt and embarrassment. Distressing emotions are stirred up, but the discomfort is simply compounded if one is aware that one is feeling and behaving like a prickly, passionate teenager or a frightened, humiliated child.

Because one's behaviour seems out of place and is unexpected, it can bring with it a sense of panic and the mind goes blank. Our adult intelligence then fails to inform us that, if the therapist were doing his job properly, such intense feelings would not have arisen in quite the same way, and we might not be feeling quite so impossibly dazed or lost. I instead concentrated all my efforts into not behaving in a way which felt strange or undignified. Resistance to giving expression to the transference may, therefore, be an attempt to resist behaving inappropriately, and to maintain some kind of dignity.

I remember, a few weeks into therapy, discussing it with a friend who told me about Freud and about how clients live out their past with their therapist. To me, it seemed a crazy idea to get angry with my analyst because thirty years ago my father was particularly hurtful. Giving vent to one's strongest feelings with someone whom one is paying can feel a little like buying the services of a prostitute.

Precisely because the therapist is another human being, the client will not be unaware that he has feelings too. Is her wish to take this into account and to be considerate another kind of transference or, quite simply, a natural, instinctive warmth? Such feelings of consideration are not without foundation in the present, since therapists inevitably find it hard at times to cope. The client may not want to put her therapist on the spot, or act in a way which seems to her to be potentially hurtful and disrespectful. When we behave disrespectfully towards another person we are in some way demeaned ourselves, but the complexity of therapy can blind us to such simple truths.

What is and isn't inappropriate transference from the past, what is and isn't an inevitable and constant part of human nature, or a valid response to the reality of the present relationship, is a minefield. The client may feel she is once again evoking irritation, ridicule, reprimand, rejection or indifference. In some cases, it may actually be the case, so her fears are not always unfounded.

If a therapist is simply a template, he may move into indifference. When he is not, he is a fallible human being who has difficult feelings too and who sometimes gets things wrong.

It may not necessarily be correct to assume that the strong emotions aroused in therapy are attributable to aspects of our other relationships. And is the practitioner sometimes unduly swayed by the fact that it is easier to deal with, for example, another's anger when we are not the cause of it? It has even been suggested that 'transference is a fiction, invented and maintained by the therapist to protect himself from the consequences of his own behaviour' (Shlien, 1984, cited in Spinelli, 1995:163).

Spinelli (ibid.) believes that the concept of transference 'allows therapists to distance themselves – and their own perceptions, emotions, issues and concerns – from the impact of direct, sometimes highly emotional, encounters with their clients'. It gives them a means of avoiding 'the possible meaning of the client's emotional reaction towards him or her as an expression of the client's experience of the current relationship'.

The therapist's behaviour will have significant consequences in the therapeutic relationship. This is what the therapist aims for, otherwise there would be no point in doing therapy. If therapists believe that they can take some credit for evoking new – hitherto unexperienced – feelings of acceptance, tolerance and understanding, for giving the client a positive experience, greater insight and self-awareness, then it follows that sometimes they should also accept responsibility for the negative consequences of their work. Yet therapists seem so often to attribute the client's negative feelings to past experience whilst, at the same time, attributing improvements to the effect of the therapy.

It might be the case, for instance, that the client feels good about herself when she's with her therapist because that is how her parents made her feel. No one can afford to make the assumption that, because she is in therapy, this cannot be the case. But do therapists draw attention to this, or are they more likely to say: 'I'm glad you're finding the therapy helpful. I'll see you next week'? And how many therapists believe that the client feels love for him simply because she has a loving nature, or because he is genuinely helping her, or because he happens to be a lovable person?

> Psychoanalysts think about the transference as a distortion of reality. It carries over from something in the past that you are attaching to the person in the present. The truth is that some current people actually fit what you are carrying over from the past. (Russell, 1992:204)

And don't some 'current people' evoke feelings in us which are not necessarily reminiscent of the past?

For the client, the combination of the relative unnaturalness and rigidity of some psychoanalytic practice – the blank wall – with an aura of emotional intensity can feel bizarre, unexpected and profoundly disturbing. The therapist may become the focus of powerful emotions, whilst appearing to occupy a kind of emotional no man's land himself. He may be idealised, seen as a fountain of wisdom, a key to doors and pathways as yet unexplored. He may become the object of an intense eroticism. But strong feelings of attachment, desire or admiration may not be brought fully to consciousness or be overtly expressed precisely because, to the client, they do not seem to fit with the reality of the therapist/client relationship, or with their respective relationships in the outside world. The client, like the therapist, has a life to live which involves considerations outside the therapy room.

Reticence and confusion will be exacerbated if the client feels she is seen primarily as a fountain of problems. One can begin to fear that the expression of any strong emotion, negative or positive, will add to this perceived perception. My fear in this respect was strongly connected to my past, but I could not see it at the time. To the client, the therapist then appears merely to pose as someone who will help us with our feelings whilst, in reality, failing to address them. This adds to rather than releases the pressure they exert.

A therapist can demonstrate his trust in the client and deepen her trust in him by acknowledging that her feelings about the therapeutic relationship have meaning in their own right. They may have more to do with the kind of person he really is and the way he actually feels and behaves, rather than because he is a surrogate. When these things are part of a dynamic and responsible encounter, the deeper waters of therapy are less likely to become unnavigable.

In my experience, therapy works when the trust between therapist and client becomes an effective and generative reality.

This trust creates and is created by a willingness to share. When we try to modify what another person says as soon as they have said it, we do not share it. So, if a therapist starts giving his opinion about the client's concerns without talking about their legitimacy, he misses out a vital first step. He presses another button, recalling a childhood where concerns were not acknowledged, where the expression of feeling was problematic, or where feelings were not a legitimate subject of discussion. He renews a sense of illegitimacy. Pressing that particular button is not difficult in a society which attaches a stigma to emotional and psychological unease.

A therapist who tries to attribute everything to the client's experience outside therapy, or to what he sees as the symbolic nature of the relationship, may leapfrog over her more immediate concerns. He not only misunderstands why the client is saying what she is saying. He implies that he is not prepared to accept her perception of or feelings about present reality, thereby sapping her confidence and triggering further negative transference. What is the point of trying to express one's feelings if one is not taken seriously?

A common experience in childhood is that of not being believed. Parents, teachers and others in authority often imply that children are being dishonest, or that they have some kind of ulterior motive, when it is not the case. We all have a tendency to tell rather than to ask our children why they behave and feel as they do. We, like therapists perhaps, may do so for the noblest of reasons, because we want to help, we want to teach them. We forget that they have their own truth, from which we can learn a great deal. The feeling of not being believed can arise in the therapy room too, subtly revived by phrases such as 'I think perhaps what you are talking about here is . . . ' or 'Perhaps what that tells us about you is . . . ', particularly when these phrases precede an inaccurate interpretation.

The client's fear in this respect may not be entirely unfounded. For example, in his discussion on openness to challenge, Peck refers to a woman who 'may speak for an hour about unpleasant childhood experiences but neglect to mention that her husband had confronted her in the morning with the fact that she had overdrawn their bank account'. Peck says that 'such patients attempt to transform the psychotherapeutic hour into a kind of press conference. At best they are wasting time in their effort to avoid challenge, and usually they are indulging in a subtle form of lying' (Peck, 1978:57).

Of course, we all avoid talking about things which we find difficult or shameful – but not, perhaps, as frequently as some psychotherapists seem to think. Perhaps the woman in this case felt it was more appropriate to talk about her childhood with her analyst and to discuss her overdraft with her husband or her bank manager. If the woman had talked about her argument with her husband rather than her unpleasant childhood experiences, would the analyst have inferred that she was trying to avoid the challenge posed by dealing with early trauma? Trying to decide what to talk about, and in what order, can be difficult, particularly if one feels that the therapist is likely to judge it in the way that he does in the above example.

If we have not been affirmed and supported in childhood, the fear of this happening again is one we will bring to therapy. The more self-effacing the therapist, the stronger the transference may be. Anxiety can further intensify the transference since, at times of stress, we are more liable to regress to more infantile ways of thinking, feeling and behaving. In promoting regression, the therapist risks splitting the client's 'child' from her adult awareness. The client may then find behaviour which is hurtful and baffling more, rather than less, hard to deal with. The practitioner may 'adopt techniques which permit an optimum level of regression' with the high-handed and somewhat perilous proviso that 'within reason, let-down can be guaranteed not to happen' (Carvalho, 1990:78).

There are no guarantees in therapy. The more impersonal the relationship, the more inclined the client may be to engage at the level of rational rather than emotional understanding. A therapist who is not entirely at ease may also tend to engage in this way, neglecting to pay attention to how the client is actually feeling. Without such attention, the most painful emotions are reawakened but remained unaddressed, at the same time, perhaps, augmenting the client's fear that there is no one who can cope with the way she feels. Internal 'splits' are reinforced and transference lives on, refreshed and refuelled. Transference feelings thus become a kind of catch-22.

Trying to work through an intense transference without skilled and caring guidance is a little like looking for your glasses and not being able to see where they are because you haven't got your glasses on. If a practitioner provokes and then mishandles transference feelings, it can be the equivalent of his treading on your glasses rather than picking them up and handing them back to you, or suggesting you try on a new pair.

In our everyday lives, strength of feeling is tempered by its context – day-to-day living. Our relationships arise naturally out of and are contingent on what we do together; feelings are held and balanced by the ordinariness of getting up in the morning and the business of the day. The ordinariness and the doing act as a kind of padding. In contrast, the intensity and focus of a psychodynamic relationship is out of the ordinary. There is no ballast of shared actions or common background, and the feelings which arise can be overpowering if the therapist does not act to diffuse them.

It can feel unpleasant being analysed by someone who hardly knows you. In the context of the therapy room, under the gaze of the analyst, I felt at times like a laboratory specimen laid out on a bench to be dissected. When I was scraping the bottom of the barrel, he seemed to stay at a safe distance, peering over the rim to lob in the occasional detached observation. In the end, I found my relationship with my analyst – which did not feel like a real relationship – more difficult than those I had gone there to talk about.

In my second experience of therapy, the relationship was intrinsically pleasant, even though the things we looked at might not always have been so. It was an adult relationship with a real, receptive person. When I consciously experienced 'inappropriate' transference feelings about my therapist, it was often when I was not with her. I did not become immersed in them and there was enough emotional distance for me to be able to tell her about them. When difficulties arose, it was often because there were problems on both sides. Every effort was made to address them openly and frankly. Who had what problem was – as far as is humanly possible – acknowledged, and we were both then able to move forward. I will never know about what she chose not to tell me, but the notion of joint exploration was an integral part of our work together.

Regardless of what the therapist chooses to see as most significant in the work, the way in which a practitioner and client spend their time together is real, and it has a concrete and powerful impact. It may be the therapist's behaviour which is inappropriate. When we neglect to pay attention to our relationships, to foster positive and constructive interactions, then they can become, by default, negative and destructive. This often happens without our full awareness.

Isn't it possible that, particularly in a psychoanalytic therapy, the relationship – the way each person behaves – is, in itself, dysfunctional? Remaining in therapy can then feel like a tacit endorsement of a practice which seems inhuman and distasteful.

When therapy is reduced to a kind of mind game, it risks becoming vandalism of the psyche. We cannot truly find ourselves in a technical relationship with a technician of the mind. If we stay in our head, our reason can work against us. When I felt confused, I tried desperately to make sense of what was happening. The more unsure I felt, the more determined I was to keep my wits about me. So I never looked at my feelings of confusion and insecurity. I was too busy trying to survive and, until then, survival had been something I had always been reasonably good at.

Feelings need to be acknowledged and appreciated before their consequences are scrutinised. Therapy is about affirming our feelings and then recognising why they can lead to problems. We need to encourage our reason to work together with a more profound sense of self, by learning to be fully aware of what is happening in the present moment. Identifying and nursing how the client feels right now, in a way that does not pathologise those feelings, is surely an indispensable part of the work.

Transference has to be felt as well as understood intellectually, but it has to be experienced in a way which is, ultimately, helpful. We understand what transference is when we reinforce the lines between the conscious and the intuitive, so that they inform and nurture each other. We need to bring to consciousness our faith in our feelings and in instinctive goodness and wisdom, as well as heightening awareness of our doubts and fears. One of our greatest fears is the fear to have faith in our own validity, and in the validity of our own perceptions. This is a fear which therapy may do a great deal to inflate.

Chapter 8

In the dark room

'I don't believe in ghosts, but I've been afraid of them all my life.'

(Charles Anderson Dana)

If the client does not feel safe in the therapy room, then her anxiety and uncertainty about the process she is engaged in can provide a fertile breeding ground for fears and fantasies. Our fears and fantasies are, of course, the very thing which the therapist hopes to evoke and work on. But if the client feels that her fears will be perceived as illusory, or as an illustration of her inadequacy, she may be reluctant to share them. Can psychotherapy sometimes drown out the saner voices of the psyche?

The idea of something can be far worse than the something itself. For example, the idea of flying frightens me at times but this changes once I am 'safely' installed on the plane. Ideas have a life of their own, they leap about and refuse to do as they are told. Truth and suspicion are like Jekyll and Hyde and, as Francis Bacon said, 'suspicions among thoughts are like bats among birds, they ever fly by twilight'.

The job of therapy is to switch on the light rather than to turn it off, but sometimes it leaves the client groping around in the dark. Accepting and honouring our fears, and seeing them as part of the jigsaw of being, makes them less threatening. If we are able to revise and reformulate what we are afraid of, we place fear in a context which makes it more manageable.

How well do we understand the nature of our fear? For example, is it always about how other people treat us, or are we sometimes frightened by the way we treat others, by our own lack of understanding and compassion? We can feel overwhelmed by the force of our emotions – both positive and negative. So it may be our own power which frightens us, as much as that of those we engage with.

It is often said that children are frightened of authority figures. They frequently are, but what exactly are they frightened of? Is it perhaps that many of those who seek positions of power are not, in their essential core, powerful – so that what children perceive is, in fact, their inherent weakness, their need to project, and it is this that feels scary? How many children would be afraid of Ghandi or Mandela?

Fear can be akin to awe, so the child who is in awe of her mother because she experiences her as powerful may also feel safe in the knowledge that her mother is strong. True strength nourishes others. By the same token, a therapist who does not feel confident may evoke a feeling of anxiety in his clients.

Whatever our childhood experience, fear is atavistic. We all share an existential fear: it is one of the ingredients of being alive. There is also the fear that can arise when we are brought into close contact with the power and mystery of the world around us. Some people are scared of thunder and lightning. I am frightened of bangs. My analyst linked this, through an event in my childhood, to what he perceived as a fear of men. Years later, I realised that the event I had described to him was linked to something entirely different. Even though I have now worked out why that particular incident came to mind, I am still frightened of bangs. Our cat Basil is the same, yet he had a blissful childhood and, as far as we can tell, is a happy, well-balanced creature.

Our fears do not only relate to our childhood experience. For example, in existential therapy, one might discuss the deep sense of anxiety that can arise from the impermanence and uncertainty of life. Scott Peck (1978:140) describes the fear that is endemic in the experience of change: 'The experience ... of being on unfamiliar ground, of doing things differently is frightening.' As he points out, our resistance might be related to the future, to our progress: 'Courage ... is the moving out against the resistance engendered by fear into the unknown and into the future.'

Fear of the unknown may be much more potent than the fear attached to specific memories of the past, and it is a fear which can manifest itself with great force in therapy. For some clients, perhaps, it is our fear of the idea of the unconscious, the concept of the shadow lurking in the shadows, which keeps us on the edge of our seat. So, if a therapist assumes that our fear is related to particular details of our past, then he may be missing the point.

Each person's capacity for fearfulness will vary, just as the power of our imagination will vary. The man under the bed who lies waiting to grab my ankles exists only in my childhood fantasy. The strength of his ability to frighten me depends on my capacity for inventiveness. The greater our inventiveness, our creativity, the greater may be our potential both to terrify ourselves and to move beyond and use positively our childhood experience. It is necessary to look at both sides of the coin in this respect.

A psychodynamic approach includes 'serious attention to the powerful effect of fantasies'(Jacobs, 1988:6). This makes it all the more crucial that therapy provides a baseline which feels tangible and sane, and an exchange which includes common sense, open- ness and humour. Fear can paralyse. So when my internal predator is out on the prowl, I need all the help I can get.

For most of us there is, in any case, a part of our thinking which is self-sabotaging. This part needs no encouragement, but I found that a psychoanalytic approach can add fuel to the flames. If it constantly questions what it is about us as human beings which is good, it also sabotages us. Krishnamurti believed that 'whether you analyse yourself, or it is done by a specialist, there is division, therefore there is already the beginning of conflict' (1978:32).

Therapy challenges my whole way of being, and this can be extremely rewarding. But there is an inherent precariousness in the work which may cause it to feel alarming. There is a difference, however, between a client who always wants to be in control and a client who wants to be assured that the practitioner is in control, that he perceives what is happening accurately, and acts without undue defensiveness.

In theory, therapy should enable us to choose rather than be governed by our defences. In practice, it can decimate them, so that our ways of being in the world no longer function. It is not simply a question of survival strategies, or of there being no hiding places. It can feel as if there is no place to 'be'.

The relationship between therapist and client is one in which, potentially, everything is called into question, everything is up for grabs. Our feelings are put under a magnifying glass. Our psychological and emotional complexities can be emphasised to a point where, if we are not careful, the head begins to swim. We collude in the construction of misleading and damaging reinventions of ourselves. The more bizarre and convoluted interpretations which are sometimes presented to the client will not be without effect. They touch our consciousness even if they don't truly belong there. So when we open the doors to fantasy and to the furthest corners of the psyche, we need to do so with caution and reverence.

There has to be some solid ground in the therapy room, so that the unthreading can begin in a place where it is possible to sort out what is real and what is largely imagined. But 'what distinguishes the psychodynamic approach from others is the way in which the relationship is understood – what is known as "the transference"' (Jacobs, 1988:12). The practitioner's perception of the client's perception will be a fact of considerable influence. If what the client says is seen primarily as resistance, or as an illusion, a projection, a fantasy – rather than as a valid statement of what she truly feels – she is on sinking sand. The procedure of therapy can, in itself, feel scary.

One of the characteristics of childhood is the child's inability to distinguish between fact and fantasy. This is a frequent source of fear and anxiety. In my experience, psychotherapy can promote a dissolving of the adult's boundary between fantasy and reality, and cause similar confusion and turmoil. When a therapist says 'You want me to . . .' or 'You wish we could . . .' with regard to the client's fantasies, he risks destroying that boundary.

There is a difference between what I actually want and what I want to have fantasies about. It is vital that the therapist does not confuse the two. There is a part of my imagination which is a playground, a playground in which I am queen. It fulfils my need to have a fantasy land, and that need may be born of creativity as well as lack or repression. Our fantasies are about exploration and experimentation and the power of the imagination. Looked at intelligently, they can reveal a great deal. But there is a difference between fantasising and thinking about our hopes for the future. If we mistake imaginative desire and put intention in its place, we turn the reality/fantasy equation upside down.

One of the most helpful things that a friend has said to me is 'It's the way it feels'. In the wake of a breakdown brought on by therapy, I was describing to him the despair I felt at the dishevelled state of my mind. The fact that my head had somehow transformed itself into a lump of overcooked spaghetti made me feel, at times, that it would be preferable to be dead. I was anxious though, to emphasise to him that I had no intention of doing anything to bring that about. He said, 'I know. It's just the way it feels.' If a therapist interprets the client's feelings too literally, he fails to make this distinction.

Is it sometimes the practitioner who gets caught up in the world of fantasy, to the detriment of his client? When my intentions were misinterpreted – for example, when I asked for an extra session at a time when I was feeling quite seriously ill – I felt uncomfortable and offended. My analyst seemed to suggest that I had inappropriate expectations, or some ulterior motive, and the fact that I wished to respect my outside relationships was not, I felt, taken fully into account. When a therapist talks about what the client wants in the therapy relationship, it can sound absurd, because one knows that it is not possible or what one expects, or even wishes, to happen in reality.

In contrast, a therapist may try to interpret what we really do want in the actual therapeutic relationship – dialogue, warmth, naturalness – as some sort of symbolic fantasy, rather than a realistic, appropriate desire and expectation. He will wonder what it means. This kind of confusion is both frustrating and profoundly disorientating. So, in practice, a situation may arise in which the therapist interprets the client's fantasies too literally – rather than seeing them in terms of what they represent, whilst he treats her 'thinking about what she would like' as an illusion, a symbolic or representative fantasy – rather than as something practical and fitting. If this happens, there are no clear boundaries any more.

Therapy can play havoc with one's equilibrium and sense of reality. In my case, I ended up feeling as if my head had been turned inside out. A lack of clarity in this respect can lead to a sort of psychic anarchy where nothing belongs in its usual place. Whilst putting things in different places might be one of the aims of therapy, it has to be recognised that some things are already in the right place and should be allowed to remain there.

A sense of chaos can come also from an accumulation of unresolved misunderstandings between therapist and client. In psychodynamic practice, misperceptions are said to be a central part of the process, thus creating a perilously precarious way to work, and making it all the more imperative that misunderstandings are sorted out. We draw wrong conclusions from others' behaviour in childhood and in the present. Present misperceptions are easier to untangle than past ones, but it is hard for the client to know whether or not her feelings are a projection unless she can discuss the relationship in which they arise. If therapy is to reduce fear and anxiety, there has to be some clarity between analyst and analysand about what is 'yours' and what is 'mine', as well as what is 'ours'.

Misunderstandings only happen when more than one person is involved, so they cannot be sorted out unless both you and I know how both you and I are feeling. For example, if the therapist is sexually attracted to his client, she may well pick this up. But she will wonder if it is imagined or real. If the practitioner feels uncomfortable about it, the client may pick this up also. She may feel unable to talk about it, however, since it is difficult to ask one's therapist about it directly.

For a client, the most important thing might be to test what is real and what is imaginary. For a therapist, what might seem most appropriate is to focus on the effect on his client of another's sexual attraction. But can he do so if this is what he is feeling? And if he feels and then expresses it, is therapy still a viable option? If nothing is said about the actual feeling, the client has no means of testing out her intuition. And is the feeling itself – sexual desire – placed in the realm of 'things that are not talked about'? The fact that it is part of being a normal, healthy adult is in some way disallowed. Discussion of it becomes taboo, just as it might have been in childhood. But whose taboo is it?

What may be helpful for the client is to know that such attraction can exist without it necessarily being acted upon. In this way, the therapy acts as a model for controlling, rather than acting on, our impulses and passions. And unconditional acceptance of ourselves includes accepting and enjoying the fact that we are sexually attractive. The attractive woman may evoke envy in some; she interprets this as dislike and, as a result, experiences herself as ugly. Experiencing oneself as not ugly is a vital part of therapy. If the attraction is, indeed, imagined, then she can look at why she wishes to create such a fantasy.

The less the therapist shows of himself, the more the client's imagination can sometimes fill the gap. For example, the therapist may not comfort the client when she is upset, perhaps fearing that this may block the expression of pain in some way, or indicate to the client that he cannot cope with it. But the client might deduce that a lack of emotion signals a kind of professional indifference. The therapist must, after all, have seen it so many times before. It is ironic that, in our day-to-day lives, a lack of response can signal an apparent inability to empathise with other people's pain.

If, in the past, the expression of pain has not been met by understanding and comforting, then reliving the same apparently aloof response can simply make the expression of that pain doubly intolerable. One wishes to avoid the whole thing happening again. So the transference is once again accentuated. Feelings of not being cared for and the fear of being hurt are brought fully to consciousness but intensify. Once again, our rawness and vulnerability are magnified.

I remember thinking, only half-consciously, when my analyst looked in his diary to make an appointment, that he was busy and that seeing me was perhaps, for him, a tiresome chore. Whether or not this was an illusion based on childhood feelings I never found out. His occasional brusqueness suggested to me that he was irritated, but I had no way of knowing whether this was because of me or something entirely separate. It would have felt very odd to have asked him if he wanted to work with me or whether he did so simply because that was how he earned a living. It is a question one would be unlikely to ask any other professional practitioner.

Perhaps it is also a question which therapists do not expect or want to be asked. Peck describes his surprise and discomfort when a client wanted to know what he thought of her. 'For this,' he says:

> I had no precedent. Telling a person honestly face to face what you think of him or her was not one of the magical words or techniques that any of my professors had taught me ... The very fact that it had not been mentioned indicated to me that it was an interaction that was disapproved of. (Peck, 1978:183)

I never asked my analyst whether he liked me, or if he cared about me. At first, it never occurred to me to do so. Later, when I wanted to know, I didn't dare ask and I wasn't sure I would have got an answer in any case. By the time I reached my second therapist, I had learnt how costly it can be to work in the dark. I made a point of checking out every tiny thing, the slightest apprehension, ambiguity, suspicion, apparent change of mood or feeling. Kate knew, because of my previous experience, how important this was to me. In any case, she encouraged me to talk about how I was feeling and it was easy to get feedback from her. The atmosphere was relaxed and friendly, and she made it clear that she was happy for me to ask questions about what she thought and felt.

Research suggests that the more uncertain the client feels about the therapist's attitude towards her, the less likely she is to benefit from the therapy (Strupp *et al.*, 1969). It therefore seems illogical for the practitioner to hold back in this respect. Yet a therapist may think that the client's wish for this kind of knowledge is indicative of a deep-seated need for approval. He may be right, but it may arise also because, in our other relationships, we usually do receive feedback about what others think of us. It comes in all kinds of ways, not just through words. For example, positive feedback might be an invitation to supper, the offer of a job, a birthday card, a hug. These affirmations make our insecurities less intense.

In therapy, there are usually no such active affirmations, and the practitioner may even dislike the client. In Jacobs's book, for example, he discusses the reluctance of his client, 'Karl', to proceed with counselling. He finds Karl challenging and he also acknowledges that he initially finds it difficult to like him. But he does not suggest any connection between this and his client's resistance. If the therapist finds he is unable to accept and feel positive about a client, he should spare them the indignity of having to pretend that this does not matter.

Perhaps there are times when the dependable, controlled counsellor senses that his client knows more than he ever has about the raw edges of life, and about the ability to skate on thin ice. In the play *Equus* by Peter Shaffer, the psychiatrist Dysart says, of his young patient Alan Strang, that he 'has known a passion more ferocious than I have felt in any second of my life, and ... I envy it'. Perhaps 'Sybil', the analyst in Chapter 6 (page 55), was unconsciously envious of her client's passion for dance. If she was, then what might that suggest about the role of unconscious envy on the part of the practitioner in general?

In therapy, the behaviour which one would normally associate with liking and caring – listening, taking an interest, showing understanding – is given in return for money. If no positive feelings are expressed, therefore, one does not assume that such behaviour is proof that they are there. On the other hand, many clients (if they are not practitioners themselves) may not realise that the more negative aspects of the therapist's behaviour – his apparent stiffness or aloofness, for example – are intended to be beneficial, part of the treatment.

In many ways, of course, a detached stance is essential. And it is often the case that we sense and recognise most sharply how we are feeling and behaving when our attention is not diverted to the response of the other person. Focusing on the latter frequently furnishes a convenient excuse for not taking responsibility and instead criticising someone else. So, in that sense, a lack of reaction can be constructive. However, it is soul-destroying when one appears to evoke no human response in another human being. An absence of response can then become, in itself, a diversion away from what the client is trying to sort out – but she may not feel sufficiently clear or confident to express this to the therapist.

Therapy is about the way we treat one another. Some clients may feel liberated by what seems to be a kind of professional passivity. Others may feel blocked by it; it is as if one is operating in a sterile vacuum. If the therapist is a blank screen, we may function at the level of the personal but without the personal, a bit like trying to learn to swim without actually getting into the water. This ambivalence can cause one to feel adrift and 'ungrounded'.

Phrases such as 'There is confusion in the room' ignore the two people involved. To me, it is like saying 'There is anger on the chair. There is sadness by the lamp.' It is as if the feelings have become disembodied and held up for inspection, an X-ray pinned on the wall. It is as if I am not there. In therapy, I need to experience myself – and to feel appreciated – as a whole person, and not seen as a case, a patient. I need to feel that the practitioner values the work we do together and gets something out of it himself.

Coping with difficulties is usually easier when we know what we have to come to terms with. So not knowing what is going on in a context which one hoped would provide exactly the opposite can leave one feeling dazed and perplexed. Not all therapists draw attention to the value and promise of sometimes not knowing.

Not all clients will be aware of this perspective, and sometimes it is neither helpful nor even relevant.

A blank screen is blank, and nothingness is hard to deal with. Sometimes we fill the void with the leftovers from previous experience, and often the leftovers we hook into are the negative, threatening ones. But sometimes it is quite simply the nothingness that is threatening – the void, the empty space which remains empty. Clients do not always project; sometimes we simply stare at the question mark. In analysis, it is our innocence which defeats us.

E. M. Forster wrote, in *Howards End*, 'Only connect!' For me, at least, the empty space of the therapy room has to be enveloped by some sort of elementary connection of sameness. Before I tried therapy, I had always derived hope and comfort from the knowledge that, although being human is problematic, it is problematic for us all. My sense of myself was inextricably tied up with a sense of being similar to others, a feeling of familiarity with what we all have to deal with. With my analyst, there was little sense of familiarity. When I once drew attention to what I felt to be our sameness, he was silent and looked faintly surprised. I felt as if there was something rather unpalatable to him about being similar to a 'patient', and this became another source of fear on my part. The context of therapy can generate fear very easily.

My analyst's interventions had little sense of there being any truths which apply to all of us. He tended to say, for instance, 'Perhaps you have difficulty in...' and never 'I think we [that is, everyone] sometimes have difficulty in...'. I began to wonder if I was riddled with unusual psychological deformities which somehow set me apart. Was I in some undesirable way different from other people, and had I failed to grasp the essentials of being a human after all? When I expressed something and then asked him if he knew what I meant, he tended to avoid saying 'yes' or 'no'. He would be more likely to respond with phrases such as: 'I think perhaps what you're talking about is...'.

My reality became less, rather than more, sharply defined. It lost its shape, its colour, its texture. It lost its sense of direction. It ventured out, seeking recognition, then found it had nowhere to go. Things which, in my terms, had some sort of meaning – even though that meaning might have needed reviewing – were suddenly called into question. Such an experience can feel threatening, even punitive, rather than gently challenging. Working with someone who is unresponsive and who behaves rather like a machine is frightening. Fear can be a mind-killer, causing us to become illogical and end up further embroiled.

One of the most frightening questions we can ask ourselves is 'Am I crazy?' The very act of going to therapy can give substance to this fear. For example, when the counsellor in 'Hannah's' case suggests they meet for several months, Hannah looks worried and says, 'Does that mean you think there's something wrong with me? Do you think I'm mad or something?' (Jacobs, 1988:67). I know how Hannah felt. When my analyst said he thought I needed precisely what I had gone there for – therapy – I also felt surprised and disconcerted.

The counsellor in the above case example reassures Hannah that he does not think she is crazy, but at the same time suggests she might be angry, and perhaps angry with him (something my analyst also said). Hannah, quite understandably, asks why that should be the case (as I should have done). But, because of a lack of time, the counsellor does not pursue it, thereby leaving the client with something else to worry about, and planting another seed of uncertainty in her mind.

Uncertainty can prompt the client to hang on to what feels familiar, rather than stepping outside to look. It will not then facilitate the drawing-out of problems which have their roots in past experience. The same circle of response or defence reasserts itself and old patterns are strengthened with a renewed urgency. Therapy then turns in on itself and becomes the opposite of health and sanity.

Chogyam Trungpa (1987:88) suggests:

> Once you begin to deal with a person's whole case history, trying to make it relevant to the present, the person begins to feel he has no escape, that his situation is hopeless, because he cannot undo his past. He feels trapped by his past with no way out. This kind of treatment is extremely unskilled. It is destructive because it hinders involvement with the creative aspect of what is happening here, right now.

Feeling hopeless and trapped is something we have all experienced. In therapy, it happens on both sides. Therapist and client may both be frightened of making mistakes, getting hurt, making a fool of themselves. Acknowledgement of shared fear can be enormously therapeutic – but how often is this expressed?

There may be times when the problem of the practitioner's fears, and of what he can or cannot cope with, is an insurmountable one. It may be that, when the therapist is frank about his limitations, it does not help at all – because he is unable to ensure that they do not become a source of further pain for the client. Ann France (in *Consuming Therapy*) describes how her analyst's inability to cope with her despair caused her to feel increasingly hopeless and suicidal. What should have been a healing relationship actually became so traumatic that another therapist had to be brought in to help the client cope with the anguish it was causing.

In her book *Folie à Deux*, Rosie Alexander (1995) courageously and with incandescent clarity gives another account of what can happen when therapy is not contained. She describes 'harrowing details of a therapy which brought her to total despair and to the very edge of her being'. Aspects of the experience of both of the above writers are painfully familiar to me, and to others I have spoken to also. For example, the phenomenon of regression is sometimes all too real.

I remember at a critical time gathering in my mind the comments my analyst had made which were chatty and spontaneous, the little glimpses he had given me of the real person. I felt like a poor child scraping crumbs from a rich man's table, and later wondered if I had been like a baby trying to internalise an image of an 'important other'. On another occasion, when I left the therapy room feeling numb and disorientated, I found I had no idea how to go about crossing the road. When I was at my worst, I could not remember how to cook; fortunately, there was no shortage of people to look after both me and my children, but this may not always be the case.

Regression is surely highly dangerous. An infant who is not looked after will simply fail to survive. If the client goes back to a place where she re-experiences the feelings of early childhood, she does so at a time in her life when she no longer has the constant nurture – however inadequate it sometimes is – that all surviving infants receive. A client who regresses still has to slot back into the world of an independent adult and continue, somehow, to thrive. She becomes a kind of mutant in whom the emotions of a

child collide with the intellect of an adult. The devastating consequences of psychotherapy gone mad can rarely be outweighed
by any later gains.

The intensity of therapy can increase rather than decrease our
fear of what is hidden, fragment rather than integrate. I began to
feel that whatever I said to my analyst would be taken as yet
another illustration of what was wrong with me. In the end, I went
through what I can only describe as the loss of a sense of my own
identity, a space in which nothing made any sense any more. I
had arrived in the therapy room feeling relatively buoyant, and
then drowned in a sea of confusion.

In therapy, our feelings are undiluted. If the therapist fails to
act as a recipient when they are expressed, then they seem even
more unmanageable, and the client is forced to reingest them in
their exaggerated form. They can then become terrifying or overwhelming. The same might apply to the negative judgements we
carry with us from the past, and any accompanying threats. This
leads to a situation where, in therapy, feelings are actually less
containable than they are in everyday life. Therapy can, by its
very nature, cause our existing fears to appear more rather than
less substantial, and throw in a few extra ones for good measure.

What needs to happen is the easy expression – from a real
human being – of an acceptance of the messy, ugly side of ourselves,
an acknowledgement that our grubbiness is a normal part of
human nature. There is then a sense of acquaintanceship rather
than distance. When the client then reabsorbs those darker aspects
of herself, which will always inevitably be there, she will put them
back in a way that is different, in an easier and less pressing place.

All our relationships challenge us to look at what we are. But
the psychotherapeutic relationship is the only one we are ever
likely to have which concentrates exclusively on exploring the
maze of our mind and feeling, on the rearrangement of the content of the psyche and on gazing into our own unknowableness.
Therapy can move the mind into different dimensions of experience. The power of the potential of unbounded exploration can be
explosive, and the chemistry of such a situation is highly volatile.
This does not mean that therapy should never be attempted. What
is does mean is that its power should be properly honoured. Professional practitioners cannot afford to play down the dangers
involved in the potency of the cocktail they offer.

Chapter 9

Burning bridges

It has been said that 'what happens in the consulting room is a function more of the personalities involved than of any explicit "approach" or "technique"'(Carvalho, 1990:80). If this is the case, then the personality of the therapist is surely a key factor. And if it is a key factor, then how does this tie in with a theory which involves the practitioner assuming the role of a blank screen? One might question whether these two seemingly contradictory positions can live happily alongside one another.

Perhaps a psychoanalytic approach suffers from an over-reliance on a theoretical model in which the therapist's personality and feelings are sidelined, on a hope that the self of the therapist does not get in the way unduly of the work the client needs to do. In reality, a client may feel very different with different practitioners.

A system of therapy cannot render the personhood of the therapist inconsequential. Yet many psychoanalysts would say 'My actual person doesn't count' (Alexander, 1995:22), believing that it is what they represent which matters most. Practitioners who don't, in practice, ascribe to this belief, might still base much of what they do on techniques drawn from that principle.

Is there a danger that such an approach might actually increase the possibility of the therapist's feelings getting in the way, precisely because they have been told to take a back seat? Perhaps the practitioner's unresolved issues are put under greater pressure if he is supposed to be a template. At the same time, his positive qualities may be left out in the cold when they could, in fact, play a greater part in the 'cure'. How many potential bridges are burnt?

The therapist is an inevitable part of what he studies. Therapists and counsellors 'are not saints, and they need to get in touch with what a client really evokes in them' (Jacobs, 1988:78). If a therapist is able to do this, then he may use it both to inform himself and to help the client see how she might affect others. From the client's point of view, the latter is a particularly vital part of the work: what the client evokes, generates and sets up needs to be allowed, understood and given space.

The therapist's feelings, conscious and unconscious, are often referred to as the 'counter-transference'. The phenomenon of counter-transference is defined in Freudian therapy as 'any disruption of the analytic attitude of neutrality' (Smith, 1996:33), though many practitioners would say that it often promotes rather than detracts from understanding; the therapist's emotional response is an essential part of the work, provided that he uses it consciously. However the therapist sees it, it is a concept with which most clients will be unfamiliar – at an intellectual level – but it is a reality which may turn out to be, at the level of experienced feeling, a major influence in the development of their therapy.

In a description of Jungian therapy, the writer cites an analysis described in *Symbols of Transformation* which Jung conducts at long distance from the psychiatrist's notes about the patient. The analysis 'ends with a negative prognosis of schizophrenia. However, a close reading of the book reveals that the real patient is Jung himself, simultaneously working through his break with Freud and, at the same time, developing his own ideas through self-analysis' (Casement, 1996:85). If this happened to Jung at long distance, how might this subtle role reversal apply to other therapists in closer encounters?

For most practitioners, the appropriate place for discussion of their feelings is usually seen to be that of supervision. In theory, a practitioner's issues will be dealt with elsewhere, in regular sessions with a supervisor or a therapist. But, in reality, is it always the case that the therapist's feelings about a particular client either contribute usefully to the therapeutic process or are safely dealt with outside it? In therapy, as in any situation, our feelings can hook us into a complex series of double binds.

In theory, supervision takes the potentially difficult feelings out of the arena in which they could have most influence. That may sometimes solve a problem, but it may also give rise to one. The fact that the therapist's feelings are not discussed with the client does not mean they are non-existent or, more important, that they do not affect the relationship. So, when a therapist asks himself the question, 'What am I generating here?', the person who most needs to hear the answer may sometimes be me, the client.

Without it, I have no means of knowing whether what I experience as the therapist's mood or his attitude towards me is imagined or whether it is simply that I have good antennae. Knowing whether or not my perceptions are correct is fundamental to my sense of my own sanity. Leaving the client in the dark in this respect can promote feelings of confusion and helplessness, whilst preserving the power that the practitioner's distance gives him. Therapy then becomes an irresponsible charade in which the client is unable to pursue the truth.

One client, when she asked her therapist about a moment she had found particularly unsettling, was told: 'If the therapist feels bored or tired, it is for the therapist to deal with.' Of course it is for the therapist to deal with, that goes without saying; but the client is nevertheless, unavoidably, involved. This attitude ignores the fact that she will be affected. It lacks an appreciation of and consideration for the client's perspective, and the therapist's arrogant insensitivity can leave her feeling powerless. She is not only prevented from clarifying a sense of unease, but may also feel that she has done something wrong by asking about it. She is shut out of her own therapy.

What happens if a practitioner does not take fully into account the possible impact of his responses and his errors? Does the academic discussion of relevant factors in the 'acquisition and perpetuation of psychological disturbance' (Dryden, 1996) pay sufficient attention to the relevance of 'therapeutic approach', 'therapist error' or 'therapist's issues'? Although there is an enormous literature on the subject of counter-transference, one might question how many practitioners are capable of putting it to good use. They may read it, discuss it in journals and talk about it with their colleagues, but do they put the expertise it represents into practice, for the benefit of their clients?

The literature on counter-transference is not usually read by clients, who will therefore not be alert to its repercussions. They may either take things personally or tell themselves, mistakenly, that the therapist is being objective – particularly if the practitioner does not own responsibility for what he brings. In his discussion of counter-transference, Menninger (1958, cited in

Aveline, 1996:376) 'lists among the items that he has "probably experienced": repeatedly experiencing erotic feelings towards the patient, carelessness in regard to appointment arrangements, sadistic unnecessary sharpness in formulating interpretations'.

When the therapist has been hurtful, does he express regret? When he is careless over appointments, does he apologise to the client, or does he use it as an opportunity to explore her neuroses regarding loss and disappointment? If he acts out instead of interpreting, does he eventually draw attention to this? And could the sexual attraction that the client may feel towards the therapist be, in part, the result of her soaking up his repressed desires? If there is an erotic tension in the air, what is its origin? It is unlikely that the client will remain unaffected by these things. So the therapist's feelings, opinions and perceptions do, in reality, 'contaminate the field of enquiry'.

It is usually the practitioner and his supervisor who determine when he is being neutral and when he is affected by counter-transference, how the two standpoints can run successfully alongside each other, and when and how counter-transference feelings should be fed back to the client. The client is not involved in such discussion. So is she required to believe that the hornet's nest of another's being is defused and tucked away – unless the therapist chooses to tell her otherwise?

In practice, counter-transference not only affects how the therapist behaves, but how the therapy room feels. Every practitioner will give out subtle, unspoken messages about what feels comfortable or uncomfortable, what is acceptable, pleasing, usual. This may be picked up by the client in a variety of ways. We feel another's presence, and its resonance can be powerful. Being self-effacing and saying very little are not the same thing. And, in a way of working in which transference is a strong factor, isn't it possible that counter-transference will also become of particular significance?

To start from a premise that the client's negative feelings are caused primarily by a kind of overspill from other relationships can seem like arrogance of the highest order. When this occurs, it is the therapist who puts himself into a god-like position, and not the client who puts him there. He may inadvertently block exploration of related issues which the therapy very much needs to address because, from the client's point of view, such discussion would be based on a falsehood, on an avoidance of what is affecting her most immediately – what is actually happening in the present.

Clients may not only get stuck because they find past memories difficult. They also get stuck if the therapist does not deal effectively with the here and now, so that more immediate issues are therefore circumvented. For the client, it may be a question of wanting to put first things first, beginning with the present, which is tangible and malleable, rather than with the past, which is uncertain and cannot be changed. 'The work of therapy is moment-to-moment awareness of what is actually taking place. It is not knowing in advance' (Diane Shainberg, 1983:174).

Professional competence means the therapist trusting in his ability to communicate what he is experiencing in a way which does not disturb the client unduly or violate her position as client, so that it will, ultimately, be in her interest. If he handles his feelings responsibly, and in a matter-of-fact atmosphere, then the whole issue of emotions which can be deeply troubling is 'dedramatised'. For this to happen, however, the therapist needs to be free of worry and guilt about his own feelings, so that he is as accepting of himself as he is – in optimum practice – of the client. But, for most human beings, this is probably a rather tall order.

Therapists can, and do, avoid dealing with difficult issues by hiding behind technique and esoteric jargon. This may happen unintentionally, since it is easy to fall back on the terms which were used when a concept was first presented to us – in this case, the terminology of a theoretical training. For example, when my analyst said, 'The therapist is in the room', I was at a loss, because I did not know what he meant. What I registered most strongly was that perhaps I was failing to respect his feelings. This sparked in me feelings of guilt and worry, and I did not know what to do.

There may, of course, be times when the client could not cope with, or would not benefit from, too overt an expression of the practitioner's feelings of bewilderment, fear, dislike, irritation, attraction or unease. But, in the highly charged atmosphere of the therapy room, they will not go unnoticed. The intangibility of electricity does not make it any the less powerful, and people who are particularly sensitive can easily get caught up in the conflicts that another is trying to avoid.

If a particular issue is not given an airing, its presence can become all the more potent. The problem is intensified because the client senses that something is causing difficulties, but does not know what it is. She is also aware that the therapist has decided not to talk about it. I came from a family where problems were felt rather than expressed, alluded to but not openly discussed. This unnerved me then and it unnerved me in the therapy room.

As every psychologist will tell you, the more we try to repress something, the more it tends to affect us. The pressure on the therapist may be considerable. In such circumstances, the asymmetry of the relationship can be as hard for a therapist to sustain as it is for a client to accept. If the client is aware of the therapist's lack of confidence, she may also feel tense and uncomfortable. Might she then 'introject' his fear of loss of control, thus fuelling her own fear?

For most clients, it would seem inappropriate to draw attention to the therapist's difficulties. She has not gone there to talk about his problems. He is, in any case, the professional, the expert, and she knows it is possible that she might be wrong. In addition, most people dislike being criticised, and so see what might appear as criticism as tactless, hurtful or intrusive. It is not uncommon for clients to feel protective towards their therapists. My analyst rarely looked happy and I began to wonder whether he enjoyed being a psychotherapist, or whether it was just me who had that effect on him.

It is important that the client does not feel that things seem to be going wrong because it is 'her fault', or because the therapist dislikes her. When things went wrong in my case – instead of 'getting better', I had a breakdown – I felt, for a long time, that I had done something 'wrong'. I felt I was letting my analyst, and myself, and everyone else, down because I was not doing what I thought analysands were 'supposed to do'.

In his discussion of 'therapists' dilemmas', Paul Wachtel (in Dryden, 1997:141) talks about the problems which arise when a client does not 'reinforce' the therapist by changing for the better. This can make her less appealing, so that if the client thinks that the therapist does not like working with her, there is an element of truth to this suspicion. 'You come to dislike the person not for his intrinsic qualities, but because the therapy isn't going as well as you would like' (Dryden, ibid.).

Our self-image is strongly influenced by how much value we feel others attach to us. This will apply to both practitioner and client. If the client is struggling, and questions the value of the therapy she is doing, the therapist might, at some level, feel less valued. He may feel guilty because he feels he is letting the client down. In practice, we are all too human. If the therapist feels threatened, what part is played by his 'adaptive defence mechanisms'?

When things are not going well, is there a temptation on the part of the practitioner to engineer an artificial increase in his feelings of self-worth by homing in on one of the client's problems, and offering her an interpretation about her own behaviour? Diagnosing the other person is a favourite pastime for most of us when we feel ill at ease, and won't the psychotherapist feel he is doing his job successfully when he identifies the client's difficulties? However, in the process, he may actually help to dig her further into a hole, because she may simply feel increasingly inept.

In teaching, interfering with the learner's cognitive progress has been called 'picking up your learners' monkeys'. The concept of the monkey, which comes from management studies, means 'the next move' in a problem-solving process (Blanchard *et al.*, 1990). The teacher, in an effort to be an effective teacher, tells the learner what to do, instead of encouraging her to find a solution for herself.

How much do psychoanalytic interpretations serve to improve the client's self-awareness and discovery, and how much do they serve to boost the practitioner's confidence, allowing him to turn a blind eye to a significant part of the dilemma – his self-doubt and what he is getting wrong? When things feel wobbly, what the client actually needs is assurance, and a shared assessment of how the therapy is going. Simple questions like 'How are you feeling?', 'Is there anything in particular you are worried about?' can do much to loosen the log-jam.

With sufficient faith, optimism and a certain levity, an impasse can become an opportunity, a breakthrough rather than a breakdown. The discussion of difficulties needs to take place 'in an atmosphere of utter honesty. To create this atmosphere, it is essential for therapists to bring to their relationships with patients a total capacity for openness and truthfulness' (Peck, 1978:60). It is most likely to take place in an atmosphere which is free of defensiveness – on the part of the therapist as well as the client.

Openness and truthfulness promote trust and act as a bridge, allow us to connect with each other and defuse the tension. For me, it is necessary to be asked how I am feeling as well as what I think. I also needed to be reassured that difficulties can be worked through. This might involve the therapist disclosing how he is feeling too, which may not be easy. Do some practitioners avoid asking clients how they feel, in case the client then asks them the same question?

In good therapy, appropriate honesty is pivotal. Appropriate honesty is not about abandoned self-disclosure, or the therapist telling the client his story, or using the client as a surrogate counsellor. It is about being open to and open about what is going on in the therapy room. It is about the therapist truly accepting responsibility for his part in what happens with his client. It is about integrity.

There may be days, for example, when the therapist feels distant for some reason. If this is not mentioned, the client may feel that her sense of estrangement comes only from inside herself. Isn't it up to the therapist to be clear about this and to say what is happening, rather than hoping that the client hasn't noticed, or that she will mention it if she finds it troubling? If he takes responsibility by owning that sense of distance, it is correctly placed. It might help the client to understand why, when the therapy room feels lonely.

If the therapist is confused or lost, there may be times when it is helpful to say so. If he shares this with his client, he eliminates the danger of her mistakenly thinking that the confusion is all her own. He also reminds himself and shows her that being lost temporarily is not uncommon and is something that can be accommodated. That way we learn equanimity. By allowing his own self-doubt, the therapist validates that of his client. We go to therapy at a point in our life when we are full of doubt, so perhaps we all need reminding of the fact that self-doubt is a healthy part of the human condition. Thomas Moore suggests that 'the shedding of heroics in the process of therapy allows for unexpected enchantment' (Moore, 1997:184).

Isn't judicious psychotherapy based on a healthy blend of objectivity and genuine involvement? But, if therapy involves building bridges, where on the bridge do we meet? The less the therapist expresses, the more the client's curiosity may be aroused. But, if she asks him personal questions, for example, 'Are you married?' or 'Have you got any children?' or 'Do you like music?', then, rather than giving a direct answer, many practitioners will probably ask her why such questions concern her. He will think about their underlying significance.

Many psychotherapists shroud their identity in mystery and then, when the client's natural curiosity and interest are expressed, infer there is another motive for her questions. In doing so, the therapist risks introducing an unfortunate change of tack, and also neglects to justify the reason for the cloak of anonymity he has chosen to put on. It is said that the more the client knows about the therapist, the less fully she will be able to experience her transference. However, it is unlikely that she will be aware of this reason and, if she cannot work through the transference in the company of a stranger, then ultimately nothing will be gained.

Whatever the relative weight of the different ingredients involved, there is another reason why the client may ask her therapist personal questions. Generally speaking, we understand best how something feels if we have lived it ourselves. So the client may wonder if the therapist has first-hand knowledge of the experiences she is describing. We may ask 'Have you ever...?' because we want to know if he really knows what it's like. He may not, and it may not matter, but that does not make the question any the less natural in a context where we do not know the person we are talking to.

A potential bridge, and one which many therapists feel should never be crossed, is that of physical contact. It is claimed that physical contact should be avoided because it can give the client the wrong signals, or because it can seem threatening, or an unwelcome physical intrusion. For certain clients, this may be the case. Nevertheless, it is sad that, even in therapy, touching is often associated with intrusion or sexual excitement. For me, touching is an important part of connecting to and relating with another person. Ironically, by refraining from any physical contact, there is an inference that it is, in fact, a problem, that it is not possible to have such contact in a way which is safe or platonic.

In some cases, part of what the client needs to learn may be that physical contact does not go hand in hand with intrusiveness or sexual harassment. And for those of us for whom touch is a spontaneous and integral part of our interactions with others, trying to have a close relationship with someone with whom there is no physical contact can cause strain. The question then arises: what feels comfortable for the therapist and to what extent is he at ease when it comes to touching others?

Practitioners seem fond of quoting the rare occasions when a female client flings off her clothes in the hope that her therapist will have sex with her. But, for most of us, making love to one's therapist belongs and remains in the realm of fantasy, not reality – just as the majority of therapists (one hopes) would consider it inappropriate to have sex with their clients.

A psychotherapist encourages the client to open up to her suffering. Then, when she does, he – in most cases – stays firmly in his chair. The client needs to feel that the therapist can cope with what she is feeling and saying, so a lack of response may at times be soothing. For some clients, on the other hand, physical contact may be the very thing she needs in order to feel safe enough to uncover and disclose what is troubling her.

In a crisis, physical contact – for example, holding hands – can help us to feel more grounded. Touch can be a simple means of offering reassurance and affection. Being hugged and held – at certain, well-judged times – can feel enormously calming and affirming. For me it has been an important part of a successful therapeutic relationship. But the client, as well as the therapist, is restricted by the rules of the practitioner's particular approach, so her wish for physical contact may be denied or misconstrued.

We live in an age where physical contact in any professional relationship is fast becoming taboo, so a reluctance to touch may be nothing more than professional protection. Therapy will always be a compromise between what feels comfortable for the client and what feels comfortable for the therapist and what, in his view, constitutes acceptable professional conduct. Ideally, the compromises we make in therapy should have therapeutic value for both parties.

Only when there are no losers can therapy be genuinely beneficial. If I pay someone to deal with and withstand those aspects of myself which are problematic, I may end up feeling demeaned by rather than freed from them. What I benefit from in therapy is expertise, understanding and awareness, backed up by a genuine ability to embrace and contain all of me – and to do so willingly – so that I learn to have that ability myself, and hence become more whole.

A therapist may uphold theories about abstinence because the theory suits his particular feelings and needs. Or he may genuinely see his professional anonymity as an adjunct to truth – as ensuring a constant focus on the client's intrinsic perspective. For the client, though, it may be experienced differently and for some, what feels like deception may have 'paralyzing consequences ... Some people can no more tolerate a duplicitious environment than they can do without oxygen' (Russell, 1992:167). We cannot breathe in the therapy room without the oxygen of truth.

'If a person is to get the meaning of life he must learn to like the facts about himself – ugly as they may seem to his sentimental vanity – before he can learn the truth behind the facts. And the truth is never ugly' (Eugene O'Neill, cited in Russell, 1992:169). If the client is to learn to like the facts about him- or herself, this is best done with someone who has already been down that road, someone who feels, as the French say, 'good in their skin'.

If the therapist is frightened that his feelings may contaminate the work, then they may do precisely that. Fear, in particular, is highly contagious. And could it sometimes be his vanity which prevents him from being fully aware of the influence of his own sensibilities, or from properly acknowledging the relevance of that influence? Is the practitioner's transference sometimes more powerful than the client's? For example, could his need for personal privacy be greater than the client's need to make him less of a stranger?

If I am too curious, then the therapist becomes the focus of attention, a tricky sort of role reversal. 'The brute curiosity of the angel's stare/Turns you like them to stone' (Allen Tate, 1971). In therapy, can both analyst and analysand be 'turned to stone' when the spotlight seems too bright? What happens when the rules simply don't work any more? In the end, psychotherapy is not a game between practitioner and client, but a relationship between two people.

Chapter 10

Survival of the fittest?

In discussion about the merits and difficulties of therapy, three people who found the psychodynamic approach helpful made the following comments. One: 'Compassion? I didn't want compassion. Tenderness has never been part of my vocabulary.' Two: 'I knew how to handle it. I was an old hand by then because I'd already been to a couple of counsellors.' Three: 'They don't treat you like a human being. That's not part of the deal.'

The third comment particularly struck me, along with the tinge of self-satisfaction that seemed to accompany its delivery. I, of course, had not been able to 'handle it' whereas the speaker in question had. She seemed proud of the fact that she had benefited from a relationship in which she felt she had not been treated like a human being. So, why is surviving such a 'deal' deemed to be an indicator of psychic health?

If a therapist removes something of his humanness from the equation, the consequences may not always be beneficial. Some clients may flourish in such an atmosphere, but what exactly does it achieve? Can it get in the way of compassion and spontaneity, and in doing so suppress our capacity to really change and grow? Such analysis may well make us more aware of our difficulties, but – having made us aware – does it complete the task by enabling us to heal ourselves and move on? Does it make us more responsible, more sensitive to others and more caring in our behaviour towards them?

Emotions deserve to be experienced and talked about in a context which makes room for and respects their 'emotionality', not one which treats them merely as 'material', as data in an enquiry. Therapy is about how we feel when we expose ourselves to an expert. It is not only what we say, or what lies behind what we say, which is important, but how we feel when we say it. So, when I tell my analyst about a secret fantasy, what may count most for me at that moment is not the significance of the fantasy but the fact that I have shared with him something which is intensely private. It is an act of enormous trust. It is what unfolds, as well as what is revealed, which touches the client deeply. The contrast between the undercurrents of such fragile feeling, which make one feel so exposed, and a practitioner hiding behind a shield of professional impersonality can be razor-sharp at times.

Is there a sense in which one needs to be insensitive when one becomes an analysand? Does it entail, for example, ignoring the effect that spitting out our pain may have on our therapist? And does it involve setting aside certain aspects of ourselves, in order for the therapist to sit comfortably in the practitioner's chair? If it does, then the process of therapy could end up being more about adapting to a contrived environment and less about achieving greater balance in one's life outside it.

We all have within us both healer and patient. But, if a therapist shows little emotion, the client may forget that he is not immune to the doubts and fears that haunt the rest of us. She sees him only as a healer. At the same time, there is a danger that the practitioner will 'locate the polarity of the "patient in himself"' in his clients. 'As a healer without wounds, [he] will be unable to engage the healing factor in [his] patients' (Aveline, 1996:377). If the client can only play the role of patient because the therapist's need to be the healer is too great, then might the client end up accommodating the therapist?

If a client in therapy is to take a responsible role, then she needs to be a 'co-analyst' in order to become more self-aware. But that may have implications in terms of the status quo in her relationship with the practitioner, and the balance of power between them. The therapist cannot get inside me and tell me how I see things, any more than an optician can get inside my head and tell me which letters I can decipher on the eye-sight chart. By the same token, who then is best placed to say what is and isn't helpful in therapy?

Discussion between client and therapist about what constitutes 'good therapy' can be an integral part of the work, and form a valuable basis for gaining greater individual awareness. The client will come to understand better what she needs in order to feel sound, what kind of attitude and behaviour works for her in the therapy room. If I am to become my own therapist, then I need to evolve a view about what a good therapist might be. The client thus evaluates the therapist, and she may also try, in her outside relationships, to behave as the therapist does – for example, to hear clearly, be more accepting, less judgemental.

For me, talking about what it means to have a therapeutic relationship was one of the most useful and enlightening aspects of the work I did with my second therapist. The question 'In what circumstances do I feel able to be genuinely myself?' evokes some telling answers. The discussion may then move on from the client's individual perceptions into generalisations about principles which might work for all of us, both within the therapy relationship and outside it.

From the client's point of view, to be asked occasionally 'Are you finding what we are doing helpful?' might open doors that had felt closed. But how willing are those who sell therapy to seek and accept such evaluation from clients? For example, documented case examples could include a commentary written by the client, so that the reader is aware of how things seemed from her perspective. But would such a contribution appear, from a practitioner's point of view, less valid, because it is not informed by a professional training? Might it threaten to undermine the therapist's professional standing, and upset the delicate apple-cart of the status quo?

The client is not a therapist and does not have the same knowledge or skills as a trained professional. But psychotherapy is both an investigation and a felt experience which is owned by both parties. A good practitioner will know about self-awareness, insight, detachment and compassion, but he does not have a monopoly on them. The therapist can choose whether to see the client's assessment as a creative factor, from which the therapy can be improved, or to see it as having another meaning.

In order to fit into the situation of being in therapy, do we sometimes stifle a part of ourselves which is inherently healthy? And is this more likely to happen with a practitioner who is attached to an image of himself as a 'successful' therapist? The Jungian analyst Peter Tatham, in a paper about the meaning of illness, points out how people are sometimes 'too successful in being, rather than becoming' so that we 'get stuck in one-sidedness and the process of individuation freezes up' (Tatham, 1988:29). Psychotherapists as well as their clients can get 'stuck in one-sidedness' – the one-sidedness of the person who puts himself in the position of 'analyser' of another. If this happens, then the client might find it difficult to achieve a balance between the positions of patient and healer in herself.

Critics of therapy justifiably point to the power of the status of experts, and most of us are predisposed to falling prey to that power: 'most of us do not want to grow up and think for ourselves. Instead, we want to be released from doubt, ignorance and uncertainty, and we want someone else to do the job for us' (Howard, 1996:132). 'It is generally much easier to seek out someone else who may be only too willing to tell us who we are' (ibid.:130).

As clients, we are attracted by the idea of the 'psychic sheep dip' of therapy, and to the notion that we can 'be born again, renewed, reinvigorated and inspired' (ibid.:132). Nevertheless, even when we are struggling to keep our heads above the water in the dipping trough, we still have an instinctive drive towards balance. We endeavour to fill the gaps, to square the circle. To do so is part of our nature. Passivity and retreat may evoke aggression and attack. When someone is unhappy, I want to make them laugh.

So the more a therapist creates distance, the stronger may be the client's desire to close that distance. The less of himself he gives to the client, the more of him she may want. This need may relate more to the incongruities of the relationship than to disturbance in infancy. If distance constitutes an element of the practitioner's power, then trying to lessen that distance may be a healthy attempt on the part of the client to redress an imbalance of power.

The relationship between a client and therapist can be a metaphor for the client's relationship with herself, and the need for internal balance. The desire for balance interweaves with and influences the tapestry of specific experiences and relationships and has a general significance. Its intensity needs to be considered in its own right, as an important variable in the process of self-regulation. The strength of the client's intrinsic need for balance will colour her response to the behaviour of others, including that of her therapist.

What happens if the client adapts to the therapeutic relationship in ways which are not to her advantage? In therapy we endeavour to relearn relationship. We relinquish our outdated map, but we also need another one to replace it, an alternative mode of anchoring ourselves to reality. If the therapist is in some way a model, if his way of dealing with things is something the client internalises, might she then take some of her humanness out of the therapy room, in order to adapt to the therapeutic relationship? If in doubt, copy the person sitting next to you. The child tries not to cry because 'grown-ups don't cry'.

It is said that: 'It is the counsellor's hope that the client will learn to regard himself in the same way as the counsellor has done...a process of internalisation takes place' (Jacobs, 1988:123). 'The crux of the matter is for the therapist (not as person in his/ her own life, but as presence) to be capable of being internalized in the patient's inner world' (Zeal, 1994:53). But what if the therapist's internalised presence is not helpful, if the way he regards the client is not beneficial? The therapist may appear negative, critical, unloving.

We all, to some degree, introject or absorb some of the qualities of those we are with. If the therapist wishes to stay in control, to be cool, calm and collected, he may also try to behave impassively, without emotion. He 'makes mental notes' about how the client is feeling. If this is the attitude that the client internalises, what happens to her feelings, and where do her passion and spontaneity go? Isn't there a danger in an implicit encouragement for the client to bypass the therapist's personhood? Might it actually work in a way which represses her compassion both for the therapist and for herself?

If the client is bright and attentive, she will soon latch on to what the therapist seems to see as appropriate areas for discussion. For instance, my analyst always seemed to perk up when I talked about dreams. So the client may begin to talk about what appears to interest the therapist and, at the same time, start to copy his style.

Historically, the fittest survive by successfully adapting to new circumstances. We are genetically disposed to doing so. We all have an intrinsic need to deal effectively with our environment because we find it inherently pleasurable. So is the successful analysand sometimes the one who becomes increasingly adept at fitting in with her practitioner's particular approach? And if this approach does not reproduce what good relationships are about, then what is the end result?

Just as children become acutely sensitive to the needs and wishes of their parents, clients can become acutely sensitive to the needs and wishes of their therapists. Children who are seeking love and approval adapt and accommodate. They make themselves what they think the other person wants them to be, which is a kind of self-betrayal. To what extent might the client regulate herself according to the reality of the situation she is in and the therapist's needs? To what extent is the context of therapy a compromise which is to her detriment?

The art of compromise can be seen both as a strength and a weakness. When the client adapts to the therapeutic relationship, it may be because she has the strength to compromise or the weakness of acquiescence. If it is the latter, her acquiescence might derive from fear, or from needing another's approval and affection, or from confusion, or from trust. When things are not going as she would wish, the client's frustration might be part of a constant, underlying wish – and an unconscious blueprint – to behave in a healthy way.

What happens when we compromise in a relationship with someone who subordinates his or her personality? Isn't this the antithesis of what healthy relationships are based on? There might be a danger that the client's ego becomes artificially inflated or that she ends up subordinating her true character too. In practice, does the client once again fit into an unhealthy relationship in the mistaken hope of becoming more healthy?

Whilst finishing this book, I read *Psychoanalysis: The Impossible Profession* by Janet Malcolm. Only then did I fully realise that it is acknowledged by many practitioners that psychoanalysis is 'highly artificial, extreme, bizarre, stressful, in some ways awful' (1980:76), that it is accepted that therapists are often characterised by their selfishness and self-absorption, their defensiveness and cowardice. There is, indeed, a positive attraction to the distance analysis affords them, to '*not* getting involved with the other person,...*not* taking responsibility for the other person's behaviour' (Malcolm, 1980:110). Critics of therapy are not the only ones, it seems, who suspect that psychoanalysis is 'unhealthy work', that 'it's work that drives people crazy' (ibid., p. 113). So, if it is work that drives practitioners crazy, what does it do to the client?

To what extent should our degree of 'wellness' be measured in terms of how well we adapt to a situation which is, in so many ways, a strange one? Psychotherapy can involve a particular type of psychic gymnastics – a fondness for conjecture, an ability to subvert the obvious and suspend reality, and a willingness to interact with someone on the basis that their 'actual person doesn't count' – which many of us discover, usually too late, is not necessarily commensurate with intelligent awareness. Is an appetite for this type of activity necessarily an indication of sanity? Is it even compatible with the achievement of greater inner congruence and authenticity?

When the psychoanalyst 'Luc Landau' says, 'My actual person doesn't count in all this', he is right in a way. But he suggests that this is because the analyst can 'represent your father, your mother, or anything else at all. It doesn't matter' (Alexander, 1995:22). Perhaps he sometimes does but, more crucially, what counts, over and above the actual person, is the quality of what is offered in therapy, and how we respond to that. Isn't it this quality, which is outside the two individuals concerned, which nourishes and helps to inform both participants?

Psychotherapy needs to be life-enhancing for all concerned. How does the practitioner adapt and survive? His well-being – like that of his clients – is surely fostered if he is able both to give and receive, and he should always be open to the possibility of being pleasantly surprised by what his clients bring. By allowing himself to be enlightened by the client occasionally, he might help to guard against feeling burnt out. At the same time, the client will then feel affirmed both directly and indirectly.

Is the successful therapist the one who adapts best to his particular therapeutic model? Or is it the one who at times actually forgets about his training? In *The Road Less Travelled*, Scott Peck says:

> Of all the good and useful rules of psychotherapy that I have been taught, there are very few that I have not chosen to break at one time or another…because my patient's therapy seemed to require that, one way or another, I should step out of the safety of the prescribed analyst's role, be different and risk the unconventional. (1978:159)

He describes how, in each successful case 'at some point or points …I have had to lay myself on the line' (ibid.).

Perhaps it is precisely those moments when the therapist acknowledges and responds to my particular need, when he 'lays himself on the line' or does something 'unconventional', that are especially nourishing. It has been said that therapy is not about 'tea and sympathy' but I will always remember the cup of tea that Kate made me at the end of a session when I felt particularly upset. In contrast, my analyst – when I misguidedly asked if we could have some coffee – declined, telling me later that he 'did not make tea and coffee for people'. Not for the first time, I felt as if I had been stupid for acting inappropriately, and I was surprised by what seemed unnecessarily curt behaviour.

An account by a client who suffered from severe depression describes the occasion when, 'feeling very daring', she asked her therapist if she might have a coffee. She says:

> This timid gesture, and the alacrity with which it was gratified… gave me confidence that I was an acceptable person who could ask for things without fear of reprimand. It did more to eradicate a lifetime of feeling too unworthy to ask for anything than any analytic interpretation could have done. (France, 1988:108)

These simple gestures are so ordinary yet, at the same time, they can mean so much. To eliminate the possibility of such ordinariness through fear of encouraging a theoretical problem, to see the concept of comfort almost as a clinical aberration, shows a lack of confidence and imagination on the part of the practitioner which is sad and self-defeating. Why is it that, in some therapy rooms, straightforward everyday acts of kindness are, as one client put it, 'about as common as hens' teeth'? In the textbooks and conference halls, how often are these moments of particular meeting applauded and encouraged?

Fortunately, many therapists do allow themselves to be tender, and no doubt many seriously question the way that they practise. For example, David Smith (in *Individual Therapy*, 1996:38) says that he has grown 'very sceptical about much of Freudian theory' and that he is now more alert to the 'destructive impact' of his errors. Unfortunately, it seems that others will never feel able to 'step out of the safety of the prescribed analyst's role' in order to act in the true interests of their clients.

As a result, too many clients will leave these encounters feeling bemused, impoverished or seriously disturbed. So how many of us have to go through the mill before it is fully realised how destructive that mill can be? And, even though the dialogue has opened up, does the notion of confidentiality – which is central in psychotherapy – work counter-productively in this respect? How much of the client's distress is actually due to the process itself?

Even when therapy is successful, what is the price to be paid for survival? Most of us benefit from having someone listen to our troubles. But in how many cases does the work become dishonest, because it fails to get us nearer to who we really are? And how might this be influenced by the fact that professional practitioners, like parents, often have a vested interest in maintaining the status quo?

Chapter 11

The compulsion to repeat – who needs what?

It is often assumed that the relationship between client and therapist will tend to mirror the relationship between the client and important authority figures in the past, in particular her parents. However, the client's behaviour in therapy may also reflect, in part at least, her expectation of what is a new, and very particular, experience. We go to therapy because – at a conscious level – we expect a therapist to treat us with respect and clarity, and not to repeat negative patterns from the past.

Everything that happens in therapy is said to be coloured by the emotional tone of the client's attitude, but how does the therapist's attitude towards the client affect the proceedings? Even if the client is not looking for a surrogate mother, father or lover, might the practitioner still quite like the idea of playing that role? If so, might this wish relate in some way to his own childhood disappointments?

What the client needs most is, simply, a good psychotherapist. In any event, she may start with the hope that the therapist – because he is a therapist – will understand her better than anyone else has. This may be what the therapist hopes too, so that both perhaps feel disappointed or angry if it does not happen. The practitioner, however, will tend to see the client as the source of any difficulties which arise in the relationship, rather than himself. Of course, he has been analysed – by someone who has been analysed. But who analysed the first analyst? And what was his 'problem'?

When therapists train therapists, do they sometimes reinforce and perpetuate preoccupations that are too specific, or the blind spots of a particular approach? What about therapy's shadow? And do practitioners sometimes see in their clients the 'faults' that their parents saw in them?

Some therapists, like some parents, make a habit of avoiding giving direct answers, but that should not deter their clients from asking relevant questions. What exactly *is* going on here?

Do you accept what your clients tell you?

Are you interested in what your clients are really like, or in showing off how much you think you know?

Do you really want your clients to feel equal to you, or do you secretly believe that some are more equal than others?

Why do you want to spend all day being anonymous, behaving like a blank screen?

Are you frightened that, if you close the distance, it might all be too much for you?

How honest do you really want your clients to be?

And are you worried that, if you are too honest, you might end up with egg on your face?

Do you enjoy being in a position of power?

What about your need for control?

Do the concepts of abstinence and asymmetry make you, rather than the client, feel safe?

Why do you wish to have intense relationships, closeted behind a closed door, in return for money?

Do you want to be the object of another's intense sexual desire?

What makes you want to analyse another, to play the role of parent, to be of such importance to those who come your way?

Why do some therapists seem so keen for their clients to be angry? Who needs to learn to forgive – the therapist or the client? Who is searching for an ideal? Is psychotherapy a part of and a way of perpetuating what Hillman and Ventura (in *We've Had a Hundred Years of Psychotherapy and the World is Getting Worse*) call 'the culture's hangup on an ideal significant other and salvation through tortuous love' (1993:181)?

We all need to find the courage and insight to free ourselves from the negative ways in which our parents have affected us, but to suggest that one's parents are toxic – an assertion which is not unknown – is poisonous in itself. Our parents might have made some hideous mistakes, but in the end they are our fellow passengers, and blaming them can only make us weaker. It is possible that some clients will have let go of their anger, or that their anger is about something other than their childhood. Can a therapist who has not forgiven his own parents accept that his client has?

In an article about a workshop he had just attended, a senior consultant psychotherapist describes how he at last felt able to let go of much of his previous 'toxic shame and ... chronic fear and body tension', to understand and forgive his parents 'for all their mistakes and imperfections', and to experience an 'acceptance of life and [him]self' (Stein, 1999). One might question how adequately his 'toxic shame and chronic fear and body tension' had been dealt with during his training analysis, and what influence it had had in his relationships with his patients. If he had been unable to forgive his parents, might that also have come into play? How had his difficulties in accepting life and himself coloured his work before he did the workshop?

In case examples, the clients' parents do not always seem to be accorded the kind of objective understanding which is, in theory, given to the client. For example, 'Miss A's' mother is described as sadistic, her father as irascible; she 'had been catastrophically failed as a child' (Carvalho, 1990:81); 'Frank's' father is described as an 'irascible introvert ... curmudgeonly' whilst Frank's relationship with his mother was 'idyllic' (Casement, 1996:98). These are the analyst's words, not the client's.

How can a practitioner make such judgements about people he has never met, and whose circumstances he does not fully understand? How can he know what the parents were really like when his only knowledge of them is gleaned from what his client says, often many years later? In any case, is it necessarily helpful to see our parents in this way? Few relationships are idyllic. And are concepts such as catastrophe and failure constructive?

Therapists sometimes suggest that clients begin with a rosy view of their childhood and then, thanks to their analysis, gradually realise how terrible it was. Are hope, faith and trust relegated to the back-burner? There are elements of love in abusive relationships, and the worst childhoods will often contain moments which are held dear. Acknowledging this is essential.

Who's repeating what in the therapy process? Do therapists unconsciously do to their clients what their parents did to them? Who, in reality, is 'acting out' the leftovers of an unhappy childhood? The therapist as well as the client projects, transfers, misperceives, has unresolved issues. Ferenzi says: 'Isn't it possible, indeed probable, that a doctor who has not been well analyzed (after all, who is well analyzed?) will not cure the patient but rather will use her or him to play out his own neurotic or psychotic needs?' (cited in Masson, 1992:129). It has been pointed out that 'the vocation for psychotherapeutic work is likely to come from at least some degree of disturbance and pathology, and from a need for repair in the analysts themselves' (Carvalho, 1990:77).

A practitioner chooses to work in the way that he does for a reason. Might he unconsciously seek opportunities to reenact the behaviour associated with his own imperfect experience of being parented – this time sitting on the other side of the fence? When he speaks to the client of what she cannot have, who is he trying to convince? Does he take refuge in the premise that the pain of the engagement is of benefit to the client, just as the abusive parent often believes that what he does is for the child's own good? And if we believe we are not the cause of another person's difficulties, then we exempt ourselves from feeling morally responsible for them.

Might a kind of unconscious complicity then arise between therapist and client in which some of the worst aspects of the parent/child relationship are relived rather than grown through? The client can reinforce and get caught by the notion of an ideal parent, inadvertently allowing the therapist to treat her in ways which are inherently hurtful. The practitioner can inadvertently reinforce the notion of a bad child, or become the parent who does not hear what the child is saying.

In his description of the Jungian approach to psychodynamic therapy, Richard Carvalho describes how the client in his case example 'managed to become quite severely ill' (1990:83). This reminds me of a friend who thought that her daughter was pretending to have a stomach ache in order to avoid going to school, (the child, in fact, loved school). The child was eventually taken to hospital, only narrowly escaping a ruptured appendix.

Why does the analyst in the above example say the client 'managed to' become ill? Is the implication that she became ill on purpose? Her illness is noted as relevant data, but the practitioner does not express in his writing any concern, or allude to a human response to it. That it merited sympathetic attention, or that the therapist might have been partially responsible for it, is not mentioned. Instead, he only seems interested in relentlessly pursuing the same distressing course of action – the 'therapy' which is having such an unpleasant effect on the person he is supposed to be helping.

Is the client's very real suffering responded to authentically or is it, effectively, ignored? Is the therapist sometimes so busy analysing it and working out what he ought to be saying that he fails to realise that the appropriate response to suffering is compassion? And if he responds to his client's confusion and pain with irritation at times because he does not know what to do, does he later explain the reason to her, and so alleviate the hurt that his response has caused? Or does he behave more like the tetchy parent who thinks that the child is deliberately trying to provoke him?

In a description of Freudian therapy, an analyst describes how a client

> tells his therapist that he is refraining from mentioning something important, and goes on to talk about trivial matters. The client uses a great deal of body language ... The therapist ... pays disproportionate attention to the client's body. The client has skilfully and unconsciously induced the therapist to gaze intensely at his body and thus enact with him an exhibitionistic sexual fancy. (Smith, 1996:34)

The therapist then 'silently analyses' the counter-transference and draws conclusions about the client's 'concealed wish to exhibit himself' (ibid.). But the client may not have been trying to 'exhibit himself'; he might simply have felt ill at ease, embarrassed by the 'something important' that he felt unable to talk about. There are many different reasons why we use body language, and perhaps what clients want is sometimes a lot more straightforward than psychoanalysts would have us believe.

The tone of some case examples is chilling. For example, Carvalho tells us his client 'maintained that she ...' (1990:83), rather than saying 'she felt that she ...', implying that he thinks her distress was in some way invalid. He says that his client frequently accused him of being patronising. Did he never consider that, on occasions, he might have been? We are all capable of being patronising at times. There seems to be a fundamental lack of humility, an absence of empathy and warmth in these clinical descriptions.

Such attitudes towards the client also demonstrate an absence of trust on the part of the practitioner. The problems of therapy are sometimes attributed to the client's difficulty in trusting the therapist but it can be the other way round. The therapist becomes the cowardly or distrustful parent – not because of the client's transference but because of his own lack of confidence or awareness.

One of the worst aspects of an unhealthy parent/child relationship is the way in which it tends to focus on the negative rather than the positive. The parent tells the child what not to do. She is given attention when her behaviour does not please. A great deal of emotional energy is invested in what are interpreted as her faults and failings. It seems to happen with even the most loving parents. Can psychotherapy also be unbalanced in this way?

Analysands tend to talk about their failures, so the practitioner may know little about their achievements. I was worried – transference again – that my analyst would think I was showing off if I said positive things about myself. Since the therapist only sees his client when she is sitting in his room, he may be unaware of the areas in which she shines. So it is not surprising if the client sometimes wonders how the practitioner sees her, if reassurance is sometimes necessary.

In acting simply as a mirror, there is a danger that the therapist will simply reflect back the negative aspects of the client's self-image, the internalised self-perception created via her parents' judgements and criticisms. A wooden manner and its concomitant lack of response can recreate the all-too-familiar feelings of apparent disenchantment and disapproval. But this time around, the adult client may no longer derive strength from the robust repair mechanisms which characterise childhood and which link in with the child's natural ability to be in tune with what truly motivates her actions.

Therapists spend a great deal of time with clients who have had deeply disturbing experiences, but this should not cause them to forget that there is another side to childhood. Children frequently have a clarity and a strength of will which extricate them from being trapped by other people's prejudices. Whilst adults theorise, they go straight to the heart of the matter. By the time we get to the therapy room in adulthood, we have usually slowed down a bit. The layers which mask and blur have had more time to accumulate, and our capacity for overcoming trauma may have weakened.

Adults frequently have less, not more, self-confidence than young people. Other people's behaviour and opinions still affect us, we have simply become adept at pretending they don't. How the therapist experiences me, the client, is particularly important because I reveal to him a great deal of myself. But his wish to provide helpful insights can feel like a subtle form of blaming and one-upmanship.

It is the fate of most children to inherit judgemental parents. But, as we grow up, we share our experiences with siblings and peers and may find that they feel the same as we do. We make other relationships, learn to measure ourselves in terms of other criteria. We may become parents ourselves and understand better why our own parents were as they were. In part, the wounds heal.

In therapy, we go back to a place of acute vulnerability, revisit old wounds. We open up in a way which is both essential and naive. So when it feels as if a therapist is being judgemental, it hurts a great deal. The client does not consciously expect him to be disapproving. When my analyst appeared to disapprove of things I had done, I felt shocked and wondered if I was mistaken. I also wondered if I was right, and felt hurt in case I was. If he was really being disapproving, then surely he wasn't doing his job very well? If he didn't disapprove and I was mistaken, then it seemed foolish to object to something which was not actually happening. I felt caught between the two equally difficult options of suggesting he was behaving out of order or saying that I felt something which, in fact, had no valid basis. Neither option seemed viable.

I did not expect to feel hurt by my analyst, but ended up feeling profoundly hurt. It is precisely because the client expects something different that the 'replay' is so devastating. Yet is this underlying factor sometimes overlooked? In her confusion, the child in the adult client might wish to 'repair the damage', to continue with the therapy. She does not challenge the therapist appropriately, and is caught once again in the trap of her own transference.

If a therapist is to be, in part, like a wise parent, then won't he be prepared to meet his client half-way? He has to give her a little of what she wants if she is to come to realise how badly she wants it. There has to be a certain amount of positive feedback and reassurance. Otherwise, the client may shut off the part of herself that seeks affirmation, because the apparent (or real) lack of esteem from the therapist is too painful.

How many practitioners encourage their clients to see themselves as strong? When I hear an 'expert' in human nature telling me this is the case, it is especially empowering. How many therapists show – in ways which are relatively easily recognisable – that they value and care about their clients? If they do not value them or truly care, then they are in the wrong job. And if they do care and don't show it, then why don't they? Are they embarrassed? If so, how can they claim to be able to help others deal with awkwardness over feelings?

Ferenzi talks about how Freud

> looms like a god above his poor patient, who has been degraded to the status of a child. We claim that the transference comes from the patient, unaware of the fact that the greater part of what one calls the transference is artificially provoked by this very behaviour. (cited in Masson, 1992:130)

The therapist does not have to 'loom' to create anxiety. Simply sitting in silence is sometimes enough.

Silence can – at certain times and in certain circumstances – be a blessing. It can also hang in the air, and glare back with an unfriendly face. This was how it felt to me much of the time. My analyst wanted to know why I had a problem with silence, I wanted to know the reason for his. Without the latter, I was unable to explore the former. To the client who feels unsure, the therapist's silence can make the space between them feel threatening and empty, and a negation of her self.

Being self-aware and feeling self-conscious are very different things, and the effect of the latter can be highly relevant to what happens in therapy. Have you ever eaten a meal sitting opposite someone who is doing nothing other than give you their un-divided attention? It is not unusual to feel like a clumsy child with spaghetti sauce all over her chin. I began to think 'I feel ill at ease, I am getting nowhere, therefore I must be doing something wrong' – just as the child often blames herself for problems with her parents. The child who has been told that she 'thinks too much' and 'shouldn't ask so many questions' is then resurrected in therapy. She doesn't ask awkward questions, she feels like a nuisance.

The contradictions of childhood are mirrored also in the contra-dictions which arise in the client's search for meaning in therapy. For example, parents often lack respect for the child's wish for privacy, to have secrets. At the same time, they may provide an insufficiently strong presence when it comes to offering effective guidelines for dealing with life. According to one account at least, in psychoanalysis 'complete candour is expected of patients' yet, at the same time, it is up to the patient to decide where to 'draw the line' (Smith, 1996:27, 33). But can the two go together? If she is to be 'completely candid', where is the line to be drawn? I found this a difficult dilemma at times.

When a practitioner cultivates the position of a distant and often silent observer, the client is given the rapt attention of someone who is partially absent. (The therapist is, after all, only doing his job.) If the therapist holds back too much, and his abstinence is not sufficiently well blended with the right degree of caring response, there is no sense of a container. This particular distillation of a combination of presence and absence may echo and heighten a sense of someone who is only there superficially, engendering the sadness and frustration children feel when they wish to engage with a parent whose attention is elsewhere. One feels unimportant, uninteresting, and therefore unable to do the work of therapy well.

The more open and committed the client is, the more she will feel this hurt and frustration, because the lack of support comes at a time when she feels particularly vulnerable, from the person to whom she has specifically turned for help and for authentic response. It comes from someone who could instead have done so much that was positive.

When the practitioner is unable to understand and help with his client's feelings, he unavoidably repeats, and even renders more powerful, similar parental failings in childhood. The client can then be left feeling humiliated and bereft. The practitioner, like the parent, puts himself in a position where his mistakes and his failures may have grave consequences.

When one becomes involved in the delicate business of caring for the well-being of another, irritation and defensiveness can easily creep in if one does not seem to be achieving the desired effect. Practitioners who set out wanting to do good can end up behaving in ways which are silly, spiteful and, ultimately, damaging. Somehow somewhere down the line things get distorted and the relationship becomes emotionally and psychologically abusive. Practitioners can then behave like the worst kind of ignorant, tyrannical and oppressive parents. If the mantra of their training pushes them into believing that their mode of accessing truth is superior to that of their clients, they risk losing sight of the goalposts – the aim of achieving a productive outcome – and of the rules for being human.

It could be argued that the psychodynamic approach actually encourages the therapist to reenact parts of the damaging aspects of the parent/child relationship. The replay takes place in the starkest of contexts, in a professional relationship with none of the underpinnings of the more tangible support that usually exists in some form – however inadequate it may be – within most families. One is having to endure the same old thing in the name of therapy, and pay for the privilege to boot.

Where in all this is the golden thread that Ariadne gave to Theseus when he went into the underworld and killed the Minotaur – the thread that enabled him to find his way out again? Establishing this lifeline at the beginning of therapy is essential. It is initiated when the therapist bears witness to the client's intrinsic strength as well as to her suffering.

The container which is the vehicle of therapy does not exist simply by virtue of the fact that one is with a therapist. It has to be created, and the trust with which we arrive should be nurtured rather than whittled away. The sense of being contained arises when we begin to feel that, this time, things really can be different. Nothing should be taken for granted. We are all vulnerable. We all need to feel that we are valuable, lovable, special and sane. We all need reassurance and encouragement, not because we are neurotic but because we are human.

Chapter 12

The problem of attachment

The question of attachment in therapy is a complex one, not least because we tend to get attached to those who get attached to us. So who needs who in psychotherapy, and what do we get attached to?

In therapy we buy a period of time in which to concentrate exclusively on ourselves. But being the sole focus of someone else's interest is a double-edged sword, both unnerving and enticing. Scrutiny may induce alarm, but the attention that a therapist offers is also seductive. The attentiveness, the intimacy, the exclusivity draw one in and mesmerise, obscuring the hazards of the emotional and psychological roller-coaster ride that lies ahead.

Therapy is self-perpetuating. It can also be addictive. But do we become addicted because of the benefits we are reaping or because we are caught, poised in wait for the benefits to materialise? When therapy does not seem beneficial, why do we continue? Perhaps it is the potential that lures, the manicured fingers of possibility which beckon and tempt. Ernesto Spinelli suggests that what may keep the client going back for more is not necessarily transference, but 'therapy's potential offering', the glimpses that we experience in therapy of an 'encounter between individuals ... which allows the client to explore and clarify and challenge him- or herself in a respectful, attentive and honest manner ... which reflects the client's stance towards him- or herself' (1995:164). It might be our natural inquisitiveness, our hunger for knowing, which determines our appetite in therapy.

We may also be drawn back by our desire to be correctly understood. After all, if the therapist cannot see me clearly, then who will? The more a therapist seems to misinterpret, the greater might be the client's need to put the record straight. So, ironically, the worse the therapy feels, the greater might be our wish to continue and to seek amelioration. Perhaps it's a little like fruit machines – the more you put in, the greater can be the desire to keep on going until you get something back. I am not usually attracted to gambling, but that was how it felt to me at one point.

I was also attached to doing what I had set out to do, to not giving up, to seeing things through. I was attached to the hope of becoming a better wife and mother, to the idea of learning and – despite my trepidation – discovery. I was attached to the need to feel that I mattered, and a desire to reach my unreachable, untouchable analyst.

We become attached to the therapist because he is another human being, and one with whom we offer to share what feels most intimate to us. Some kind of bond is bound to develop, simply by virtue of the fact that two people meet regularly and do serious work together. My analyst both floored and fascinated me. He gave me his undivided attention, inferred that we might climb mountains together. He offered exploration, but then de-activated my compass.

The roots of our attachments may be multifold. The client's attachment to the therapist might come from a transferential need for his approval, inflamed by the dubious logic that, by not giving someone something they want, they will then stop wanting it. And is there a sense in which some clients are attracted by the complex reinterpretations of themselves that analysis offers, because such interpretations make them feel they are more inter-esting people? With my second therapist, what attracted me back was my need to understand, and the sense of both space and containment which she gave me. In humanistic types of therapy, it could be an attachment to the affirmation that the therapist appears to offer.

It is said there is a danger that, if the therapist is 'really warm and nice to clients, it leads many of them, as well as [the therapist], up the garden path' because they become dependent on him (Ellis, in Dryden, 1997:9). In my experience, the therapist's being 'really warm and nice' does not necessarily foster dependence, or involve his being overindulgent, unwise or unrealistic. Never-theless, most therapists will rightly emphasise the importance of helping clients to accept themselves unconditionally, so that they become less dependent on the esteem of others. But is the therapist best placed to facilitate greater independence?

Perhaps psychotherapy homes in on that most basic human need, what the poet W. H. Auden says is 'true of the normal heart' – 'the error bred in the bone of each woman and each man', the error which makes us crave what we cannot have – 'not universal love, but to be loved alone' (from *September 1, 1939*). And isn't this 'error', the need to feel unique and special, bred in all our hearts – the therapist's as well?

Issues of attachment and dependency are relevant to the therapist as well as to the client. Whatever the approach, the client is dependent on the therapist, and the therapist is also dependent on the client. He needs the fee his clients pay him and is, in most cases, dependent on them for his income. We all tend at times to resent those on whom we depend so, on a bad day, any therapist would be forgiven for resenting somewhat the demands of his clients.

Can a way of working which emphasises transference foster an unhelpful dependency and an equally unhelpful counter-dependency? To what extent, for instance, is the practitioner dependent on his clients' esteem? Perhaps there is a risk that his need to feel of value may get in the way. The therapist will be dependent on his clients' ability to change, just as teachers are dependent on their students' ability to learn. He is also dependent on their need for his help, the very thing which he works towards eliminating. Is there a temptation for the therapist to go on looking for problems in order to keep the client, and for the client to go on looking for problems in order to keep the therapist?

It is our attachment to particular ways of being which prevents us from growing. A practitioner, equally, may be strongly attached to a specific way of working, a way which may not always be appropriate or beneficial, so that sometimes the client needs the therapist to change, in order to be able to change herself. It could be that both analysand and analyst are frightened of leaping into the unknown, that both of them prefer to cling to the wreckage of what they have known in the past.

The therapist, as well as the client, may lose a sense of perspective both about the work and about his own importance, so that the therapy 'freezes up'. There can be 'a kind of grandiosity that is often embodied in the attitudes of therapists that they can be all things to all people' (Wachtel, in Dryden, 1997:144). Such an attitude might divert attention away from the centrality of the client's everyday life and relationships.

In *Consuming Therapy*, Ann France describes how, at the beginning of her therapy, she talked about 'the pressing problem' of her relationship with the person she was living with. Her therapist told her that she was really talking about her relationship with her (the therapist). France contends that this interpretation is not an unusual one in therapy. I remember my analyst suggesting that I was curious about him at a time when I rarely gave him, personally, a second thought outside the therapy room.

What might often be of relevance, particularly at the beginning of the work, is how the client feels about being in therapy. This does need to be discussed, and it may be very different from how she feels about the therapist as a person. The client may feel considerable trepidation at the idea of counselling or psychotherapy. She may be embarrassed by the situation which has driven her to the therapy room, and about the fact that she has ended up there. It is quite possible, for example, to dislike doing therapy but, at the same time, like the therapist with whom one is working. It is necessary to distinguish between feelings about therapy and feelings about the therapist, and if the practitioner personalises everything the client says, he fails to make this distinction.

An insistence that the client is really referring to the therapist when she is talking about something or someone else is, at an immediate level, inefficient and impractical. It may prevent her from talking about the problems she actually wants to discuss, so that her short-term concerns are effectively ignored. But doesn't it also carry with it a dangerously undermining undertone? Instead of being encouraged to see herself as an independent adult, is the client fed back an image of herself as someone whose psyche is inextricably entwined with that of her therapist? Rather than help her to see herself as separate, the practitioner does the opposite.

Why does this arise and who is trying to recreate what? Is it always the client who wishes to restore the 'symbiotic parental relationship'? Might a therapist sometimes have an unconscious need to have such a relationship, or to manoeuvre himself into a position in which he can contend that any negative views his clients entertain about him have no substance and are merely projections?

There is a worrying whiff of both insecurity and conceit in a therapist's readiness to see himself as the central point around which everything the client says pivots. In practical terms, he risks sidelining not only the client's everyday difficulties, but also her more long-term aspirations – 'the hero's journey'. His true role is that of a facilitator, but the concepts of transference and projection might feed a disposition to see himself, and what he represents in the mind of the client, as the crucial focal point of the work.

In some cases, a focus on the therapist may occur in any case, to a greater or lesser extent, particularly perhaps in a relationship between a female client and a male therapist. The need for male approval is strong in many of us. For any woman, finding a man who listens to her intently for fifty minutes is bound to evoke surprise and delight, whoever he is. The therapist may appear to offer a cornucopia of support, understanding and a subtle unspoken intimacy. It is an emotional dynamic which can easily slide over into an unhelpful attachment and betray one's best intentions. Family and friends may feel usurped or threatened by such a seemingly bounteous and private relationship.

As the literature points out, 'the stereotypical notion of trans-ference is that the client falls in love with the analyst' (Jacobs, 1988:102). But what a practitioner might see coolly as part of the treatment can be the opposite of beneficial from the point of view of the unwary client. A make-believe love affair which is one-sided, paid for and by appointment may seem more humiliating than healthy. For someone who is alone and without close friends, the therapist may become disproportionately important. And, if the client has a partner and children, such feelings are not to be taken lightly.

The client does not live in a psychotherapeutic vacuum. What Freud referred to somewhat glibly as the patient's having to 'accept falling in love with her doctor as an inescapable fate' (Freud, 1915; cited in Malcolm, 1980:12) may have negative reper-cussions not only in terms of her personal sense of stability, but also in the wider realms of her life outside – the very thing she is hoping to improve. So, if the client falls in love with the practi-tioner, what happens then? Does she leave, or does she stay and 'process' it? Is it possible to have a professional relationship with someone in such circumstances, or are the two incompatible?

How are therapists affected when their clients fall in love with them? Are the client's feelings seen as a stage to be worked through? If so, this might infer to the client that something as seminal as her capacity to love is seen as misplaced and in need of correction. It is important that the therapist respects and honours the delicacy and acute rawness of the client's emotions in such cases.

Do practitioners remain immune to the client's strength of feeling, or are they drawn into its provocative intensity? Are they frightened by it, or do they derive satisfaction from it? Is it humanly possible to avoid feeling bolstered by such adoration? Or might the therapist try so hard to avoid feeling gratified in this way that he ends up giving the impression that the client's feelings are of little importance to him?

The problem of attachment may be viewed radically differently by the person sitting in the practitioner's chair and the one sitting in the client's. A practitioner will be familiar with the phenomenon of 'transference love' and may consider it to be a central element in the therapy. From the client's point of view, it may come as a surprise, and it is difficult to see such strength of feeling – if that is what arises – simply as a means to an end, viable in terms of its temporary utility. Highly emotional and intimate relationships are not usually a means to something else, but an end in themselves. We work on the difficulties they throw up because we wish to sustain the relationship – it forms part of the central fabric of our lives. In contrast, we usually engage with a professional practitioner in order to avail ourselves of certain skills, and not in order to have a intense, personal relationship with him or her. So what may be, for the therapist, an accepted part of the process can seem, to the client, an unwelcome, additional and complicating problem.

The pain that falling in love with the therapist can cause should not be underestimated. One might question how many practitioners have the ability to handle the erotic transference sensitively and successfully. The therapist needs to appreciate how important he is to the client, yet be unattached to feelings of his own importance. If he is to enable her to feel free of undue attachment to him, he will look constantly beyond the limited relationship he has helped to create. The client's deepest and most intense attachment may be to the process of discovery, and the journey towards 'individuation' – subjects which deserve all her passion and intelligence.

What the client is most dependent on during this journey is the practitioner's integrity, his willingness to extend himself, to lay himself on the line, and the authenticity of his 'devotion to the pursuit of truth'. I am dependent on the therapist not so much as an object of my love or hate, but as someone who is willing and able to be open, honest and responsible, and to change and grow alongside me. I am dependent on his commitment to truth.

If a therapist sees the past as being the main cause of 'current behaviour', he may be ill-prepared to move into the uncharted waters of what might come next. Therapy exists in the present and it is also about the future, about experiencing new emotions, about the fulfilling of potential. It is an opening of doors which had been partly closed, an encounter with the unknown. And what we do not know can sometimes seem more threatening than dealing with what we know.

Therapy, then, is an initiation into newness, a kind of rite of passage. In her discussion of Jungian therapy, Ann Casement refers to the significance of such rituals and to a 'reincorporation into the world but with a new identity' (1996:91). If, in therapy, we reincorporate ourselves into the world with a new identity, then our boundaries will go through some profound realignment. By being open to the possibility of change and being committed to that process, the client's boundaries crumble, much as they do when we fall in love.

'Lovers need to know how to lose themselves and then how to find themselves again' (from *By the River Piedra I Sat Down and Wept*, by Paulo Coelho). And so it is in therapy. In Coelho's novel, he tells us: '*Son los locos que inventaron el amor*. The song was right: it must have been the lunatics who invented love' (1997:35). To make the most of therapy, we might have to become, at some point, less sane than we were when we began. When this time comes, we need something real to hang on to.

The therapist's most important role is to be a real and loving midwife, rather than a fantasy mother or father or lover. The midwife (the French term 'sage-femme' also means 'wise woman') helps us in knowing when to hold back and when to push forward, when to conserve our energy and when to call on our deepest reserves. The wise woman helps us to breathe through the pain, so that it is manageable rather than overwhelming. She helps us to get the timing right. Living well has to do with good timing, with being in tune with life, so that we move with its rhythms rather than against them. Good therapy helps us to hear the music and enjoy the dance.

What we need when we are feeling frightened and foolish and angry and hurt and confused and ashamed, and when we are feeling excited and curious and elated and wild, is a steadfast, consistent and caring companion. We need an ally who will walk beside us hand in hand and peer with us into the unknown. That person might, at times, be the object of our fantasies but, over and above everything else, we need an anchor, someone who will help us to feel secure, someone who trusts enough to believe – and to enable me, the client, to believe – that what we are essentially about is fine. When we feel panic and fear, we need to hear: 'This is not all of you. This is just the place you are in at the moment, and things will change.'

If the therapist feels safe, if he is ready to go out on a creative limb occasionally then, in partnership with his client, he might add to our collective understanding and be enriched by the experience. Attachment to a particular theory can restrict and restrain, engendering tunnel vision and a dangerous narrow-mindedness. A genuinely therapeutic environment is one in which mystery is welcomed and becomes the territory. The unknown takes its rightful place as a site for exploration. It then loses its power as a prompter of discomfort. The most accurate – and sometimes reassuring – explanation might be that there is no obvious answer.

If the practitioner is too attached to the past, he looks back at what we have come from, rather than thinking in terms of what we are moving towards. He sits at the edge of the client's experience and labels as neurosis what could be providential; he fails to identify that which is redemptive, and that which simply is. 'Freud never saw the possibility that therapy could be a prelude to a passionate love-affair with Mystery. The pathologizing of the unconscious makes it frightening'(Claxton, 1994:158).

The true therapist has a broader perspective, and an ease which enables him to both contain the client and make space for her. In doing so, he allows her to grow and move forward. And by holding and sharing a belief in our individual and collective wisdom, he will enable his client to touch whatever it is that transcends us all.

Chapter 13

When 'therapy' traumatises

Therapy is about how we feel when we seek help for our self. When a client takes that step, she will be greatly affected by the way her request is dealt with. According to one psychoanalyst, analysis is 'an operation. It rearranges things inside the mind the way surgery rearranges things inside the body' (Malcolm, 1980:108). If it is an operation, then it is on the heart as well as the mind.

If we open up to someone and place our trust in them, we give them the power to wound us deeply. If we begin to rearrange the contents of our mind, there are considerable risks. So perhaps the suffering engendered during psychotherapy is not only about making the unconscious conscious, about the experience of previously buried anguish. The newness of the context of being in therapy gives it the potential to improve things, or to do the opposite. The factors which characterise the work of some psychotherapeutic practice can combine together to forge themselves into something which is a long way from what was originally intended, and which becomes fragmenting and traumatic rather than helpful.

The shifting sands of therapy can be dangerously unsafe. Therapy can evoke both intense feelings and unfamiliar states of mind, sometimes even pushing the client into an altered state of consciousness. Such experiences may have more in common with a bad LSD trip than with the notion of healing. The dismantling brought on by analysis can tip over into disintegration and leave the client feeling unstable and at sea, mentally adrift and emotionally ransacked.

When one goes to a therapist, one needs clarity and support, and not the equivalent of a psychological quiz game entwined

with an emotional endurance course. Yet isn't much of the behaviour embodied in an analytical approach the *opposite* of what we
normally associate with lucidity and caring? Conversations with
other clients suggest that some practitioners can and do behave in
an odd and astonishingly heartless fashion. It is little wonder if the
client then becomes abstracted or distraught. Yet many practitioners
appear to persist in their belief that the resulting anguish is not
of their own making and is, in any case, advantageous in the
long term.

Do some professionals promote encounters which are intrinsically eccentric and disagreeable, then fail to see that their folly
breeds further folly? How many clients are aware of the effect of
psychoanalytic techniques before they begin therapy, or of the
huge emotional investment and upheaval therapy involves? Most
of us are not. What may happen in reality is that another unpleasant and demoralising experience is added to the client's life history.
Any gains which are accrued then carry with them an expensive
price tag, and the client may be left in a worse state than when she
started. Existing insecurities are sharpened and new ones added.
Associated feelings of hurt and shock are then revived.

In his book *Waking the Tiger*, Bernard Levine argues that ways of
working 'that encourage intense emotional reliving of trauma may
be harmful ... There is a good chance that the cathartic reliving of
an experience can be traumatizing rather than healing' (1997:10).
When we feel traumatised, we freeze. In freezing, we enter an
altered state in which no pain is experienced, and our capacities to
respond effectively are overwhelmed. How confident can practitioners be that their clients will always work through, rather than
simply relive, early emotions and experience?

The source of our difficulties may not necessarily be easily
recalled and then – possibly – exorcised. They may be associated
with seams of emotion which ran through childhood. Certain ways
of working, coupled with human error on the part of the therapist,
might produce too vividly some of the common denominators
which are unsettling in childhood, recurrent elements which
underlined individual events.

Such themes might include not knowing what is happening;
not feeling in control; a paucity of genuine communication and
understanding; a lack of feeling affirmed, valued or supported;
feelings of rejection or abandonment; a misinterpretation or

apparent pathologising of our emotions and experience; and the fear that those emotions will engulf and overwhelm us. These things are likely to arise at some point in any childhood, but the client's memory of them may not be sufficiently distinct for them to be earmarked and identified.

If they arise again in therapy, might they actually freeze our capacity to use the therapy relationship as a vehicle in which to make sense of them? One cannot afford to ignore the significance of the context in which the reliving occurs. The client had trusted the therapist and had assumed that the work would be of benefit, so such repetition feels both upsetting and incongruous. A claim that the therapist is simply tapping into past problems – and therefore has no personal role to play when the client feels hurt and confused – can feel like an additional twist of the knife and is, in any case, debatable. In the context of any other relationship, such a claim would appear nonsensical.

The themes outlined above can be disturbing *per se*, in childhood and in adulthood, whatever our past experience. The capacity to inhabit a whole spectrum of mental states and emotion is part of the human condition, so there is not some cut-off point at which everything becomes attributable to past events rather than present ones. In any case, our ability to overcome what has been blocking us will depend, in part at least, on the opportunities which are offered in the present.

No one would deny the significance of early life, or the value of understanding the cause of the habits we have evolved. The notion that present and past are connected is indisputable but, as a guiding methodological principle, it may not always get us very far forward. Does it necessarily benefit the client, promote good practice or lead to responsible therapy?

Is it expedient to work on an assumption that everything that happens in therapy is caused by something that has happened before? Is it even a sound premise? 'That clients can and do experience strong emotions towards their therapists is beyond doubt; that the source of these emotions is best explained via trans-ference, however, remains an open question' (Spinelli, 1995:163). Whatever their source, the powerful emotions aroused in therapy may be distressing and disabling rather than curative.

Therapy will promote the remembering of past feelings; but it will also create a chemistry of its own. And could it be the case that a client who has not had a particularly traumatic childhood has developed fewer defence mechanisms, and is therefore less able to cope with the stressful idiosyncrasies of the blank screen approach, than someone who has had to develop a thicker skin?

It might sometimes be the therapist's behaviour which is a source of difficulty. In the field of learning, it is recognised that it may be the teacher, not the learner, who is responsible for feelings of incompetence and inadequacy and for a fear of failure (Williams and Burden, 1997). If one takes the view that psychotherapy 'has more in common with an educational experience than a form of medical treatment' (Cooper, 1996:56), then it is important to take into account how we learn. Surely we learn best in the context of a supportive, meaningful relationship rooted firmly in the here and now? But such a relationship may not develop if the therapist remains stuck in his belief that everything is 'the outcome of ante-cedent conditions' (Farrell, 1981, cited in Cooper, 1996:43).

Am I anxious or at ease now because of past anxiety or ease, or because the present is making me feel anxious or at ease, or is it both? Whatever the cause, experiencing something as unhelpful in the past should not disqualify one from suggesting it is unhelp-ful when it is encountered in the therapy room. And perhaps there are things which are problematic in therapy which have not, generally speaking, been a significant factor outside it. There are few other situations in which the feelings and behaviour of one person are so intensely scrutinised – at least, by someone who makes of point of remaining, effectively, a stranger. So doesn't therapy sometimes reveal, sometimes replicate, and sometimes create the feelings and behaviour that arise there?

Feelings of incomprehension, for instance, can induce anxiety in any situation. Children often feel scared when they don't under-stand what is happening, and they can cope with a lot if we take them into our confidence. Therapy can feel scary or safe for exactly the same reason, irrespective of the past. In my case, not knowing had, at times, been a source of fear and anxiety in child-hood, as well as in more recent times, in events involving my children. In my first experience of psychotherapy, the process I was engaged in began to make less and less sense to me. The lack of structure and my analyst's inscrutability had considerable effect, but it was not one which was to my advantage.

Unease can also arise in a relationship with someone who does not seem to accept what we tell him, even if he does preface what he says with 'perhaps'. We cannot then be clear about our confusion. If it is true that we don't know what we think until we hear ourselves say it, then the first step in therapy needs to be to get a more accurate idea of what we think we think. Changing our feelings and perceptions, and then moving on, will come second. If there is no recognition of the validity of the client's feelings, or of their most immediate cause, this may replicate precisely what was missing in the past.

The client can, inadvertently, begin to assume an essentially passive, powerless role if her behaviour is talked about in isolation. She is someone to whom things are done. A therapist might tend to play down the significance of the actions of others – working on the basis that he can neither judge nor change other people, he can only help the client to change. He focuses on her feelings. The asymmetry of that focus can seem, to the client, like an asymmetry of responsibility; she may feel she is entirely responsible when things are problematic. This emphasis leaves out or marginalises a notion of joint responsibility within a relationship. It also neglects the parallel and equally important reality of the effect of the client's personality and actions on other people.

Taking responsibility includes fully realising the impact we have on others. So isn't a truly therapeutic relationship one in which we experience and understand how we affect another, and in which our challenge is both accommodated and confronted? In childhood, we frequently feel we have little control over or influence on the behaviour of others and on the course of events. Might a feeling of powerlessness be similarly generated by a therapist? By remaining apparently unmoved by the client, he may actually make her feel impotent.

My analyst's copious silence, and his lack of receptivity when I expressed unbearably painful emotions concerning our relationship, cut me to the bone marrow. I felt that my feelings had been crushed by a large granite boulder. 'It is the failure to get through to other people and to elicit a response from them that is at the source of much emotional disturbance' (France, 1988:180). Such failure, and its concomitant emotional disturbance, can feel more acute in therapy than in everyday life.

It is argued that any lapse from analytic neutrality impinges on the client's freedom to discover her true feelings. However, the absence of a reasonable human response may, to the untrained client, appear bewilderingly false or seem like emotional insensitivity of almost psychopathic proportions. It therefore, in itself, will provoke a reaction in the client – feelings which then, equally, may divert her away from properly exploring the particular issue she wished to focus on.

One of the aims of therapy, of course, is to provide a context where, in theory, our behaviour does not produce the usual negative consequences. So perhaps a lack of response is overlooked by many therapists as a severely damaging negative consequence. Just because the therapist remains sitting in his chair and does not actively abuse his client, his behaviour is not necessarily helpful.

In theory, the client chucks everything at the therapist and he invites her to come back next week and do it all over again. But the encounter can be dysfunctional if it appears to soak up the impact of her feelings and behaviour to a point where the relationship ceases to be either credible or constructive. It is equally counterproductive if it fails to incorporate and reflect the positive effects of what she brings.

A therapist will endeavour not to be shocked by what his clients tell him, but he should not give the client the impression that her personality and her feelings – especially her feelings about him – are of no importance to him. If feedback is too clinical, the client can feel she has become, within the therapy relationship, a kind of object, a non-entity. Her feelings and behaviour have no consequences – the position of the psychopath. It seems to her that, as far as her therapist is concerned, she does not touch him, she does not exist.

Do practitioners sometimes forget how negating this stance can be? One is obliged to try to make sense of a relationship where neither person can be truly present, where each plays a kind of game – a game which can become a maddening experience, in both senses of the word. The two protagonists inhabit an unreal place of hypothetical inconsequentiality. And, if the client feels that the therapist is immune to her, she may fail to take proper responsibility for her part in the relationship.

Our actions, of course, are not without consequence, even in therapy. The psychoanalyst Brearley (1996) describes the ways in which a patient 'nudges' , 'invites', 'provokes' others, including the practitioner, into various roles. But the therapist is not a textbook and he does not always simply note this fact and draw attention to it. Sometimes he may actually play some of these roles. He may really be insincere, pompous, patronising, uncomprehending, authoritarian or defensive.

Because the client, and not the practitioner, is the focus of attention, such tendencies can flourish, unchallenged. For example, a therapist may appear condescending, the client may feel inadequate. She subsequently looks at her feelings of inadequacy and fails to consider whether or not the therapist is acting with grace – and the effect that has on her. If she feels intimidated, she may not see when he is being unhelpful and defensive. An insinuation that she does not trust can divert her away from disagreeing with the practitioner, or from recognising when he is being intransigent or opinionated. By sidelining the problems which the therapist contributes, the client's difficulties are not properly contextualised.

In his discussion of psychodynamic counselling, Jacobs points out how the practitioner will inevitably 'fail' the client 'by not listening, by not understanding, or by making the wrong interpretation'. He says that 'none of this need spell disaster (providing the counsellor is not afraid to bring these losses and disappointments into the open)' (1988:117). But the therapist does not always bring them into the open. He may even be unaware of his failures. He may refer to them using therapy jargon which mystifies the client, or simply allude to them in order to see how she responds.

If the client does not pick up a therapist's more abstruse cues then, instead of returning the ball to his court and waiting for him to act, she may jump over the net and attempt to scoop it up herself. This echoes the situation of childhood where a parent fails to take responsibility, to have clear boundaries, and so the child – and later the client in therapy – then carries a disproportionate load of guilt and anxiety. The client, like the child, might be the recipient of mixed messages, which then serve to blur her vision even further.

Inappropriate interpretations and negative projections can be extremely destructive. The client may find herself adrift in a sea of uncertainty, because the concept of the unconscious means that nothing is irrefutable. She becomes a compendium of interminable and often indeterminable possibilities, something which can easily create feelings of apprehension and alarm. These feelings are conjured within a relationship with someone who aims to be a blank screen on which a series of conjectures flicker.

In my experience, what may transpire in practice is that the practitioner tries to impose certainty on what can only be speculative – the past, whilst refusing to bestow any certainty on what is experienced as tangible – the present, and the present relationship between therapist and client. A sense of not being in control may be exaggerated in such a nebulous context, particularly if one's usual ways of behaving and communicating no longer seem to have a place. We may then fail to identify a significant source of our 'dis-ease'.

I began to feel that affection, humour, irony and everyday talk were somehow unacceptable. I remember the occasion when I arrived late for a session because there had been a hold-up on the road. I apologised and explained what had happened. My analyst looked at me in silence, which made me feel as if I was the one who had done something odd.

If we engage, on a regular basis and in an intense fashion, in an encounter which is not based on a shared set of assumptions about how we interact, then an activity which is, in any case, uncertain and unpredictable risks becoming seriously destabilising. In addition, it is naive of therapists to claim that everything they say is merely a suggestion. They, more than anyone, should know that the client's perception may well be different, and that this is particularly relevant if the therapy churns up strong transference feelings.

An absence of feeling validated can pull the rug out from under the client's feet. It is hard enough to do therapy with someone who is positive and affirming. If the therapist does not care about the client, or does not show that he cares, the encounter may feel like little more than an academic exercise, with nothing to underpin it when things become difficult. When therapy recreates and amplifies old problems, it reinforces fear and pain rather than dissolving it. Instead of healing wounds from the past, it simply rubs salt into them.

What underlines all these mini-deaths is a failure to connect. I venture into the therapy room and have all kinds of doors slammed in my face. If what we are, and the words we inexpertly grasp at, seem to be rebuffed, then it is another death. The client's true self is not vindicated. In therapy, in particular, 'disbelief slaughters' (from the poem *Angel Wings*, by Brian Patten).

If a practitioner makes a habit of not being 'too human', sacrificing genuine interaction on the altar of analytic theory, then the techniques of therapy can make the atmosphere begin to feel unreal, and the therapist equally becomes increasingly unreal. This takes place at a time when the client is already likely to be under extra pressure from strains in her everyday life. In my experience, the mind can begin to tip in therapy; a sense of normality and a sense of self gradually become eroded.

The process of integration of the self involves becoming more fully aware of our strengths as well as our weaknesses. My analyst rarely alluded to my positive qualities. He focused on drawing attention to my problems, accentuating perhaps, in my mind, a previous sense of not being valued. He seemed to think that I had had an 'abusive' childhood. I had never really seen it that way and it was not a label I wished to attach to myself.

The destructiveness of such an attitude is highlighted in the book *The Soul's Code*, where James Hillman talks about how we 'dull our lives by the way we conceive them'. He says:

> Because the 'traumatic' view of early years so controls psychological theory of personality and its development, the focus of our rememberings and the language of our personal story-telling have already been infiltrated by the toxins of these stories. Our lives may be determined less by our childhood than by the way we have learned to imagine our childhoods. We are ... less damaged by the traumas of childhood than by the traumatic way we remember childhood as a time of unnecessary and externally caused calamities that wrongly shaped us. (Hillman, 1997:4)

What I am is all that I have. Even if I have been 'wrongly shaped', there is nowhere else to go. What matters is the capacity to be true to oneself and to face life's problems with openness, dignity and creativity, and with due consideration for others. Therapy is about making the best of what we have. But do some practitioners encourage us to see ourselves as tainted, defective, as victims rather than effective survivors?

A friend described how, if she arrived at her therapy session in a good mood, her analyst implied that she was pretending to feel happy in order to avoid her problems. Even with a relatively cheerful therapist, there is a danger that 'the very focus on oneself...is, *per se*, a depressive move' because we concentrate on 'What's wrong with me?' (Hillman and Ventura, 1993:231). Before I tried psychotherapy, I felt happy to be me. 'Therapy' can take that away and, when it does, it feels like a kind of rape of the soul.

In an article about trust, the therapist Susie Orbach says: 'The hurt of trust betrayed is often what can propel a person to seek therapy'. The hurt of trust betrayed can happen to the client *in* therapy too. When therapy simply rubs salt in old wounds, then the client feels 'in shock, uncomprehending, faced with an internal reckoning about who they thought the other person is...and their own naivete'. Psychotherapy, too, can force clients to 'forego the ease with which they walked through the world, viewing their openness now as a quasi liability' (Orbach, 1998a).

When we go to someone seeking understanding and, in the gradual unfolding of our story, are not met, seen and understood, it is a sharp and confusing rebuttal. It has been said that 'whenever our own truth is denied, ignored or invalidated, we experience the greatest fear we can ever know: the threat of the annihilation of our self' (Dorothy Rowe, in Masson, 1992:17). The resultant shock waves will have a force of their own, and perhaps also flow into the undercurrents from previous disturbing experiences.

The dictionary defines shock as 'a violent impact; a shaking or unsettling blow; a sudden shaking or jarring; a blow to the emotions; outrage at something regarded as improper; a convulsive excitation of nerves' (*Chambers 20th-Century Dictionary*). When things go wrong, that is how therapy can feel, and it is the fact that therapy, of all things, can feel this way which produces another shock and makes it a kind of triple whammy. The client reexperiences past difficulties, feels hurt by the therapist, and in the ensuing psychic anarchy cannot understand what on earth is going on.

Shock numbs, our awareness is skewed, leaving us distanced from what we truly feel. In therapy, this makes us less able to express what we need to express – thus making it more difficult for the therapist to help us. The client's mind may have taken on something of the chaotic and transient nature of a house which has become a building site, and so neglect to intervene in its usual way to bring things back to a more even keel.

When we start the process of unpeeling the layers, we frequently work from top to bottom: we look at our 'false', more superficial, motives and perceptions first. In doing so, we may focus on our fears about reality, neglecting what is more substantial and essential. We accentuate what is, in the end, 'less real' rather than what is 'more real'. I began to think that my analyst thought that the layers were all of me. Perhaps he was the mirror that reflected my fear that this might be the case, slowly corroding my habitual self-confidence.

If our thoughts and feelings seem less rather than more manageable, at a time when we had hoped that things would improve, it increases unease and ambivalence. My analyst told me that what I said was valuable, but to me it seemed like 'an aimless ramble' (Aveline, 1996:366). Too much free association can become debilitating; Jung suggested that it merely leads the client back into the complexes which already imprison her. I rambled into quicksand, from which I could not extricate myself.

What if, in the course of this diffusiveness, this word-spinning, the client reflects or even soaks up what the therapist is unable to deal with in himself? Clients will have varying degrees of absorbency – both in the past and in the present – and their permeability may be highly relevant to what transpires in therapy. If the work is coloured by the therapist's unresolved issues, and this is not clarified, then the nature of the problems and their exact location get lost.

In theory, 'when confronted with an impasse, the therapist should first consider how she or he has contributed to it, and redouble efforts at understanding' (Smith, 1996:35), but in practice he may be unable to steer a course out of the fog. If the therapy seems to be out of kilter, and the client does not understand why, there is a danger that she may begin to imagine that whatever it is that is wrong is something in her which is so deeply repressed, and therefore so terrible, that she must have greater problems than she had ever supposed. In my case, I redoubled my efforts to be a 'good' analysand, to think about my inner reality, to discover what was 'wrong with' me.

Psychotherapy can be powerful stuff. It can stir us up, and then slap us down for suddenly wanting what we have spent a lifetime learning to live without. The metaphorical slap in the face stings, leaving the client feeling high and dry, trapped by the inevitability of human nature. In therapy, a lifetime's desire, hope, confusion and distress are condensed rather than diluted by time. And it can seem that all the work we have put in during that lifetime to evolve a way of being has, in fact, come to nothing.

Everyone has their breaking point 'under abnormal degrees of stress or in situations where there is some inhibition against the deployment of their adaptive defensive capacity' (Carvalho, 1990:75). Psychotherapy can be a good example of a stressful situation which inhibits the deployment of our usual ways of being – defensive or otherwise.

For me, the therapy room began to feel like a pressure cooker, and eventually I lost a sense of self. My instinctive response was to try to understand what was happening, but the harder I tried, the more confused I became. My analyst encouraged me to think about my 'inner reality' and this started to take on a momentum of its own. But then, when I began to become seriously disorientated, he appeared to go into reverse. When I talked about my inner reality, he focused on my outer reality. Perhaps he was endeavouring to put on the brakes and stall a crash but, at the time, I felt we were talking at cross-purposes and that I must somehow be failing to grasp what was happening.

It seemed to me that, for some reason, I could not 'do' psychotherapy, and I felt stupid, baffled, curious and afraid as a result. When there was a break in the therapy, I felt as if my analyst had emptied my mind and thrown its contents all over the floor, then stood by expecting me to clear up the mess. A relationship which I had assumed would not be problematic – the 'therapeutic' relationship – was suddenly so full of problems.

My wish to feel closer to my analyst was interpreted as an attempt to be inappropriately intimate with him. As a result, I found it even more difficult to talk to him about what I was experiencing; it seemed either too personal or too weird. My psyche seemed to implode, in a constellation of heights and depths I have never experienced elsewhere. Everything seemed overwhelmingly significant but nothing seemed quite real. I felt wonderful and terrible, powerful and impotent, full of love and full of fear, all at the same time.

When one's 'current integrated state' falls apart, it is necessary to 'tune into' the meaning and purpose of what is happening if one is to emerge from it and grow: 'A descent into the darkness will...initiate the search for meaning' (Tatham, 1988:31). Tatham discusses the process of self-regulation and change and Jung's belief that the psyche 'pulls itself up by its own bootstraps' (ibid.:26). 'The meaning of illness is what you make of it. But the essential thing is that you do make something of it' (ibid.:33).

For a breakdown to become a breakthrough, its potential as such needs careful handling. But, at times of rapid shifts of consciousness, the places we move into may be inaccessible to those who are with us. The therapist will not always be able to follow where the client is going and, if this is the expectation of therapy, then it is an impossible one. What he can do, however, is to open his heart and hold out his hand. 'Analysis should train the heart, but then the heart must be present...And how do you train the heart?' (Julian David, 1997). When we descend into the darkness in therapy, or veer out of orbit, we make something of it if the therapist is capable of doing so also, if he has the heart, and the stomach and the backbone, to really stand by the client, if his own psyche and the system he uses are sufficient for the task.

My first experience of therapy, the hallucinogenic state I went into, and the painful impasse in which the therapy finally ended, proved to be more harrowing than anything in my past. Other traumas, however difficult, had seemed somehow• to have a place, but this felt entirely out of place. My analyst saw it as an 'intense transference'. My husband and children saw it as a frightening change in someone who had until then been relatively stable and easy-going. For me it felt, for a short time, as if I had gone permanently crazy, and that petrified me. Such a breakdown can have deeply damaging reverberations that reach into the client's work and career as well as her personal life.

In my case, it was my family and friends who provided a container when I was no longer able to cope. I tried, sometime later, and clumsily and falteringly, to discuss with my analyst the reasons for this trauma. He said he could not tell me, that it was for me to 'reexperience my negative feelings'. This felt like an instruction which I had no idea how to set about following. I had still less understanding of how it would help my current disintegrated state. The internal chaos I was caught up in bore little identifiable or obvious resemblance to anything that had happened to me before. And losing one's mind is a uniquely terrifying experience.

With my analyst I felt I had made a fool of myself because I had behaved so strangely. Some of his comments served to increase this feeling, and what we said to each other seemed to add to rather than sift through misunderstandings. I decided not to continue, fearing that staying might increase the crossed lines, embarrassment and turmoil. But, by then, the damage had been done. For the first time in my life, I experienced panic attacks, constant nights of sleepless confusion and an eerie loss of self-confidence. Later came a profound and gnawing sense of sadness. 'Forsaken', someone said, and that was how it felt. Alexander (1995:139) speaks of being 'overwhelmed by a feeling of ineffable sadness'. Ann France describes therapy as a 'perilous enterprise' (1988:243).

When I made the decision to terminate the therapy, I was unaware of the baggage I would carry around in its aftermath. I was left with a nagging need to salvage something by making my peace with the person who had unintentionally caused me so much anguish. A further attempt, much later, to reach some understanding failed.

In his absence, my analyst – an ostensibly reserved, dignified and unintrusive man – became someone whose magnetic pull was as inescapable as the moon's. It was as if I had unzipped myself and he had climbed inside. It was a presence I both desired and resented. A friend laughed and said it was 'a bit inevitable . . . like orphan geese'. She said it would fade. But there was something unique and special that I had lost. That quiet, private place inside my head, a place of contented reverie, now had a sitting tenant.

My first experience of psychotherapy left me feeling deeply troubled and wondering what exactly is the 'expertise' of those who sell it. Does the psychotherapeutic establishment provide its practitioners with the opportunity to engage in a series of powerfully influential, and potentially destabilising, relationships without having the means to manage them effectively and without taking proper responsibility for their consequences? Counsellors, analysts and therapists play with fire, and too often it is the client who gets burnt.

Chapter 14

The straitjacket of analysis

It has been said that psychoanalysis is only suitable for the 'psychologically fit'. One could argue, on the other hand, that someone who is psychologically fit may find little merit in it if the encounter seems hidebound and lacking in warmth, and that a fit person may well have grave doubts about the processes and interpretations that some practice involves. That doubts about a certain therapist or style of therapy may only become manifest when it is too late might be to do with the client's tenacity, along with a pressing awareness that we all have plenty of room for improvement.

One of the most absurd, insidious and disempowering notions in psychotherapy – and also one of the seemingly most compelling – is that, if you challenge its value, it is a sign that you need more therapy. Such parochial circularity trips us up and prevents us from getting any further forward. In the end, we must all recognise the problem – that humans are messy and that life is a steep learning curve; but perhaps we are frightened that, if we reject something which is offered as being of assistance, then it is tantamount to refusing to acknowledge the problem. The two, of course, are entirely separate. So-called solutions are not necessarily solutions at all, and may even perpetuate the problem.

Nevertheless, faced with the idea that therapy can, in itself, be a deeply traumatic experience, many professionals fall back on the assertion that no therapist can *make* a client feel a particular way. In practice, we affect each other deeply, which is why the profession of therapy exists. Theories of childhood development are based on the way in which parental behaviour influences their children. But the interconnectedness of all human beings goes on, it continues to touch and shape us throughout our lives.

A suggested contract between client and consultant at a complementary health clinic in London asks the client to agree to the following: 'In requesting professional consultation, I understand that to be successful I must be entirely willing to... acknowledge that my feelings, thoughts, images and desires – conscious or unconscious – ultimately determine the course of every action and relationship in my life'. Would it not be more accurate to say that our feelings and thoughts *help* to determine the course of every relationship since, by their very nature, our relationships involve other people?

In an article on holistic healing, the writer points out that scientific opinion now recognises the interrelatedness of space, motion, energy and matter. He suggests that 'the state of any one person's balance is reflected in his or her electro-magnetic field and can affect not just his or her own health and well-being, but that of others in the immediate vicinity' (Worthington, 1990).

The idea that no one can make you feel anything is open to debate. Although such a notion may be an inspiration to some, it has another side. It can actually double the pain one experiences, because it can feel accusatory rather than liberating, implying that one is foolish to feel upset. It then simply adds to one's discomfort rather than alleviating it.

It is a notion that might encourage us to believe that, when we are affected by others, our responses are somehow invalid. We are naive, unreasonable, too sensitive. We then direct attention away from the concept that each of us has a responsibility to act in ways which are not hurtful or disrespectful and that, when we fail to understand, or to be kind and considerate, we play a key role in the pain which is felt by the other person. We play down the merit of tenderness, receptivity and sensitivity, forget that it is what we do with our feelings, rather than the fact that we have them, which tends to cause problems.

Certain behaviours are, by their very nature, disturbing, so it is healthy to feel disturbed by them. The onus of responsibility is then on the perpetrator not to behave in that way, rather than on the receiver to analyse his or her feelings or not to feel hurt. Yet the emphasis often seems to be the other way round. For example, if I exploit someone who is particularly generous, he may well be blamed for being 'too nice', thus shifting the focus away from me, the person who initiated the interaction. The generous person is left feeling he is at fault; the exploiter continues to behave in the same cynical and inconsiderate manner.

An essential part of finding greater understanding is learning to notice when we soak up and take on other people's projections, fears and problems. In therapy, it can sometimes feel disloyal to talk negatively about another person, particularly when the therapist has never met that person, and when he or she has no opportunity to put their point of view. Learning to talk with respect about what we dislike in other people, to describe what happens in a relationship rather than imply it is the other person's fault, is a skill which is poorly developed in most of us.

When we are talking about a relationship we find difficult, it is helpful to have the validity of one's feelings acknowledged by hearing the therapist say, for instance, 'I think it is very hard sometimes to be with someone who is silent and unresponsive.' But, if those things which the client finds hard in her everyday relationships also correspond to the things she finds hard in the therapy relationship, then will the therapist be able to help her to evaluate them objectively?

Dealing with feelings in a balanced way needs to include a consideration of what they are prompted by, a putting into context, so that one can evolve a more appropriate sense of proportion. Rigorous thinking about the way we behave and the implications of that behaviour may be seen as a philosophical rather than a psychological matter. But it is necessary to learn how to make judgements and, at the same time, how to do so without blaming or being vindictive. If this is not part of the discussion of therapy, we risk creating a kind of vacuum in which we ignore the inherent power of a belief in the ethical. Evolving sound values helps to give us a sense of direction, a 'moral compass'. If we try to 'process' problems rather than describe them, is there a sense in which we become amoral?

Therapy should be about maximising the positive influence we can have on other people, as well as minimising the negative effect that someone else has had on us. When we focus on the consequences of what is done to us, rather than on what we do, are fortitude and generosity marginalised? Empowering each other cannot be achieved unless we are able to believe that 'if we

choose to do good things, it is not because we are trying to overcome our sense of badness, but because being loving and kind and
helpful and all those things that we call good gives us pleasure'
(Dorothy Rowe, in Masson, 1992:22).

We ignore the importance of kindness and civility at our peril.
It is through our pain and anger that we reinstate them in their
rightful, central place. If we cultivate a way of being where nothing
is a problem, where we feign or favour indifference, if we cease
to be offended by that which is offensive, then isn't that, in itself,
pathological? And can the other side of that particular coin be a
position where we slide out of a responsibility towards others and
cultivate a certain thoughtlessness because, if the other person is
offended by our actions, it is their problem?

Can therapy encourage us to be selfish when we do not wish to
be? Is the importance of serving others left out in the cold?
Michael Ventura describes how his therapist told him that his
grief at seeing a homeless man was really a feeling of sorrow for
himself. 'Dealing with it means going home and working on it in
reflection...and by that time you've walked past the homeless
man in the street' (Hillman and Ventura, 1993:12).

This reminds me of a time when I was describing to someone
the pain I felt at seeing my daughter in distress. 'You see your
own pain', my interlocutor said. I smiled weakly and, not wishing
to offend her earnest desire to help me, mumbled 'Yes'. Later, I
thought what an absurd comment it was. Yes, I remembered the
heartache I had felt after a similar event in my own childhood.
Yes, I felt considerable anguish myself over what had just
happened. But what I saw very clearly when I looked at my
daughter was her pain. It hurt to see her suffering.

To analyse our response to another's pain as some kind of
projection is criminal. It endeavours to obliterate that which
causes us to reach out and embrace one another in a way which is
spontaneous and heartfelt. We cut off Eros, 'the part of my heart
that seeks to touch others' (Hillman and Ventura, 1993:12). As
Hillman says: 'What about the world's soul?' (ibid.: 51).

Can psychotherapy cheapen what might be a common denomin-
ator of love, aligning it too closely to romantic idealism or Oedipal
longing, analysing it into a corner where it is labelled as misplaced? When therapy does work, does it sometimes push its
consumers towards a certain, narrow self-centredness, falsely

perceived as strength? There is a world of difference between a healthy self-awareness which enhances our interactions with others, and self-absorption which distracts from and impoverishes relationships. Can self-reflection become unproductive self-obsession? Therapy is valid only if it is ethical. What we become is an improvement on how we were only if it adds to, rather than detracts from, the collective pot of what is good about being human.

Yet loving kindness can be pathologised in an analytic setting. For example, an acquaintance who works as a counsellor once told me about a client who 'had a problem' about wanting to help people. I found it somewhat ironic hearing this from someone who had chosen to earn her living trying to help people, but I know what she means. The wish to help can sometimes be compensatory, inappropriate, intrusive or disrespectful. (Perhaps it can be in therapy too . . .) Nevertheless, a spontaneous desire to help is surely, in itself, healthy.

This particular client had seen his counsellor walking to their meeting place in the pouring rain one day. He told her at the beginning of the session that he had wondered whether to offer her a lift. There is, of course, a problem about boundaries between client and practitioner which puts both in a difficult position at times. But the client's instinctive reaction when he saw his counsellor – to want to give her a lift, because she was getting wet – was normal, pleasant, considerate. Yet, when he expressed it, it led to a discussion of one of his 'problems'. And what actually happened was that the counsellor got soaked, while the client drove by in his warm dry car.

Is there a sense in which both practitioner and client can become victims – victims of the circumstances they have created, of the way in which the practitioner works? The analyst is trained to be a blank wall for projections, he isn't trained to be kind. The analysand complies, believing that what is taking place is good for her. Both put on a straitjacket which denies the heart. So does being an analysand mean that one is in some way disenfranchised when it comes to generous and courteous behaviour? And can we never offer a psychotherapist a lift in the rain?

In responding to the invitation to analyse ourselves, can we collude in the process of our own sabotage? Might we actually lose faith in our own validity, believing that we are at a disadvantage because we have not worked our way through someone else's version of what it means to develop? Might we simply be continuing the process of denying our true selves which brought us to the therapy room in the first place? In twisting ourselves into the straitjacket that psychotherapy can be, we may cut ourselves off from our vitality and creativity, become estranged from a deeper sense of self and of the world around us. It feels a little like eating chalk whilst being told it is cheese. We are so busy trying to know, we prevent real knowing.

How many therapy rooms are places where the client is really free to be herself? In his discussion of the abuse of power in therapy, Mark Aveline draws attention to the dangers involved if the therapist adopts an aloof, all-knowing stance:

> From a detached position – which may be bolstered by viewing all the patient's communications as manifestations of transference and, as such, only needing to be put back to the patient for his sole consideration – the therapist is tempted to be a bystander in life, vicariously involved but spared the pain and puffed up by the patient's dependent approval. Progress towards separation and individuation is obstructed. (Aveline, 1996:377)

When a therapist makes a point of not being real, we stare into the masked face of a false self, reach out to hold a hand which is heavily gloved. So might the false self of the client then click in and claim centre stage, in an effort to meet with its equivalent in the other – thus leaving her true self muffled in the wings? Falseness, at a time when one most needs the opposite, lends to the experience a counterfeit nature. Perhaps it is this inherent incongruity, and its resultant sense of shock, that can cause therapy to be so destructive.

If the therapist puts himself behind a screen in the belief that, in doing so, what he offers his client is space, he is in danger of denying her the greatest gift of all – a sense and recognition of our shared humanity. Is it too often the case that 'in analysis, there is no sense of solidarity, of two people who have come through some tragedy still alive but wounded in similar ways' (Masson, 1992:129)?

Healing cannot occur unless there is a sense of well-being in the therapy room. A sense of well-being comes from connecting – with the natural world and with our fellow human beings. Notions of mutuality, of finding meaning together, of each person having something to give in a relationship are an essential part of the process of moving forward fruitfully. The capacity to both give and receive is an integral part of a feeling of balance. A confirmation that what we are is worth sharing encourages us to be generous. I remember the surprise I felt the first time Kate thanked me – because, she said, she learned from me – and the ensuing sense of my own value which it gave me. I found the fact that she thanked me immensely moving.

In therapy, we may give up a lot, but something we need very much to hold on to is a sense of worth and dignity. It is this that has to be honoured over and above everything else and which has to come before the principles of any specific school of therapy. There is an important kind of dignity in reciprocity. There is an important kind of sanity in not playing games and in mutually valuing a sense of shared vulnerability, honesty and responsibility. A healing relationship is one in which authenticity and grace are paramount.

It is only when the therapist gives the client the benefit of the doubt that he will allow her the space to restore herself. It is only when we feel free of other people's erroneous perceptions that we can stop for a breath of fresh air and take stock. If an adherence to a particular theory takes precedence over an adherence to truth, the client is oppressed, the practitioner loses his way and both are squeezed into a straitjacket.

Knowledge is a tool, a means of enquiry, but it can only serve to help the client in an atmosphere which allows genuine enquiry to take place. The value of theory – provided it is the right theory – cannot be discounted, but it needs to be used discerningly. If it is overemphasised, it can become deadening and irrelevant. It puts us all in a box before we begin. In the end, the only real authority psychotherapy can claim lies in its ability to operate from a basis of uncertainty.

'The significance of therapists' uncritical allegiance to, and reliance upon, a particular theoretical model, unfortunately has not been given sufficient attention by the majority of individual therapists or by many of their training institutes' (Spinelli, 1995:158). The client might also be damaged by an inept and inadequate application of a potentially suitable therapeutic approach.

In Alexander's account of her experience of therapy, she says of her analyst: 'he was like a child playing with a nuclear bomb' (1995:123). Her traumatic experiences went beyond neat categories of psychoanalytic interpretation, and beyond the very limited abilities of those who helped to instigate them. Her account reflects the conclusion that 'psychotherapists do not know what they are doing and cannot train others to do it, whatever it is' (Howarth, 1989). Mair (1992) suggests that practitioners who do seem to be able to help people do so because they have managed 'to outgrow the handicaps imposed by their training' (cited in Spinelli, ibid.).

Does training someone to respond in a certain way mean that, in practice, they may actually become less responsive? Can training become a kind of cloning process? Of course, it depends on the training, and on the personal qualities of each individual practitioner. Therapy is about my answers to the question, 'What does it mean to me to be alive?' It is also about the therapist's answer to the questions, 'What is it that makes being with me for a certain time each week beneficial to my clients? What is it that I, personally, am able to offer?'

Does psychoanalysis concentrate too much on the apparently repressed desires of infancy? Is it perhaps the analyst rather than the client who is preoccupied by the sexual, the oral, the anal, with orifices and breasts and penises? The client Ann France, for example, describes how her therapist, 'Simon', 'was always trying to remind me that he had a penis' and 'tried consistently to make me see him as a man ... as a potentially desirable other'. She, on the other hand, 'thought it was more useful that he offered me a receptive space, in which we could jointly create something' (France, 1988:99). Alexander's analyst suggested that she was 'afraid of the male penis' and of being 'penetrated' by him, whilst in reality she would have been delighted to have sex with him (Alexander, 1995:104). Another client described to me how her therapist said 'again and again' that he was sure her insecurity was caused by the repressed memory of a sexual incident, even though this explanation made no sense to her. My analyst seemed convinced that I was frightened of men, even though that was not my feeling.

The above examples have in common an insistence on the part of the practitioner which none of the clients found helpful.

Indeed, Alexander says 'It infuriated me because it showed such a lack of understanding' (1995:104). There is a dangerous corrosiveness to an emphasis from the practitioner on what he sees as a problem. His interventions may have a harsh or accusatory tone which pushes the client into a corner; there seems to be an almost sadistic quality to the coerciveness of some of the interactions which take place.

In contrast, by opening up a problem and looking at it in a broad and constructive fashion, the client is coaxed out of a corner, offered space and movement. Emphasising difficulties can simply make us feel more imprisoned by them, and finding reasons – even when they are the right ones – does not always provide a solution or allow us to move forward. For example, trying to determine where or how something originated may be far less helpful than simply looking at the patterns of our behaviour and trying to understand their meaning. 'Rational explanation . . . is no substitute for insight – the latter term being more akin to "personal awareness" than intellectual knowledge' (Jacobs, 1988:37).

Knowing why I do something does not necessarily help me to stop doing it. We can often trace the source of our problems back to aspects of our childhood; we discuss them with friends and family as well as in therapy. Simply parading the causes of pain around in a sterile, cold-blooded analysis, however, may do little to enable us to heal the wounds. If what is felt is the hurt and confusion of the child, rather than something which changes the way the hurt and confusion is experienced and perceived, then the straitjacket tightens.

In my experience, when I am nervous, or taken by surprise – and the psychoanalyst's infrequent interventions can come as a surprise – I tend to agree even if I don't really agree, or I respond defensively, trot out the familiar, standardised recipe. Later, I may realise it was not a true reflection of my feeling. When I do not stop to focus and reflect, I may not see what truly belongs to me. I give a conditioned response, rather than a more natural and authentic one. I remain in a straitjacket because I log into my ingrained habits, and the opinions I have been exposed to, and I experience them as me.

If the therapist suggests that everything the client does is directly related to him, or to her attitude towards the therapy, this can increase the straitjacket's stranglehold. For instance, if the client is late, it is not – in the eyes of some practitioners – because there was a last-minute panic at home trying to find her son's football boots, or because there was a traffic jam. It is a possible sign of resistance. The unpredictable or inevitable aspects of the client's world are not respected as such. Yet it is necessary to cherish the ordinary enough to leave it alone.

The analyst's 'blinkers' may be an aid to focus and attention, but they may also get in the way of all-round vision when that is what is needed, squashing essential elements in the client's experience and making them smaller. For example, interpreting the client's capacity to feel love and empathy as being in love with the therapist may reduce its significance. Such experience has to be seen and understood at a number of different levels. Perhaps the claim that psychotherapy is a process whereby the bland teach the unbland to be bland (cited in Masson, 1992:245) is sometimes justified.

If we are put into a straitjacket, we are totally dependent. When we are in a position of dependence, we tend to behave like a child rather than an adult. So could the regression which often takes place in therapy be actuated as much by the straitjacket as it is by our need to 'process' the past? If the client is not treated like an intelligent adult, then she may end up not behaving like one. And such outcomes are not always therapeutic.

When we feel unsure what to do, we may either freeze or fall back on what we know. But when the practitioner falls back on a psychoanalytic model, it may not offer him much. As the scientist Ian Stewart said, of an entirely different topic:

> Control systems can behave chaotically ... if they are over-driven ... the whole system thrashes, spending nearly all of its time reacting to its own errors and very little time reacting to the reality it is supposed to be controlling. (Stewart, 1995)

Because the focus is always on the client, the system becomes pernicious, feeding the problems it highlights and leaving the client carrying the burden of responsibility.

Is analysis itself irrational in its dependence on theory? Does the 'science' of psychoanalysis rely too heavily on surmise? Can it, in so doing, complicate matters unnecessarily? Does it also confine and narrow us down, obscure the importance and solace of instinctual wisdom? Does it focus on the masculine side of our nature, and not enough on the feminine? And isn't the potential of our imagination more powerful than the demons of the unconscious?

In the book *The Moon and the Virgin*, Nor Hall (1980) 'questions the damaging interpretations of the imagination and of the unconscious which diminish our concept of the feminine'. Estés (1992) talks about how 'woman's genuine nature has been repressed ... by a value system that trivialises emotional truth, intuitive wisdom and instinctual self-confidence'. Can the theory and practice of psychotherapy also trivialise these things, bypassing some of the essentials of our nature and thus restrict rather than release us? An appreciation of the transpersonal, the transcendent, and the kind of understanding which is illustrated, for instance, in *Spiritual Emergency* (Grof and Grof, 1989) is part of our soul-searching. The impact of the society we live in is also surely important.

It could be argued that, in much psychotherapy, the basis of the work is dangerously incomplete. In addition, therapists might fail to exploit fully what their theories do offer them, to put into practice what they write and lecture about. For example, Hillman claims that, although Jung explored the concepts of collective psychology, of synchronicity and the collective unconscious, they 'are ... rarely employed in practice', thereby diminishing the possible application of Jung's work (Hillman and Ventura, 1993:59). How many therapists have the depth and breadth and ability to do justice to the work? Theoretical knowledge is meaningful when it is genuinely relevant to the client's experience and used by the therapist in such a way that, in practice, it results in progress.

I recently discovered, in a text about the process of individuation in psychotherapy, that:

> One danger is that of breakdown when archetypal activity is very strong and the patient may be overwhelmed with contents from the collective unconscious. Another danger is that of identifying with the mana-like power of these contents ... Jung points to Nietzsche's identification with the ... prophet Zarathustra. Depression is another consequence of the individuating process. (Casement, 1996: 88)

This description helped me to make sense of some of my experiences, as did the reference to the 'Rosarium' (ibid.:95) – a series of ten pictures seen by Jung as representing, for example, concepts of 'the naked truth', of trying to hide one's 'shadow' and of an intense desire for connection. Yet these concepts were not – as far as I can remember – used either by my analyst or (later) his colleagues, who seemed to feel that it was my past which was most relevant.

In Casement's account, the proviso is made: 'If the analysis survives this stage . . . If the analytic container can withstand all the difficult feelings up to this point'. Is it, in practice, too big an 'if'? What sort of problems ensue if the analysis does not survive? What 'symptoms' might it cause in the client, and how can she be helped? Perhaps we need more theories – about therapy's contribution to psychological disturbance. What about the shattering chaos and pain, and profound insecurity, that psychotherapy can lead to?

Casement does not discuss what happens after the analysis breaks down, or how the client might then feel in such an event. Nor does she refer to the client's world outside. What is the average husband, wife or partner of the client to do whilst the 'archetypal transference', or 'the erotic transference', is running its course? What are they to make of it when 'the analysis deepens', when 'the two protagonists are joined together in working towards greater consciousness', when they struggle to forgo 'physical gratification', then go through 'death-like feelings' because of this 'sacrifice' (Casement, 1996:95)? And is the client to assume that the practitioner's partner remains unaffected by such intensity?

This is only a 'symbolic conjunction' but, nevertheless, the therapy here takes on a significant and powerful life of its own. Again, an absence of attention to the client's everyday life can make a mockery of her intention in coming to therapy in the first place – of the wish to improve existing relationships. And what happens if the client runs out of money when the analysis has only reached picture four?

The writer above points out that, in Nietzsche's case, there was a lack of conscious integration which would have grounded him. She also emphasises, however, that 'the analyst needs to withstand the temptation to "explain" what is happening and to give reassurances to the analysand' (Casement, 1996:95). The analysand, nevertheless, needs some kind of guidance. I remember trying to talk to my analyst about the collective unconscious but feeling that I was getting nowhere. I am not clear about who said what at that time, but what I do remember is the confusion, and the impression that what I was experiencing was abnormal.

My experience was messy, complex, unexpected and – for me – profound, but I felt it was not honoured as such, and the analysis ended at a point which was critical. I felt saddened and demeaned by the attitude of my analyst. Regardless of what he thought in private, and what he might have discussed with his supervisor, his stance towards me seemed to reduce the meaning and potential of what I had been through.

The anger which is expressed in therapy may not necessarily be provoked by the past. It may be disappointment and frustration in the face of what feels like a personal failure or a professional misrepresentation – because the process we are engaged in is not achieving what one hopes or what it claims might be achieved, because of the discrepancy between what is said in theory and what actually happens in practice. It may be an instinctive rejection of an over-insistence on the relevance of the past, and of the paucity of sheer reductionism. What happens when the wrong theories are applied? The 'rightful and clear anger' to which Clarissa Estés refers might be the anger that any of us would feel if we were put into a straitjacket.

Ann Casement describes the stages of 'a classical Jungian analysis'. So do the clients of Freudian or Kleinian analysts behave differently – because they are with a Freudian or a Kleinian? Or is an analysis essentially the same experience, interpreted in different ways? If our experiences in therapy vary depending on what type of therapist we go to, then what does this tell us about the influence of the practitioner and the model he is using? Where does that leave the client's unique and individual truth?

How wonderful it would be if all psychotherapists and counsellors had the sort of freshness and eagerness for life embodied in this piece by Ben Okri:

When we look out on the world with all its multiplicity of astonishing phenomena, do we see that only one philosophy can contain, explain, and absorb everything? I think not. The universe will always be greater than us. Our mind should therefore be like Keat's thorough-fare, through which all thoughts can wander. It should also be a great cunning net that can catch the fishes of possibility. (1997:19)

Therapeutic therapy is about freedom, freedom to be fully our-selves, to be all of what we are right now, this minute. It involves a loosening of the tightness of fulfilling a role. It involves the client being able to act both as a person and a client, and the therapist being able to act both as a person and a therapist. It is about each accept-ing and acknowledging both of these in the other. 'It is impossible to truly understand another without making room for that person within yourself' (Peck, 1978:159). This works both ways. I can put my analyst into a straitjacket just as he can do that to me.

Only when each person moves freely can we become as well as be. This involves a willingness on the part of both therapist and client to take off their familiar attire and try on something differ-ent. It involves making shifts. But there has to be a balance between movement and stability. If I am too much of a client and not enough of a person at a time when my analyst is too much of a person and not enough of an analyst, then each of us might end up both waving and drowning. When things go wrong, what then can be done to pull something of value from the wreckage?

Chapter 15

Responsibility

A fundamental problem in all relationships is our failure to understand, acknowledge and accept responsibility for what we have helped to create. A truly therapeutic relationship is therapeutic not only because someone listens and helps us to see things clearly but because it is one in which the other person owns and takes full responsibility for what they bring.

It is extremely difficult to be clear about where the responsibility of the therapist begins and ends. It is extremely difficult to answer the question: 'To what extent might psychotherapy be in some way detrimental to certain notions of mental health yet still be a valid endeavour?' Do we have a sufficiently clear and common understanding of what we mean by mental and emotional health and of what might be beneficial or detrimental in this respect? The answer is probably 'No'.

What seems to be fundamental, however, is that, whatever our degree of psychic ease or unease, the aim of going to a therapist is to alleviate suffering and not to increase it. Sometimes, however, the discomfort of therapy moves into pain and turmoil to such an extent that this aim gets lost. The client becomes less, rather than more, able to manage her life successfully. Psychotherapy then provides 'a rich soil for creating deep and lasting misunderstandings, and even greater misery' (Masson, 1992:44).

If psychotherapy has inflicted its own wounds, the client has the right to expect that fact to be acknowledged. Practitioners who choose to deal in relationships carry particular obligations regarding awareness and accountability. If we put ourselves in a position of offering to serve others, it matters very much what we do. We carry a responsibility to act in good faith. It is our responsibility to care.

When the effect of therapy on the client is more destructive than constructive, hypothesising about the transference is no more than a convenient red herring which appears to offer the practitioner a relatively straightforward and reassuring explanation. For the client, whether or not her suffering is transference is academic. What matters is whether, in the end, therapy is helpful. Do the concepts of transference, projection and resistance become labels which invite practitioners to evade looking at questions about how psychotherapy can harm rather than help? Do therapists then fail to address the ways in which something that is offered as a means to better psychic health can actually instigate the opposite?

The ever-present box of Kleenex is testimony to the accepted fact that the majority of clients will feel upset at times during therapy sessions. Nevertheless, most of us go into therapy in the hope that, overall, it will make us feel better in some way. Who evaluates what 'feeling better' means and how? Since greater awareness is often accompanied by an increased capacity to feel pain and vulnerability, the equation is a complex one. How do we balance the disruption which is an inevitable and necessary part of therapy against the gains which may accrue?

How, in addition, does the client balance her own needs against those of the people she shares her life with? And does the therapist always bear in mind the importance of the wider picture? His intervention will also have repercussions for the client's family, friends and work colleagues. The therapy room might feel like a space capsule, but life goes on outside it. It is perhaps a moot point, but the profession of psychotherapy is part of the society in which it operates; it does not exist in isolation. The political and philosophical questions which can arise from this fact are not easy, but cannot be ignored.

If intense feelings are aroused in therapy, but then not properly resolved, it may be that the client becomes more disturbed. She may act out those feelings in her everyday life more forcefully, resulting at times in greater dislocation in her relationships rather than greater harmony.

What happens when clients move on to become practitioners themselves? How does their unfolding transference affect their clients, and does it have a bearing on those issues which are brought into focus? Is someone who has just been through his or her own analysis in the best position to try to help others, or can their work sometimes become too much a continuation of their own therapy?

Generally speaking, when therapy goes well and the client feels she has benefited from it, it is common for therapists to point out that progress has been made because of the client's willingness to examine herself and make the effort to change. No one would dispute this, but it is reasonable also to say that that change has been facilitated by the efforts of the therapist. If he had played no significant part in things, he could hardly justify his fee.

Why, when therapy appears to be detrimental, does the same principle seem sometimes to start wriggling away? When I become a client and pay a therapist, does that act grant him a kind of immunity? Does it mean he is suddenly incapable of causing emotional and psychological harm? The client is likely to be acutely sensitive to the therapist's views and behaviour, because what she tells him is private and precious, and because he is in a privileged position when he is invited to share such things.

The psychoanalyst David Smith writes: 'Failure to progress in therapy may be due to therapist, to patient, or to both ... more frequently, the lack of progress can be attributed to therapists' errors' (Smith, 1990:33). The client, however, may well be unaware of this. Despite the textbook acknowledgements of the relevance of therapists' mistakes, what happens in practice? How many therapists actually say this to their clients? In practice, there is no other profession in which the practitioner is so well equipped to attribute a lack of success to the client's problems rather than his own. And there is no other situation in which the client would so easily allow herself to be dumbfounded by this assertion.

Whatever the problem happens to be, a therapist can always respond with the view that that is precisely what the client needs to deal with. Whether it is a problem which would arise for that client in any relationship is another matter. In the end, if she wishes to continue with the same practitioner, she will have no choice but to try to find a way through. But who most needs to change – the therapist or the client? The essence of good therapy is to find ways of moving forward, rather than simply to point out a problem. If a therapist assumes an inherent pathology in his clients, does this belief allow him to hide behind their difficulties? And is he clear about how such an assumption is helpful to the client, where it comes from and why he subscribes to it?

Practitioners may not find it easy to accept responsibility for behaviour which is damaging. In any case, it is difficult to define 'damage' or to be sure of its cause. But the therapist's natural human inclination to look elsewhere for an explanation might be reinforced and augmented by certain aspects of the training. Isn't this training, in many ways, about creating a predisposition *not* to take responsibility for the way the client is feeling?

In many professions, the feelings of clients are taken on board in order to improve the service. The psychoanalyst, on the other hand, is trained to think that the feedback he receives from his client is what the client needs to work on. Psychotherapy is the only profession where the practitioner can be insensitive, evasive, patronising, arrogant, discourteous, self-righteous or just plain wrong and where the client's observation of this can be taken to be an expression of her problems, evidence that what she really needs is more of the same therapy. It is a kind of closed loop.

The way we experience things in therapy is not always a reflection of how we experience them in the more realistic contexts of our daily lives, and therapy may tap into untested and sometimes mystical seams of energy. It is also a business contract, and the making of any contract should include negotiating rights. The negotiating rights of the client within the therapeutic contract must be disentangled from the notion of transference, or that notion can misrepresent both therapist and client and impoverish the relationship between them.

Therapists rightly emphasise the client's personal responsibility in the therapeutic contract, but they cannot ignore the other side of that particular coin – that the client also has rights. The client has the right to expect that, in her dealings with her therapist, universal rules about integrity and healthy, humane behaviour are not usurped by the theories and rules of psychoanalysis. If basic principles are violated, as they inevitably will be at times, it may be a problem because the ground rules have been broken, and not because the client is neurotic. 'The crucial need of the patient is to be understood, valued, loved, respected by the therapist as an equal, fellow human being. This is irreducible, it is not simply transference' (Lomas, 1973:133).

If this 'crucial need' is not met, then does therapy do more harm than good? Does the concept of transference encourage practitioners to break one of the ground rules – that we have a responsibility to own what we contribute when something goes wrong? In therapy, this is crucial because, for the client, it has to do with that most fundamental of fundamentals – our perception of our sanity and of our ability to function well in the world.

The asymmetry of the relationship should work for rather than against the client when there is particular confusion or distress. The therapist has the greater experience of what happens in therapy, so the onus of responsibility is on him. But does his professional expertise sometimes blind rather than illuminate him?

Of course, a therapist is not responsible for what a client brings from her past or from her everyday life, but he is responsible for the way he evokes and deals with her feelings within the psycho-therapeutic relationship. This is what his professionalism is about. It is what we pay for. For example, taking responsibility for feelings of tension or confusion can be a vital first step in dissolving the discomfort and then beginning to repair the damage. It allows us to deal with our embarrassment and opens the door to repairing damage which has been done elsewhere. When the client is unable to dig herself out of a hole, she needs the therapist to move towards her in some way and try to suggest a means of progressing.

Therapy is about courage, but not just the courage of the client. The courage of the therapist is axiomatic. There is no clear boundary between professionalism as it is defined in ethical guidelines, and professionalism which depends on the character and moral strength of the practitioner. It is the latter which, in the end, matters most. There is perhaps no other profession in which the personal integrity of the practitioner is the equivalent of a basic professional tool. But, as Laing says (in a dialogue with Roberta Russell about what we can and can't buy and sell): 'We're talking about emotions and oneself, and they aren't a commodity and you can't sell them' (Russell, 1992:224).

And isn't this part of the problem? We cannot purchase what isn't there. What, in the end, makes therapy therapeutic is not to be bought or sold. Perhaps what real responsibility comes down to is the ability to act unselfishly, in a loving way – or, at least, to do so as far as we are able. Some practitioners might find it odd or even faintly amusing if one asked them if they loved their clients. They are, after all, professionals, doing a job of work. But what does professionalism in therapy amount to? Doesn't the effective therapist act in a loving way? If so, does this not amount to love?

And aren't we expecting rather a lot if we think this can be reproduced on a daily basis in return for a fee?

The courage to love one another well includes endeavouring to be aware of and, when necessary, drawing attention to, all our limitations. If this does not happen in therapy, then the client's expectations and the psychotherapist's theory can forge a lethal combination which hijacks reality and hurts them both. It is the responsibility of the professional to take into account not only his personal weak spots, but also the dangers and shortcomings of the way that he practises, and to be ready to take a fresh view of things. If it is a lot to ask, it is no more than therapists expect of their clients.

In discussions of therapy, the centrality and potential effect of the therapist's model and behaviour are detailed primarily in terms of their positive outcome. But their disruptive and potentially harmful impact merit equal attention and awareness. Are practitioners sufficiently well-informed about the possible destructiveness of their work, and the different psychic dimensions that may be experienced within it? The only case examples I have seen which chart the course of a harmful therapy are accounts which are written by clients. So who is taking responsibility for what?

An eminent psychotherapist recently commented to me that, in his view, it is up to the client to get out of a therapy which isn't working. If the client cannot do that, he argued, then she should take responsibility for that fact, unless there was some quite clear offence. This premise is perhaps more obvious in our personal relationships, but when we pay someone for a professional service, isn't it rather different? If the therapist who said this knew how it felt to be in that position, he would realise that in practice it is far from simple. When things seemed to be going wrong, I thought it must be me who was getting them wrong and I was in no way sufficiently clear-headed to do very much about it. I had underestimated the power of therapy, was like a rabbit caught and frozen in the headlights.

If we have been told often enough that we should accept what we do not like and what does not suit us, we may well do the same in psychotherapy. It is a question again of the closed loop. If we simply work on the basis that we do or don't 'feel better' at any one point during the therapy, that could be misplaced or oversimplistic.

If, for example, a psychotherapist employs a professional person, to what extent is it then his responsibility, as the client, to evaluate whether or not that practitioner is working well? If, as a client, he were in a position to do so efficiently, he might well not have needed to seek the services of a qualified professional in the first place. Unless mistakes along the way are glaringly obvious, it is only when the work is finished that we can properly judge the outcome. At what point, in therapy, do we evaluate the outcome? In any case, what is and isn't damaging or abusive is not always easy to define. Part of the problem we face is that we are student, patient and customer all at the same time.

Many clients who find themselves in 'therapeutic' relationships which are, in fact, deeply disturbing do take responsibility – soul-searching, talking to friends, even consulting other professionals, trying to weigh up the relative merits of leaving or staying. When I tried to make a responsible decision to leave a process which had destroyed my ability to function normally, I was told by my analyst that I would not return because I was angry with him and wanted to punish him.

It may take a particular kind of toughness to stand up and leave. It is difficult to question someone if the consequence is always a response directed back at one's own difficulties. When I finally decided to stop seeing my analyst, he told me in a letter that he was sorry I 'did not feel able to continue'. Once again, I felt like a failure. The friend on page 13 was told the same thing by her analyst when she decided to leave. In neither case did the practitioner suggest that it might have been a judicious decision. Neither did they acknowledge that perhaps it was they too who were 'not able'.

If a therapist maintains that it is up to the client to decide what is and isn't helpful, then how often does he back this up in practice? Does he actually say things like: 'I think you're probably right to finish. I think I've been getting things wrong'? And how often does he add 'and, before you leave, let's briefly try to talk about why perhaps things haven't worked out well'?

In principle, the client is responsible for determining when to end therapy. At the same time, some practitioners seem reluctant to allow their clients to exercise fully that responsibility. For example, France describes how, when she decided to finish working with her therapist, 'Simon', he 'made me feel I did not have the right to declare unilateral independence...He claimed he did not think it was good for me to be allowed to control my own therapy in this way' (France, 1988:236). It is not uncommon for therapists to encourage their clients to continue when the client expresses the wish to stop. Perhaps, on occasions, they are right to do so.

What we mean by 'progress' in therapy must be subject to a variety of interpretations. How much suffering do we need, and how far down the road do we go? One could argue that terminating relationships which are not easy is not necessarily a sign of progress. It also takes a particular kind of courage to stay when things do not feel comfortable. It may be that the greater the discomfort, the more potentially we might learn. So the client who chooses to continue to work with a therapist she does not feel at ease with is, in some ways, taking the work more seriously than her counterpart who shops around. Sometimes the cost of terminating the therapy might be greater than the cost of continuing. If an impasse could be overcome, the benefits might be considerable.

How long does one wait? How many times does one try? Do I walk out at the first sign of aloofness, the first time there is a misunderstanding? Do I leave because therapy isn't working or stay because it is bringing up issues which I find difficult to deal with? And, if I stay, will the therapist be able to deal successfully with those issues? If I feel the therapist does not understand me, do I look at why the misunderstandings are arising or find someone with whom I feel a greater affinity? If I do not feel contained, do I look for a more suitable container or do I try to take the problem fully on board and work on my need for containment? If I feel in chaos, do I go back into it or try to close the door on it?

If I do leave, what does that mean? That I am discerning or that I am a coward? If I 'fail' as an analysand, then what does that tell me about myself? Perhaps I am 'unhelpable', irredeemable. If I alienate the person who is theoretically 'unalienatable' – the therapist – what kind of monster am I? The familiar clichés nag in the head. Do I always reap what I sow? Does the wheel always turn full circle? The old dark terrors push their way forward. Transference turns psychotherapy on its head.

How do I, the client – or how, in the end, can anyone – distinguish with any certainty between those things which are caused by the flaws of the system, or by therapist error, and those things which are caused by transference and which, with persistence, might be resolved? These are complex and difficult questions. The adult in me struggled long and hard with them while an abandoned child wept tearlessly in a corner. Is it possible for the client to make a reasonably objective assessment of the situation, or to distinguish between a therapy which feels difficult and uncomfortable but which might be of eventual benefit, and a therapy which feels helpful and reassuring but which will not initiate any significant change for the better?

The contention that the client must take responsibility if she has not been able to get out of a relationship which is not working is valid up to a point, but it leaves out the all-important matter of the therapist's responsibility. It is also somewhat insidious if it comes from a practitioner who encourages the transference and thereby puts the client in a position where her judgement may be more impaired than usual. In any event, if the therapist implies that the therapy isn't working because the client is unable to deal with relevant issues, and if the client believes him, then for her it makes no sense at all to get out.

This seems to me to epitomise both the double bind I got myself into and the ambivalence which pervades much psychoanalytic thinking. It is a way of thinking which encourages us to reinhabit the child within, then maintains it is our own doing when our responsible adult becomes submerged. It pushes and prods us into exploring the darkest corners of the psyche, simultaneously saying that it is up to us to decide where we go. It acknowledges that the therapist influences the client and, at the same time, maintains that the client can choose the ways in which she is influenced. It endeavours to justify the most pernicious use of a therapist's power – the power of withdrawal. He abuses that power when he withholds relevant information or refuses to accept joint responsibility for what takes place.

The practitioner cannot have it both ways. If he offers himself as a professional, as an expert, he cannot shrug off the responsibility that that automatically carries with it. By the very nature of his title, he will have considerable influence over his clients. He cannot conveniently put aside the issue of his influence if the outcome of what he offers is negative or if the client makes an unwise decision. Therapists claim that therapy offers a context for exploration which is safe and sure and in the next breath point out that, of course, all relationships contain risks for their participants. Both these contentions may be true, but the practitioner cannot opt at random for whichever one happens to suit him at the time. The complexity of appropriately placing responsibility reflects the dilemma which haunts us all – the parallel existence of our separateness and our interrelatedness, and the struggle to enable them to complement rather than fight with each other.

Whatever our struggle, investing in therapy is a significant commitment to endeavouring to come to terms with that struggle. It is not like buying something in Marks and Spencer, trying it on and then taking it back if it isn't right. We don't walk smartly out and go to another shop. When we leave a therapy which has not worked well, we leave behind a failed encounter, not an unwise purchase. We go into the encounter carrying our heart on our sleeve, our hope about ourselves on open display. When things go badly wrong, we leave it in a state of consummate confusion and pain carrying, in many cases, a bundle of heightened and unresolved feelings.

When therapy is not successful, it is often said that this is because some practitioners and clients are not well-suited. In practice, there are no obvious procedures in place to help clients to find a suitable therapist.* And how ready is the therapist to turn clients away, on the grounds that he feels he is unable to help them? I was advised to exercise care when choosing who to see, but what criteria should one use, how is one to know if they are the right criteria, and how does one apply them?

A friend told me – rightly or wrongly – that most psychotherapists looked solemn, said little and worked in a somewhat impersonal fashion so, although I found this hard, there seemed to me to be little point in changing to someone else. I did not know about 'negative fit' (cited in Aveline, 1990:384), or about the hazards – and

---

*At the time of writing, the UKCP (United Kingdom Council for Psychotherapy) is, I believe, in the process of writing a leaflet to help clients choose a suitable therapist.

the force and intensity – of psychotherapy. I do not know if mine was a case of negative fit, or whether my analyst thought that it was, but I suspect that if, when I first went to him, he had said he did not think we could work together, I would have been hurt and alarmed. I think I would have been reluctant to try another practitioner, for fear that I might be rejected again. Other clients, of course, might have a tougher skin.

I had no way of knowing that things would end as they did. My analyst had been recommended by a close friend, who was herself a therapist. He does good business and, as I sit here writing this, he is probably sitting in his room with a client who finds what he does very helpful. One of his many satisfied customers (herself a counsellor) told me my problem was that I was 'too naive and trusting'. Perhaps I am, but going to therapy is a leap of hope and trust. If the client did not have any trust in the therapist, she would not be there in the first place. I had no reason not to trust my analyst; I don't believe he is an inherently untrustworthy or uncaring person.

Many clients, perhaps, trust their therapist unthinkingly. But what choice do we have if he remains a stranger? In *The Case Against Psychotherapy Registration*, Richard Mowbray argues that accreditation and 'official recognition' can lull potential clients into a false sense of security and suspension of judgement: 'It encourages them to defer to the authority of the practitioner and the institutions...that give him credibility – to "leave their brain at the door"– in a way that fosters dependency and a letting down of appropriate self-protective guards' (Mowbray, 1995:130).

Because clients and therapists differ so much, various series of criteria have been suggested by which a therapist might decide whether or not a client is suitable. But many of these factors must be tricky to assess since they will apply to us all to a greater or lesser extent. For example, what exactly does the ability 'to give a self aware history' or to 'recall memories with their appropriate effect' (Coltart, 1993) mean? How many therapists would satisfactorily meet such criteria? If we were all ideal clients, then would we be candidates for therapy? Is the fact that practitioners think in these terms indicative, in part, of the paucity of what is on offer?

The term 'psychotherapy' covers a variety of approaches used with a huge range of clients: those seeking 'self-actualisation', the worried well, and those who are considered to suffer from a re-cognised psychological disorder. These distinctions are not always easy to make. Making them may not even be useful or necessary if one starts from the premise that, in any exchange aimed at increasing the well-being of a client, certain basic human values should underscore the work. The distinction could, on the other hand, be an important one in terms of the central question of the responsibility of the client – if I am mentally ill, then am I entirely responsible for my behaviour in therapy? And might the label 'ill' actually engender in a therapist greater compassion and a more accommodating attitude?

It has been said that the public needs to be better informed about therapy, but isn't such discussion part of a responsible therapy relationship? It may be that it is practitioners who need to have a more realistic perspective. Shouldn't it be the case that any encounter with a competent, well-qualified professional practitioner – someone who is sensible, intelligent, compassionate and understanding – will, generally speaking, be more beneficial than detrimental in the vast majority of cases? Certainly this was the basis on which I went into therapy – naive though it may have been.

Even if a kind of initial 'compatibility' procedure for prospective analysands and practitioners could be evolved, it would still be subject to the same kinds of misunderstandings and misconceptions which arise in any dealings between human beings. It would be severely limited by the fact that the client is not clear about what she really needs, that even a professional practitioner cannot be clear about what another person needs either, and that this causes problems. The circle repeats itself.

It may sometimes be the therapist who decides that he does not wish to work with a particular client or that, in his view, further therapy with him would not serve any useful purpose. In such cases, the client needs and deserves some sort of explanation. His declining to provide one can leave the client 'feeling that the psy-chotherapist has identified in [her] some flaw which renders [her] hopeless and incurable. The cruelty of this act is not even seen, much less condemned, by psychotherapists' (Dorothy Rowe, in Masson, 1992:15). If a professional practitioner tells a client that he does not think he can help her, it will almost certainly induce alarm, unless there is proper discussion and reasons given.

To say simply that some analysts and analysands cannot work together is quite likely to leave the analysand feeling that she has been found wanting in some way. The therapist is a professional person who has, after all, been trained to work with people who are having difficulties, and who is therefore equipped to deal with a wide range of human peculiarity. In any case, it is not, in itself, an adequate explanation when problems arise and is an avoidance of looking at what has actually taken place. It in no way addresses the fundamental issue of the harm therapy can cause, and the varying degrees of unhappiness that might trail in its wake. Practitioners often point out that analysis frequently involves considerable anguish, but at what point does the 'cure' become, overall, worse than the illness?

It has been said of psychoanalysis that 'sometimes it works, sometimes it doesn't'. But, when things do not go well, it is unrealistic and irresponsible to suggest that no change has taken place. If the client decides to leave after a few sessions, and remains largely unaffected by the experience, that is one thing. But there is a difference between an absence of progress and actual damage being done.

The therapist must take responsibility for his part in the process. This has to be set against his need and right to earn a living in a way which does not make unrealistic demands on him. Again, there has to be a balance. How well does the present system of psychotherapeutic practice achieve this balance and meet the needs of both practitioners and their clients?

Why is it that, when challenged, some psychotherapists seem so easily to lose sight of the target – the welfare of the client? In his laudable desire to be non-authoritarian, a therapist should not abdicate responsibility for the services he sells. If the contract statement on page 145 is valid, then how might this apply to the practitioner? Why doesn't the 'consultant' sign a similar declaration?

When things go wrong and people are badly hurt, we have an obligation as human beings to try to understand why. If we are cowardly and duck the issue, then nothing is learnt. Choosing a profession in which an important part of your role is to listen does not mean that you relinquish a responsibility to speak. From the client's point of view, there are no real safeguards. We are dependent on the intelligence and integrity of the psychotherapeutic profession and, in the end, its willingness to be accountable.

Chapter 16

Accountability

'There is hope in honest error, but none in the icy perfections of
the mere stylist.'

(Charles Rennie Macintosh)

When a person chooses to become a counsellor/analyst/therapist,
he puts himself in a particular position of power, and that carries
with it a particular obligation to be accountable. The psychotherapist Paul Wachtel says: 'The task we take on is in some ways a
terrifying one' (Wachtel in Dryden, 1997:151). It can be terrifying
for both practitioner and client, so it is important for the client to
know that the question of accountability is one that the profession
takes seriously. Sometimes therapy becomes part of the problem
instead of offering some solutions.

Accountability involves being responsible and honest, but if the
way in which therapy is structured works against this happening,
then unaccountability is built into and reinforced by the very
nature of the practice. James Hillman, in *The Myth of Analysis*,
talks about how 'we have become victims of therapy and its good
intentions – and the analyst can get off scot-free by ... ascribing the
destruction of the involvement to the magic word "transference"'
(1992:37). Some psychotherapists might argue that a client's
breakdown is somehow an acceptable – even desirable – part of
therapy.

The concept of transference absolves the therapist neatly from
all responsibility. He can avoid engaging meaningfully in a challenge to his behaviour by remaining silent or simply by implying that the client's difficulties are entirely of her own making.
Incompetence is invisible because there is only one spotlight, and
it is always on the client. When things go wrong, this may be

taken as a demonstration that the client needed therapy, rather than an indication that therapy can be harmful.

Unaccountability can flourish in the profession of psychotherapy because the work takes place unobserved, in private, behind a closed door, and usually without any proper record being kept. Unless the client regularly discusses what takes place there with somebody else, she has no 'objective' feedback about it: 'therapy is not subject to the natural regulation of the scepticism, and even incredulity, of outsiders... This gives the therapist great power and consequently exposes [him] to great temptation' (Aveline, 1996:377). In theory, clients should be protected from malpractice and incompetence by professional training, accreditation procedures, practitioners' ethical codes and by the process of supervision. In practice, the client in therapy is not protected and puts herself in a potentially risky position.

At the time of writing, supervision is not always mandatory in the UK and, in any case, it can never be entirely objective. A therapist will tell the supervisor what he wants him to know and will, inevitably, describe his perceptions in terms of his own experience. Therapists are likely to choose a supervisor who follows the same model as they do, and who will therefore reinforce their particular beliefs and way of working. Crucially, the supervisor never actually meets the client and never witnesses the relevant sessions.

One way of supervising might be for the supervisor to become a client, so that he can experience what being in therapy with a particular practitioner feels like. The problem with that, of course, is that his experience would be different from mine. And the therapist might start to suggest to the supervisor that what the supervisor thinks the therapist needs to work on is, in fact, what the supervisor (his client) needs to look at.

However imperfect the system, at least, when things are going badly, a therapist can turn to his supervisor for support and guidance as well as, perhaps, to his own therapist. He will also have other clients, some of whom will probably tell him how much he has helped them, so he will not feel that he has failed in all aspects of his work. A client, on the other hand, is unlikely to have had numerous experiences of therapy. For her this is a singular event, and one in which she invests her whole self. When a client has been traumatised by therapy, where does she go?

A response which springs to mind is 'a psychotherapist'. Some may avoid this, partly because of the time, emotion and energy – and money – that therapy consumes, and partly because there is no guarantee that things will turn out differently. In reality, practitioners vary a great deal, and things do turn out differently, so much so that it is surprising – and confusing for clients – that they all give what they do the same label of 'psychotherapy'.

Even in a successful new therapy, however, most therapists will be reluctant to be drawn into a discussion about the behaviour of another practitioner. Indeed, they are likely to be under an ethical obligation not to discuss the work of another therapist, and 'an analyst should not speak ill, professionally or personally, of a colleague or group of colleagues to an analysand' (taken from the ethical code of a registered psychotherapy organisation). It is therefore difficult for a client who has had a traumatic experience with a therapist to discuss this fully with another therapist. Those who have the professional expertise to understand and help to alleviate such trauma are, in theory at least, prevented from offering helpful insights because, in this case, it would be unethical to do so.

With persistence and the right therapist, further therapy can, nevertheless, be helpful. But, inevitably, the relationship will be different, and different emotions and attitudes will come into play. In my experience, it will never entirely undo the damage done by a previous therapy, or necessarily lead to a complete understanding of its cause. Why is it that psychotherapy can induce such extreme emotions and bizarre states of mind in people who had, until then, behaved relatively normally?

Even if further therapy can help to resolve some of the client's problems, this still does not address the question of accountability. It is unlikely that psychotherapy has fewer unsatisfactory practitioners or gets things wrong less often than any other profession. Given the delicacy and complexity of the work, it is probable that more mistakes will be made here than in most other fields. 'There are big risks involved when you work with systems' (Mackay, in Dryden, 1997:124).

Yet we hear relatively little about the aftermath of unsuccessful cases. The inherent confidentiality, coupled with the worry that 'if you're going to a therapist, you've really got a problem', discourages discussion and openness, so aggrieved analysands do not, generally speaking, form support groups, wave banners or write to their MP. They do not share their experiences, so opportunities to break the circle of self-blame do not abound.

It has been said that 'therapy and the therapy relationship itself can be examined for its own trustworthiness both literally and in the fantasy of the individual. Here, issues of inequality and power are part of the discussion rather than side-stepped, glossed over or patronisingly assumed' (Orbach, 1998b). But are they? In reality, difficult issues are not always part of the discussion. If the therapist chooses not to talk about them, there is nothing the client can do.

Psychotherapy, of course, has been institutionalised in the hope of ensuring good practice and accountability. But do those institutions protect the practitioner at the expense of the client? When therapy is challenged, who is supported and who is sacrificed? What happens to the theoretical aim of 'a caring commitment to the client' (United Kingdom Council for Psychotherapy guidelines)? Who comes first and who, in practice, pays the price? 'Paradoxically, the institutions in our society often seem to encourage the very opposite of what they are supposed to be about' (van Deurzen-Smith, 1996:173).

Ethical codes cover specific issues regarding conduct, for example, fees and confidentiality, and obvious misdemeanours such as physical or sexual abuse. But therapists hurt and damage their clients in ways which go beyond a physical assault or inappropriate sexual relationship, and which are perhaps more difficult to recover from. If such damage occurs, it needs to be acknowledged and then understood. These things cannot easily be encoded in a list of ethical requirements, but they nevertheless need to be allowed for. They can only be addressed in an atmosphere of openness, unpretentiousness, creative thinking and trust. If they aren't, then therapy ceases to be an ethical profession.

A client can seek help and question a former therapist's behaviour behind the closed door of someone else's therapy room, but this does not mean that questions of responsibility and accountability have been properly addressed. Those who wish to take their pain and their dissatisfaction further will probably have little idea of how to go about doing so and, in any case, may well get nowhere.

Some professional organisations offer a mediation procedure in an effort to help accommodate occasions when a therapy breaks down. But when I eventually decided to contact my analyst's professional body to ask for their help and their opinion, I did not get very far. I was very nervous when I made my phone call, and all the old demons about being a nuisance and not being heard danced down the telephone line. I requested a meeting with my analyst and a mediator but was told that this could not be accommodated. I could, if I wished to, write to the group's Ethics Committee.

The person I spoke to was courteous and kind, but his suggestion that expressing my feelings to them might make me 'feel better' both failed to recognise the fact that I had hoped to find some answers, and also had the effect of marginalising the possibility of his colleague's competence in my case being in question.

I did not want to make a formal complaint. I wanted my analyst – or, failing that, someone who had spoken to him about my case – to acknowledge that he was partly responsible for what had been a terrifying disintegration, because my feeling of being entirely responsible for the resulting mess was so hard to bear. I also wanted to understand better why things had gone so wrong, to know if he and his colleagues were familiar with the state I had got into. A label or two would actually have felt quite reassuring.

Having a breakdown is always a shocking experience. But, for me, having a breakdown in the context of therapy was especially disturbing. I had gone to pieces during a process which I had assumed would help me to cope better with life, not make it more difficult. Because of the seemingly anomalous context, it was doubly frightening and upsetting, and it utterly shattered my faith in my own equilibrium. It seemed to me that I had managed to crack up despite being in therapy. No one had told me that psychotherapy itself could unhinge the mind. It was this particular confusion, shame and hurt that was never addressed either by my analyst or his colleagues.

I had experienced at first hand the weird states and turbulent extremes that therapy can produce – and therefore 'know' quite a bit about it. But, at the time, I did not know what was happening to me. I had no intellectual knowledge of the stages and processes of what was, after all, called 'therapy'; and the creative potential of the experience was not immediately obvious.

It took a long long time to climb out of the black hole I had fallen into, and I am still learning about what I experienced when I was in there. It was only when I started to work with a therapist who was willing to discuss the dangers of therapy, when I read about psychodynamic techniques, and then later learnt about other clients who had had similar experiences, that a sense of sanity finally returned.

In her account of one-to-one therapy, Rosie Alexander describes how she eventually made contact with others who had had negative experiences in therapy and, only then, felt understood. She calls it 'a quantum leap forward' after the 'Alice in Wonderland type of exchanges' she had been having with practitioners. She says 'I felt a terrific sense of deliverance when I realised that I was no longer alone, no longer a unique being from another universe' (Alexander, 1995:141).

The suggestion from my analyst's colleague that writing a letter might be the most appropriate course of action once again left me isolated and struggling through the same psychic quicksand. It continued the process of excluding the other side of the story. And, for a client who feels that her therapy has been badly handled, it is extremely hard to know, let alone state succinctly and clearly in a formal letter, what is most relevant. Putting my letter together was a dauntingly long, lonely and difficult process. It was also, as I later realised, a waste of time, as no one was prepared to go into the detail of what had happened.

The issue of mishandling or incompetence – difficult, perhaps, to define – is not, in my experience, covered by ethical codes and is therefore not one which a therapist's colleagues are prepared to discuss with a client. I received a brief reply acknowledging my confusion and distress but saying that, as there had been no breach of the group's ethical code, there was 'no case to answer'. The questions I had raised were 'outside the remit' of the Ethics Committee. They were sorry I felt I had had an unsatisfactory experience and wished me well in my work with my new therapist.

Within whose remit my questions were I have never discovered. Yet the practitioner's personal limitations are highly relevant in therapy and, 'while critics ... have principally focused on therapists' physical and sexual abuses of power ... far more subtle and devastating abuses are provoked when therapists are not sufficiently cautious and critical of the theories or models they espouse' (Spinelli, 1995:158).

My situation, it seems, was far from unique. For example, in an article in the *Independent* (19 April 1992) about the problems of counselling and therapy, a client – 'Jennie' – describes her psychodynamic counsellor's unpleasant and destructive behaviour. Jennie ended up feeling far worse and she complained to the British Association for Counselling (BAC). She was told that her counsellor had not transgressed the BAC Code of Ethics. Jennie's psychiatrist and her health authority agreed that she had been harmed by the treatment she had received, but there was no such admission from the relevant professional body. What was felt to be the practitioner's bullying and irresponsible callousness were not recognised. Her attitude, Jennie was told, was 'just the format of the counselling'.

It seems it is not only clients who get nowhere in such situations. When the therapist Angie Perrett tried to help a client who complained about unethical sexual conduct, she felt that practitioners 'protect themselves from discussing the issues and acting responsibly'. As a result of her wish to seek justice, the client 'felt re-abused by the whole experience'. Ms Perrett's behaviour was then called into question: 'a diversionary tactic where claims about breaking confidentiality and bringing the professional body into disrepute are threatened' (Perrett, 1993).

We pay therapists to help us to understand why problems arise in our relationships. But when problems arise between a client and a practitioner, silence descends on those who are, in theory, best placed to help throw some light on the matter. Many therapists maintain that it is impossible to evaluate competence in something as complex and intimate as a psychotherapy relationship. Yet therapists evaluate the effect of other relationships unstintingly. And any professional practitioner must at least try to look at where his predecessor went wrong if he is to help to deal with the resulting problems.

It would surely be beneficial all round if relevant insights and feelings were shared. I was told, however, that representatives of my analyst's association 'cannot comment on the work of a colleague'. Who, then, will? The practitioner is spoken to in confidence by a colleague – another closed loop. Once again, the person who most needs to know – the client – is excluded from the discussion.

However sincere a therapist, he will inevitably see what happened from his point of view, and he will naturally be concerned to keep his good name and credentials within the psychotherapeutic community. His colleagues, similarly trained, are likely to share his perspective. Professional – and personal – pride, and identification with one's fellow practitioners will frequently play a part. Here, as well as in individual therapy, do the therapists' 'own internal security measures operate to maintain blind spots and protect self-esteem from sobering realisations' (Aveline, 1996:386)?

To the client, the pledge in the Ethical Guidelines of the United Kingdom Council for Psychotherapy that 'all psychotherapists are expected to approach their work with the aim of alleviating suffering and promoting the well-being of their clients' can seem empty and hypocritical. Who is there to call them to account when this pledge is broken? The practitioner who is emotionally or psychologically abusive, or who simply gets things horribly wrong, is safe in terms of the outside world. The evidence against him is intangible because it lies inside another person.

A balance needs to be struck between the proper right of clients to have their concerns dealt with effectively and sensitively, and the need for the time and effort of practitioners and their colleagues not to be spent inefficiently. However,

> psychotherapists ... have shown a marked resistance to taking critical feedback from users seriously. Psychotherapists in particular have a tendency to discredit negative consumer feedback as being tainted by psychopathology or the distorting impact of transference. (Pilgrim, 1996:15)

If the client's perception has been 'distorted' by the impact of transference aroused during therapy, then isn't the fact that her judgement has been impaired rather than improved, in itself, an indictment of the process she has been offered? Isn't the whole point of therapy to reduce rather than increase an inability to be objective? Perhaps positive feedback is sometimes distorted. And, if therapists are not prepared to listen to the 'users' of therapy because what we say is 'tainted', what does that tell us about their faith in their clients' validity?

How many clients who have questioned their therapist's efficacy have gone unheard? The client is the only one who can give substance to that question, but how can she do so convincingly without dialogue and without help? When things go wrong in therapy, and no one is prepared to talk about why, the general public is right to question the integrity of the profession.

The practitioner may feel that it is simply not appropriate to discuss his truth with me since I am the patient and he is the professional. He remains loyal to the rules of his system of working. But doesn't that violate the ground rules about how human beings should treat each other? If one has been through a period of intense confusion and transformation, it matters to be able to discuss the meaning of it all with the person most directly involved, and the therapist's feelings and behaviour are likely to be highly relevant. An expression of regret would mean a great deal. But if the client's devotion to truth is greater than that of her therapist, then psychotherapy becomes a brick wall.

In an article in the journal *The Psychotherapist,* Robert Young (1997:6) points out how 'healing splits requires the taking back of projections and working through them'. This applies to therapists' projections also, and it needs to be taken fully on board by practitioners. Fiona Gardner (1997:8) describes how the therapist may 'fail to hear what is really being said ... act out instead of interpreting. If we feel insecure we may act defensively and in justifying ourselves overly reassure or speak sadistically.'

For a client who has had a seriously undermining relationship with a practitioner, it would be immensely reassuring to hear that, when the therapist feels insecure, he may find himself 'in a sadistic interaction with a client, in an attempt at mastery of [his] own discomfort' (Gardner, ibid.) – because such an explanation makes sense. It would be comforting and enlightening to be told by the therapist concerned that 'all this may happen without our conscious awareness, and we may not sense our patient's consequent distress' (Gardner, ibid.). Such things provide an explanation for otherwise baffling or hurtful behaviour, an explanation which does not leave the client feeling she is at fault. But how often do therapists tell their clients these things? Instead, it seems, they tell each other.

It is salutary to read these reflections in therapists' professional discussion and to see that they are at least acknowledged, but it is both tragic and absurd that they are so rarely shared with clients. If therapists leave out a vital part of the therapy equation, then the picture which they paint for the client is a false one.

Some therapists have a tendency to conduct themselves as if they belong to a secret society, a society which does not need to follow the usual norms regarding efficiency and cordiality in its dealings with the public. Was George Bernard Shaw right in suggesting that 'all professions are conspiracies against the laity'?

When responsibility for misinterpretations, muddle and despair is not acknowledged, the client can be left feeling alienated and further disempowered. When the therapist remains silent, it is an act of immense cruelty which can chip away at her sense of self, and her perception of her own sanity. Does psychoanalysis do to the client what the parent unwittingly does to the child? Does it bestow upon her its own limitations and difficulties, and ask her to accept them only as her own?

A short while ago, at a conference on psychotherapy, I got into a conversation at lunch one day about accountability in the psychotherapeutic profession. The therapist I was talking to – well-known and well-respected – told me about a client who had sued him because he had wrongly interpreted her case and then written about it in a publication. I was interested to know how the therapist feels in this situation – that is, when he gets things wrong. He acknowledged that his client had been right but, nevertheless, said she was 'completely loopy' and cited as evidence the fact that she had written a six-page letter. When I asked him whether it mattered to him, he laughed and said 'It certainly did matter. It cost me a thousand pounds!'

When I wrote to the relevant umbrella organisation to express my unhappiness about what had happened in my case, they did listen to the feedback I gave them. They wrote back to say that they had taken my comments seriously and would be reviewing their procedures in cases such as mine. To my surprise, the letter also said that a meeting would be arranged between me, my analyst and a mediator. Over six months later, however, I was informed that such a meeting was not possible, but was offered instead a meeting with the members of my analyst's Ethics Committee.

I was told the meeting should not be seen as a 'reopening of the complaint against' my analyst, so there seemed little point in asking the questions which I wanted to ask about what had happened. The mediator began by suggesting that the meeting should last for fifty minutes because it would be difficult for them to listen for much more than that – which made it feel rather like a therapy session, though they did agree to my request for more time.

I was told that my analyst could not meet with me for insurance reasons, because I had made a complaint. (I had not used the word 'complaint'.) The anomalies in what I had been told were never clarified, and I felt baffled as well as hurt. I had made it clear that I had no wish to take him to court and the last thing I wanted was money. In any case, I had been told repeatedly there were 'no grounds for complaint'.

My analyst's colleagues said they acknowledged my pain and that they had learnt from our exchange. But what I wanted them, and my analyst, to do was to acknowledge the part played by both people involved, and to offer some insights into why things had become so unmanageable. This they could not, or would not, do. No one mentioned the responsibility of the therapist. No one said 'strange things can happen in the presence of another. Sometimes, despite our best intentions, different ethics and morals come into play' (Gardner, 1997:8). I had to turn to the professional journals to find such 'official' acknowledgement. Again, these insights are directed towards other therapists instead of to the person who is at the receiving end – the client.

In a profession based on honesty and truth, it all seems rather hypocritical. And how impartial, how neutral, can practitioners be when they are looking at the behaviour of someone who is a colleague, or even a personal friend? How likely are they to put the client first? I wondered how the report of my meeting with my analyst's colleagues would have read had it not been written by one of his fellow analysts. For example, it referred to my 'very very deep and extreme feelings of anger', something which I had neither felt nor described at the time.

In my case, it was the fact that things were never openly discussed, and that, apparently, I was not believed which I found so disturbing. What hurt me most was that my analyst never expressed any regret. And there is a world of difference between the statement in a letter from his professional group, 'We are sorry *you felt* you had an unsatisfactory experience' (my italics), and the simple and straightforward acknowledgement, 'We are sorry you had an unsatisfactory experience'.

In a recent book on complaints and grievances in psychotherapy, the author says that 'there is rarely room for mediation in a complaints matter'. She argues that, if an apology is offered, 'the complainant may begin to makes a series of demands of the practitioner which are unacceptable to him or her or the insurers, and perhaps also unacceptable to the organization concerned' (Palmer-Barnes, 1998:94). 'The complainant' may, but this is not really the point, and it is a shame that the client is not given the benefit of the doubt. Even if the client does make unreasonable demands, no one is obliged to go along with them. It does not alter the fact that an apology should be given in any case, simply because apologising is the courteous, responsible and decent thing to do. The client, unlike the professionals, has no choice if the procedures of the organisation concerned seem 'unacceptable'.

Despite an acknowledgement in the book of how painful complaints and investigations can be, practitioners are nevertheless advised that 'letters should have a formal tone and language... [and] be as brief as possible' (Palmer-Barnes, 1998:173). I remember the painful irony of the sentence 'the matter is closed' in letters I received. For the client, the matter may not be 'closed' emotionally and psychologically so this, along with, for example, 'we believe no further discussion will be helpful', can seem a particularly insensitive choice of language. For therapists, this tone is apparently seen as fitting. From the client's point of view, it can make the blood run cold.

I wonder occasionally what the writers of these neat phrases actually feel when they write them, and I wonder about that fabulous line at the end of *King Lear* when Edgar says: 'The weight of this sad time we must obey; speak what we feel, not what we ought to say.'

In a letter to me after our meeting, the comment was made: 'It is sad that you experienced the situation as distressing.' I agree. It was sad, very sad – for me, for my analyst and, of particular importance, for my husband and children, who had had to live for a while with someone who was dangling on the edges of the moon. But, in the context of a professional service for which one pays, 'sad' seems a curious choice of adjective. And the phrase 'you experienced' could suggest that anyone else would have found such a situation unproblematic.

It is more than simply sad when things go wrong. So why do clients accept this kind of thing when therapy has been detrimental? And who decides what is and isn't harmful? A major problem, of course, is simply the unfathomability of the human mind and, therefore, of what therapy is about. But is the client's reluctance to speak out also because we feel ashamed of ourselves for having sought the therapist's services in the first place? And, in any case, if there is something wrong with me, what should I expect?

The role of shame, for many clients, may be poorly understood by professional practitioners in this respect. The view, as one client put it, 'that it is only weak, stupid and pathetic sorts of people who seek therapy' is not uncommon. The client will be aware of this view and may even hold it herself to a certain extent. This presents an additional hurdle for her to get over when she begins therapy, as well as during it and, most pertinently, if she ends up feeling worse. Some clients feel that it would be a shock to those who know them to discover that they were doing therapy, and they therefore have no one with whom they can talk about the distress which it has led to. If they feel ashamed, they are less likely to seek support and advice from others. And, when we have invested so much of ourselves, and put so much trust in someone, it can be hard to admit that we might have been wrong to do so.

The client may well have mixed feelings about the practitioner, a difficult combination of attachment and anger, and those feelings may prevent her from thinking clearly about her rights. A client told me that she was frightened of complaining about someone who knew all her darkest secrets: 'I was worried about my analyst finding out that I had complained, because I had told him so many personal and embarrassing things.' It is rather like the abused child who feels ashamed because of another's behaviour, behaviour which is never openly addressed and discussed. Does the client, in effect, 'hold' the 'blame' which rightly belongs to the professional?

In terms of accountability, psychotherapists should be treated like, and behave no differently from, anyone else who offers a professional service, even though things are often intangible and uncertain. For example, in teaching – another uneven and complex profession – there are clearly delineated, stepped procedures for dealing with dissatisfaction and complaints, and an important distinction is made between conduct and capability.

In contrast, therapists maintain – at least, when they are talking to a client – that they cannot judge the competence of another

practitioner. I was told by a trainer of therapists that ethics com-
mittees do not exist to make that sort of judgement and that 'it
would be a tyranny' if they did. So to whom should clients turn?
And on what basis does this particular trainer make judgements
about his trainees?

If professional practitioners have no means of evaluating competence, what then is the definition of a 'professional'? And how
can psychotherapists evolve appropriate training, supervision
and accreditation procedures? In these situations, the quality of
the therapy offered is closely assessed. So why is it not possible to
use similar criteria to address cases of poor practice in practising
professionals?

In private, practitioners do acknowledge lapses in competence.
But, in my experience, this will not be shared with the client, who
may then be left with the impression that the therapist was not, in
the eyes of the professionals, at fault. At the meeting with my
analyst's colleagues, the 'impartial' mediator – another analyst, and
chair of another relevant committee – told me that my analyst
was 'very well respected in the profession and did co-supervision'.
I already knew he was 'very well respected'; that was why I had
gone to him. Hearing this did not help, it simply made me feel
worse.

Some argue that, 'in an area that should be concerned with the
individuality of the client above all . . . standardization of practice
is akin to throwing the baby out with the bath-water' (Mowbray,
1995:150). From the point of view of the consumer's safety, however, accreditation and registration procedures are not without
value. Therapists need to be aware that their qualifications may
skew the client's perspective, but this does not in itself negate the
worth of a good professional training. What the client wants,
above all, is not standardisation but accountability. If therapists
were truly accountable, then that in itself would surely help to
ensure good standards of practice.

When therapy has been the opposite of therapeutic, the client
needs and deserves both an apology, and informed and balanced
feedback. Neither was, in my case, forthcoming. The apology
belongs in the realm of good manners and good citizenship, the
explanation more in the realm of psychology. Therapists need
to apply their expertise more assiduously to the negative consequences of their own actions, and to consider their procedures

also in terms of justice, fairness, and efficient and responsible communication.

Palmer-Barnes (1998) describes the impasse which, in her experience, usually ensues once a complaint has been formalised, so that mediation at this stage is rarely successful. But clients need to know in the first place that mediation is an option, and to be given all the relevant information about possible ways forward. Otherwise, how are they to know how best to proceed? This kind of information is not, in my experience, made easily available to consumers of therapy. My requests for such information, and for clarification of what I had been told, were ignored, and a letter to the Governing Board was not answered.

If the practitioner is unable to talk about what went wrong, then this could be done by a genuinely independent mediator who has spoken to the practitioner concerned and who *is* prepared to comment on what has happened in discussion with the client. The value of linking cause and consequence is usually emphasised by therapists – so why should psychotherapists and counsellors be exempt from this process? Freud said that the best way to shorten an analysis was to get it right. This might also apply to the way that problems and grievances are handled.

It is sad that we seem to live in an age where the question of practitioners' accountability has been emphasised to a point where it is actually reduced – to the crude level of standardised, oversimplistic codes and insurance policies. Are therapists frightened of saying to their clients, 'I got it wrong. I'm sorry. I'm willing to talk about why' – which is all that many of us want? If they are, this leaves us all in a straitjacket and blocks the way to understanding.

If, when therapy goes wrong, the practitioner fears he might be sued by his client, then what hope is there for the truth? The client has to trust, and so does the therapist. Otherwise, we are all prevented from engaging in a process that would help to repair the damage and make everyone feel better. In therapy, 'the survival of the therapist, and the understanding of what is being encountered . . . are both central to the patient's ultimate recovery' (Casement, 1994:133). If accountability is reduced to the villains-and-victims mentality of the insurance broker, then therapy will not move forward. Legislation and formal contracts can undermine the very principles one is trying to safeguard – those of willing partnership and, ultimately, understanding and agreement.

In the end, true accountability is a private matter. It belongs in shared discussion between therapist and client about mutual misconceptions and about the nature of what has actually taken place. It is only through such discussion that things can change, so that mistakes are used to advance understanding and, in some measure, heal both the wounds they have caused and the deeper wounds they have opened. Wounding also happens in layers.

The emotional impact and intense loneliness of an 'unresolved' relationship with a therapist should never be underestimated. Neither should the length and depth of its reverberations, or the sense of profound inadequacy which it can invoke. There is a sense of shock, rejection, betrayal. One is left with the worry that perhaps one has been too naive, an idealist, and in some way stupid for not having realised that therapy is a risky business. There is also the indefinable feeling of being stranded in some halfway house between reality and a dream.

If the client is involved in a process of identifying – and, where appropriate, apologising for – what has been hurtful and destructive, it can provide the basis for invaluable lessons in letting go of guilt and blame and for pulling something worthwhile out of the mess. This, after all, is what therapy is supposed to be about. The client would automatically be an equal and her contribution genuinely valued and utilised. Such opportunities, at the right moment, would create not only a greater sense of sanity but also a space in which forgiveness can do its work.

If such openings are not available, error is hidden and pathologised, instead of being used fruitfully. Psychotherapy does not 'own its shadow'. Progress is not made. And we miss the point of what it means to grow, because we omit one of the most centrally healing experiences which two human beings can have – to bring something positive out of the ashes.

Yet, if therapy wishes to be seen as a profession, and if it is to deserve that title, then no one can afford to ignore the dilemma that 'If analysts are expected to learn from their mistakes, this must necessarily be at the patient's expense, which leaves us with an ethical problem' (Alexander, 1995, translated from Maud Mannoni).

Chapter 17

The healing art?

If we psychoanalyse psychotherapy, what do we find? Perhaps some psychotherapists need to take themselves a little less seriously and their profession a little more seriously. Perhaps some schools of therapy need to grow up. Isn't the principal problem with much counselling and therapy that it simply isn't good enough to do the job properly? And is an analytic approach, in the hands of many practitioners, too often based on false reasoning, unsound thinking, and a lack of humanity – offering a barren framework in which to explore who we are?

When therapy distorts the ordinary, we risk losing sight of compassion, clarity and logic, and instead perpetuate a feeling of illegitimacy. In distorting passion and imagination, we risk missing glimpses of the extraordinary. If therapy sexualises the sensual and pathologises desire and creativity, it is poor soil in which to grow. It limits and unearths us rather than replanting us with deeper, wider roots. The soul cannot thrive if it is imprisoned or overlooked.

The discussion has to include universal aspects of themes such as love, courage, responsibility, power, will, intimacy, change, choice and freedom so that it deals with what it means to be human and puts pathology on the sidelines. Because therapy is a learning process, the roles of anxiety, expectation, aspiration and attitude need to be seen from a broad perspective. The physical experiencing of our emotion – linking our feelings and our bodily sensations – is often also part of an increased awareness.

Being knowledgeable about psychoanalytic theory is not the same as having a deep appreciation, and an acceptance, of the poignancy of the human condition. Can psychodynamic therapy lean unevenly towards the negative rather than the positive, and thereby leave out an essential balance and become undermining? If therapy is to be therapeutic, it should be true to its dictionary definition of 'pertaining to the healing art'. Therapy, like life, is a paradox and the art lies in containing the paradox.

It is said that the aim of therapy is not to make us happy. Nevertheless, its purpose is surely to bring about some sort of worthwhile change. But, if concepts of psychological disturbance form the basis of an exchange between two people, how will that affect what emerges? How psychologically healthy are those who deal in psychic health and how much do they infect rather than help others in the course of their dealings? What constitutes an authentic and healing response to suffering? Isn't there a horrible coldness sometimes in the dubiously named 'therapeutic hour'?

Perhaps therapists, like their clients, need to pay attention to the ways in which they repeat old, negative patterns – and to be more discriminating in their use of what their predecessors have done, of what is best left in the past. Goethe said: 'All the thinking in the world will not bring us to thought. We must be right by nature. Then thoughts jump up like the children of God and say "Here I am".' Moments of truly therapeutic encounter are those that feel 'right by nature'. They are a far cry from the moments of madness that psychoanalysis can promote.

Few would dispute that our unconscious conflicts might cause us to behave destructively, or that seeking insight into those conflicts is work worth doing. But we are often unconscious also of our finer nature, of the simplicity of an attachment to truth, a desire to connect, a striving for happiness and fulfilment. Some therapists maintain that 'we can each tolerate only a certain degree of self-knowledge' (Smith, 1996:34); 'humankind cannot bear very much reality' (Brearley, 1996). How can such a negative view of human nature be purposeful and empowering?

Another psychotherapist expresses surprise at his sudden realisation, during a weekend workshop, that 'healing does not apparently have to be all misery-filled' (Stein, 1999). He says that, when he arrived for the workshop, he was 'hopeful and determined to give it [his] very best shot', but felt that he was 'fighting for [his] life . . . scared stiff that [he] . . . wouldn't make it' – just as I had felt when I first started therapy.

What are we all so frightened of? Why is self-knowledge so often seen as painful, when it can be enlightening and expanding? It needs to be seen also in positive terms and, ultimately, as a gift rather than as a burden. Our unconscious, our intuition, the unknown reaches of the psyche can be enablers, rich sources of possibility and hope.

The notion of the unconscious frequently conjures visions of darkness and demons, an awesome kind of lurking psychic cancer. In psychoanalysis, the very concept of 'unconscious' can, in itself, have pernicious power. It enables one person to say just about anything about another person's psyche and to add: 'but, of course, you aren't aware of it. It's unconscious.' It's a bit like the emperor's clothes. No one dares say it isn't true because, if something is unconscious, then no one knows for sure. The client can then be left with a series of potentially intolerable unknowns hanging over her head like the sword of Damocles. It is this that is so distasteful, and not necessarily – as some therapists claim in response to criticisms – that Freud's ideas about our unconscious feelings are, in themselves, unpalatable.

If we are to respond to therapy in a way which makes us more healthy, then we need to be seen in our wholeness before we are fragmented into analysable chunks. If we are to grow, it is necessary to widen our ways of seeing ourselves and the world around us. It is better to 'search for truth with an open mind and an attitude of wonder rather than fitting the client into pre-established frameworks of interpretation' (van Deurzen-Smith, 1996:166).

Therapy may be more about what was not done in the past than about what was done. In that sense, it is a grieving. When we grieve, we need solace. When we uncover the pieces of the jigsaw that were hidden, they need our blessing. It is the blessing and the solace and the making of keys that is the work of therapy.

It is the abandonment of the notion of cure that finally 'makes the cure', because it leaves us with something which can bed down, fill out and help to nurture the future. 'The most authentic thing about us is our capacity to endure' (Ben Okri, 1998). We make progress by learning to confront our concerns with awareness, but also by renewing our faith in our viability, in our ability to survive.

Therapy can become a parody of what its proponents like to believe it is if it nudges us away from respecting the 'essential,

transcendental inaccessibility' (Russell, 1992:6) of another, if its
practitioners are deafened by theory to the soundings of the heart,
if something which is offered as a service to humanity becomes a
kind of magisterial evangelism. The quest for understanding cannot
succeed when one person believes that he can take a ride through
the maze of another's psyche, get off at any point and know more
or less where he is.

Are those in the profession of psychotherapy and counselling
perhaps too ready to believe that 'therapists who hand down their
interpretations like they were the truth, who tell patients what
to think or pronounce on what is really in their heads (or hearts),
are caricatures' (Orbach, 1998b)? How do they know what their
colleagues are like when they are in the therapy room?

My analyst certainly told me what he thought was in my heart
and my head. What do clients think about these so-called 'caricatures'? Many might disagree with Orbach's statement, finding that
therapists all too frequently pronounce on 'what is really in their
clients' heads'. From the client's point of view, there is a world of
difference between someone who allows, receives and holds and
then enlarges awareness, and someone who sits in silence waiting
to give a psychoanalytic interpretation.

The profession of psychotherapy unfortunately does include
those who believe that they know what other people really think
and feel. We all make this mistake, of course, we do it all the time,
but it becomes particularly dangerous when it is given the
benediction of the status of the expert. One writer, for example,
appears to claim that he is able to say when parents do or don't
love their children (Peck, 1978:60). He seems not only to make up
his own mind about how people he has never met felt, but to expect
his clients to agree with him. It depends, perhaps, on whether one
is considering our actions or our emotions, on how we define
love. Definitions will vary, and no one has exclusive rights over a
definitive definition.

When arrogance and insensitivity are apparent in the work of
therapists it is, because of the nature of their profession, particularly chilling. When we put our trust in someone, they inhabit
a position of privilege, and to marginalise the importance of
courtesy, tenderness and compassion can rarely be justified. The
emotional distance that training may engender can become precisely that which prevents a climate of true understanding. And

does it tempt us all to forget that, if we use our collective ignorance and confusion to move forward collectively, then everybody gains?

It could be argued that psychotherapy must be good because so many people 'buy' it. But what does this actually tell us? We all appreciate being with someone who listens, but many of us have less and less time to give to listening, so perhaps this is one reason why there is a demand for those who do so for a fee. And is it also because an increasing number of us are willing and ready to look at why relationships go wrong, and want to do something about it?

Ironically, the literature on therapy – usually written by therapists – often fails to demonstrate a consideration of the client's perspective. For example, reference is made to those who 'flee from' the therapy room because they cannot bear to look at themselves. Do such writers forget that their flight might be prompted by other considerations, that the problems of therapy might often stem from the nature of the practice, or from the psyche of those who choose psychotherapy as their profession? And wouldn't it be practical to evolve ways of working in which fewer prospective clients felt inclined to flee?

When clients express dissatisfaction, what is the reaction? For example, in response to Stuart Sutherland's story of his harrowing experiences in a psychiatric hospital, the psychotherapist Jeff Roberts suggests it is a 'hard luck story' (Dryden and Feltham, 1992:186). Remarks from professional practitioners which would seem, to most of us, nauseating, farcical or even somewhat deranged (see, for example, pp. 172 and 175 in the same volume) are described by Roberts as 'thoughtless, silly, foolish, unjustified', or he uses the somewhat euphemistic term 'wild analysis' – though he does acknowledge that they may also have been destructive and sadistic. What might strike a layperson reading this account is that the analysts described there are not simply being incompetent, they sound like very odd people.

Sutherland felt angry about the way he was treated, and maybe his anger was about more than mere incompetence. When, for example, he spoke to an analyst about his wish to feel protected by his father, what was offered to him (Dryden and Feltham, 1992:172) was a concept that must have hurt and shocked him deeply. It is this violation of innocence which is the greatest crime committed in therapy, the condemnation of the true nature of a client's feelings and intention. The clear voice of the child is scorned and repudiated by the 'expert'.

What the practitioners in Sutherland's account said – however 'wild' it may have been in this particular case – represented the way they think, a way of conceptualising which, presumably, derives from their psychoanalytic framework, since a non-analyst would be unlikely to think along such lines. One wonders how many people are subjected to similar 'explanations' but – unlike Sutherland – do not say anything to others because they fear the interpretation may be true and then feel ashamed. An interpretation that I found particularly paralysing was that I enjoyed 'making trouble', but I did not mention this when I wrote to my analyst's professional group because I was afraid they would assume it was the case, and that the credibility of everything I said would then be undermined.

Roberts says that Sutherland's account is not an indictment of psychotherapy but 'of the quality of personnel he encountered'. So what happens when an unfortunate patient is caught up in such an encounter? Sutherland is described as having been 'extremely unlucky' in meeting up with 'poor psychotherapeutic practice' (Dryden and Feltham, 1992:190). How poor does such practice have to be before its perpetuators are moved out of harm's way? And maybe the 'bad workmen' of psychotherapy might sometimes be justified for blaming the tools that they believe equip them well.

The reaction of certain professionals to critics of psychotherapy is surely proof enough of a frequent absence of real professionalism. For example, in a comment on Jeffrey Masson's arguments in *The Tyranny of Psychotherapy* (Dryden and Feltham, 1992), the psychiatrist/psychotherapist Jeremy Holmes maintains that Masson is a 'helpless and traumatised child' who lives in a 'perverse and faecal world in which everything is smeared and besmirched' (cited by Johnstone, 1998:211).

What does this tell us about Holmes's 'neutrality', about his respect for those who hold opinions different from his own, about his view of his fellow human beings, and about the way in which he responds to challenge? Is this the kind of person one would want to turn to in a crisis? It is difficult to have faith in the intelligence or integrity of those who express themselves in this way.

Why do some therapists react so angrily to those who criticise therapy? According to Fromm-Reichmann, quoted earlier, when we 'get upset or angry about an interpretation, this is usually indicative of its being correct' (1950:151, cited in France, 1988). How might this apply to therapists who react defensively to criticism? And if their anger is, in fact, perfectly justified, then might it not be the case that the same is sometimes true of clients who get angry?

Holmes refers to Masson's 'fury and bitterness', to 'the outpourings of an unbalanced man' (Dryden and Feltham, 1992:29ff.). I found *Against Therapy* most helpful during my recovery from 'therapy'. It gave me the confidence to question my therapy and, in doing so, regain some faith in myself. Masson and Rowe write with a strength of feeling which I found heartening and which, in contrast to the cold abstraction of some descriptions of therapy, seems both reasonable and humane. It is more difficult to attach such adjectives to some of Masson's critics. Is this how practitioners talk about a critical client when they are chatting to a colleague?

Clients, of course, will never know what their therapists say about them when they are talking to fellow professionals. It is interesting though, to adopt the position of observer with the therapists in view. For example, I once attended a series of talks given by a local group of counsellors. I found the atmosphere rather cheerless at times, but assumed the solemnity was in keeping with the subject matter. The audience did laugh on one occasion, however – when the speaker made a joke about one of her clients, though I was heartened to notice that not everyone seemed to find it funny.

Although the literature suggests that practitioners, almost as a matter or course, respect their clients, the comments they make in practice – and the fallibility of human nature – would suggest that, in reality, this is not always the case. To strive to open up to someone who does not genuinely want to 'receive' us can feel, in itself, demoralising – regardless of the nature of the client's specific difficulties.

If a client has not found useful what a therapist has on offer, it is not necessarily because she has not realised how useful it is. Perhaps, quite simply, the therapist is not very good at his job. Perhaps he cannot provide what counts most. Training is a waste of time if the practitioner lacks the right personal qualities, above all if he lacks real courage and sincerity. Respect and kindness matter. So does integrity. We do not need 'knowledge without character', 'science without humanity' (two of Ghandi's 'seven social sins') because they are not helpful.

'Such is the complexity of the analytic process, and the depth of our ignorance about the working of the human mind, that... opportunities for error are endless' (Smith, 1996:35). Given how damaging such errors can be, does this not suggest that an analytical approach in which the concepts of interpretation, projection and transference are central may, on balance, not be an efficient psychotherapeutic orientation? Should we not laugh a little more loudly at the absurdity of some psychoanalytic interpretations? And, if the emphasis during exchanges in therapy is always on the subtext, what does that do to the minds of those who spend their professional lives in such encounters? What does it do to the client?

Therapy should be a gentle and supportive exploration, not a corrosive excavation. Yet some therapists seem to need to drag it down to the level of an endurance test, a penance, a chamber of horrors. Do they actually believe that that is what life is about? And why do their clients sit there loathing much of it but continuing nonetheless? Is it because they both fall for the tired old line that if the client feels bad then the therapy must be working?

Psychotherapy should not lack grace. 'Analysis' has to go along with something more loving and creative. Therapy should be a celebration of the richness and dynamism of the psyche and of the ways in which we overcome and move beyond those parts of childhood which were less than happy. Children's acceptance and tolerance might be born not of a desperate need to feel loved but of love itself, of a capacity to adapt and of a sense of the world as a place where our different ways of being and doing will inevitably at times jar.

There are two sides to everything. When one's pain is not seen, when one is left to dust oneself off and start all over again, then, in some shape or form, that is what we do. When our needs are not met then, of course, it has its effect, and sometimes that effect is extensive. But we may also learn about acceptance, self-sufficiency, tenacity and inventiveness. Resilience is valuable and should not be confused with defensiveness. Isn't a capacity for overcoming difficulties something we appropriately – not inappropriately – 'transfer into the adult environment'?

It is a love of life which counts most. And it is a love of life, 'life's longing for itself' (Kahil Gibran) which carries us through the pain. It is a love of life which therapy should promote. There is something that outstrips the murkier waters of analysis and the trawled-up voices that threaten occasionally to deafen us as we struggle to make sense of them. It is that something else which each of the protagonists in this bizarre scenario needs to sense and hold.

Analysis is destructive if it underestimates what it is to be human. We go back generations, millennia. We are mysterious and magical. We are mind, body, heart and soul. We are more than a simple reductionist equation of cause and effect. If psychotherapy is to be an honourable profession, it must honour and nurture our essentialness, the part of us that endures, the unanalysable what-you-are-made-of, what Hillman calls our 'ore, rocks, that make for character' (Hillman and Ventura, 1993:30). It must salvage the sacred and honour our sacredness.

Analysis is diminishing if it becomes insipid, if it forgets that we need our pain and our anger in order to interact creatively with each other and with the world around us. If the neutrality of analysis takes us out of any kind of controversial engagement, then it does us all a great disservice. Satish Kumar once said that you 'have to fall in love with the world'. Doesn't that include keeping the raw edges a little bit raw? We need our anger and we need our pain. Our collective sensitivity must not be supplanted by technical 'expertise' expounded behind a closed door.

An awareness of our own pain can hone our souls to a better sensitivity. We need to understand our pain and remove some of its sting, but we should not endeavour to process it away. Even if it could be tipped out in a neat parcel on the therapist's floor, we may not benefit from such purging. The question is to use it well. 'The more we discover the different degrees and different aspects of our own unhappiness, the greater our capacity to sympathise instinctively' (Brian Keenan, *An Evil Cradling*, 1993).

It is instinctive rather than theoretical empathy which touches another human being. Therapy is therapeutic only when it is without pretence. It is instinct which is offended when the therapist does not speak from the heart, but only from a system of thinking. We know instinctively when another person is open to our otherness.

Our anger too has a role to play. There are times when anger clarifies rather than blurs, and rage, like love, is not always blind. Anger can move us from inaction to action when action is precisely what is called for. Let us always 'rage against the dying' of intelligent rage, and against practices which are trite and heartless. Perhaps we need our anger more than ever before, to direct it towards the systems which betray us all. The way that some practitioners treat their clients – in the name of therapy – is nothing short of outrageous. And, as one environmental campaigner remarked: 'If you're not outraged, you're not paying attention.'

> ... we live in unnatural times.
> And we must make it
> Natural again
> With our singing
> And our intelligent rage.

(From the poem *For Ken Saro-wiwa* by Ben Okri)

Chapter 18

Will you, won't you...
won't you join the dance?

The therapist, the analyst, the counsellor have become the witch doctors of the modern age, dream doctor, dream twister, heart surgeon with a scalpel of words. There is great danger in giving such power to those who may not use it wisely.

The following quotations summarise two very different approaches to the practice of psychotherapy:

> I suspect that the more Freud understood about the workings of the human personality, and the causes of particular problems, the more difficult it was for him to stop explaining to his patients what was wrong with them. This is a perennial problem for the psychodynamic counsellor. (M. Jacobs, *Psychodynamic Counselling in Action*, 1998)

> ...a good summary of my approach to therapy: sit down and forget everything you know. Be present...I can't presume to know how to help anyone...Each person is a mystery. The response to a mystery should be entirely different from that to a problem...At the very least, we can add the goal of enchantment to all kinds of therapy. (T. Moore, *The Re-Enchantment of Everyday Life*, 1997)

As a client, I would prefer to work with a therapist who is 'present', and who believes in mystery and enchantment, rather than with one who thinks in terms of 'what's wrong with' me and believes that he has the ability to explain it to me. Many clients might find the perspective of there being something wrong with them offensive. I do want to feel, however, that my therapist knows something which I do not know, and which will be of benefit to me. I would also want a therapist who is attracted to the mystery of life rather than to what David Smail has called 'the alienating dogma of "experts"' and its resulting 'process of mystification' (Smail, 1987).

Everyone knows at least something about human nature. So isn't the first task of the therapist not to explain but rather to find out what the client already knows? And isn't it more honest if practitioners use and describe what Freud, Klein and Jung postulated as no more or less than their own understanding of the views of three 'experts'.

There are some things, on the other hand, which do need to be explained. The client may benefit from an explanation of issues which are relevant in the work she is doing, but which she has no way of knowing about unless the therapist tells her. Practitioners cannot afford to be too secretive regarding either their own feelings or the dangers and contradictions of certain types of practice. In some cases, holding back can amount to deception, and 'deception is not perpetrated without a price' (Russell, 1992:152).

There were certain things in my past which, had they been repeated by the psychoanalysts in my case, would have been of great benefit to me. My parents acknowledged that, in bringing us up, they had often got things wrong and hurt us as a result. There was no pretence between us in that respect. For many clients in therapy, certain behaviour is incongruous, bewildering or hurtful at the moment it is experienced – whatever its theoretical or actual outcome might be in the long term – and it would seem that the affect of absorbing that particular punch is not always fully appreciated by practitioners.

How many clients look back on their experience and wonder if, on balance, it was worth it? My first experience of therapy led me to a place inside which was in many ways extraordinary. But it was a place that also frightened me because it became chaotic and overwhelming, and because I did not understand what was happening. Overall, it left me with a pervasive and lingering sense of fragmentation, distraction and anxiety. If those feelings were the residue of past experience, then I have yet to discover, remember or relive their roots in a way which lends support to such a view. The memory of the trauma to which the therapy led, however, remains and, in particular, the hurt it caused.

Had I not left when I did, the subsequent feeling of being both mentally dislocated and emotionally skinned alive might have been less intense, but who can say what might have happened if I had stayed? For me, it was not only having my intentions misconstrued, and the absence of an acknowledgement of what genuinely took place, which left me feeling devalued and denied. It was also the absence of an opportunity to try to turn the experience into something more positive.

It is difficult to evaluate my second period of therapy because it was initiated and coloured by the first, and the fact that my first therapist was a man and the second a woman cannot have been without effect. It did not entirely succeed in dissolving the hangover of unfinished business, but it was, I believe, a worthwhile experience. The work was fruitful because it was done with someone who, most of the time, was genuinely able to contain what I thought and felt, and who was never arrogant or defensive. It took place in a context which seemed clear and healthy, and I felt I was genuinely liked and respected. What I cherish most is that our encounter was gracious, and it inspired me to strive to be gracious, to make graciousness my goal.

I try to be more conscious in my relationships, though I have not changed as much as I had hoped I would. I also question whether therapy necessarily provides its clients with 'newer, more effective ways of coping . . . as the textbooks suggest' (France, 1988:237). I have found that being more aware of my insecurities has not always been helpful. Where lessons begin or will lead is hard to pinpoint and, as time goes by, I wonder sometimes whether it was necessarily good to lose all of the things which have changed. My sister tells me: 'You're not as much fun as you used to be before you did psychotherapy.'

As far as the past is concerned, it has been my children who have brought back into my awareness much of what it means to be a child. When the writer Laurie Lee's daughter was born, he wrote: 'I see her leading me back to my beginnings, reopening rooms I'd locked and forgotten, stirring the dust in my mind by re-asking the big questions – as any child can do.' My daughter too, fierce and fragile, has been a 'bright-eyed pathfinder' (from *The First Born*, by Laurie Lee).

In therapy, it is the client's life – not just her psyche – which is in play. Because the stakes are high, an assumption that to enter psychotherapy is to enter a process which will be beneficial needs constantly to be challenged. But to say that the practice of therapy should be abandoned altogether means that we risk renouncing something which might offer us a great deal.

Good therapy should enable, instigate, enliven, provide its clients with useful tools for careful and generous living. A context which is free of judgement, which brings instead discrimination, awareness and an understanding that is fresh and invigorating, can renew and inspire what is best in us. A context which evokes division and denies the connectedness and interdependence that characterise all human relationships can chip away at a sense of authenticity, of one's presence in the world and of the importance of other people:

> We suffer pain because we damage each other, and we shall continue to suffer pain as long as we continue to do the damage. The way to alleviate and mitigate distress is for us to take care of the world and the other people in it, not to treat them. (Smail, 1987)

When we analyse our feelings, do we also take care of them, or might we intellectualise them to a point where they are actually devalued? Can we become too conscious of our feelings, thoughts and actions, then run the risk of losing our energy and enthusiasm, and an essential spontaneity? If we are wary of a preoccupation with the treatment of dysfunction, acknowledge what we are as well as what we could become, and if we shrink the fear of challenging injustice in our lives, then we might dare to begin to believe in greater possibilities for happiness.

Because of the complexity and uncertainty involved, the profession of psychotherapy must be seen as a perilous one, necessitating a particular degree of skill, humility, vigilance and care. The only justifiable reason for becoming – and remaining – a counsellor/analyst/therapist is that one is genuinely able to do something to alleviate suffering.

It has been said that many therapists 'are scared shitless of making mistakes' (Ellis, in Dryden, 1997:12). Can we do good work with someone who is 'scared shitless'? Do practitioners need to redefine and realign what is meant by vulnerability and strength, detachment and involvement, caring and professionalism, so that they are enabled to work in a way which is more effective and which enables them to feel more comfortable? And won't we only move forward if psychotherapy's 'mistakes' are ploughed back into a shared understanding, then recycled for the benefit of therapist and client and, in the end, of those whose lives they touch?

This cannot happen when one human being puts himself in a position where he analyses another, and when another human being is prepared to let him do so. If there is any truth in Marshall Rosenberg's assertion that 'all analysis of others is a tragic expression of our own unmet needs', then should the professionals give a little more thought to the ways in which therapists', supervisors' and trainers' 'unmet needs' might colour the whole procedure?

'Ultimately, it is the essential human longing for truth that redeems' (van Deurzen-Smith, 1996:171). How can we know what is true, and what might amount to a sell-out of the self? Perhaps we get nearest to it when we listen to something that goes deeper than thought. 'One is reminded of truth by the pangs of one's conscience, which may expose one's evasion of reality. A sense of courage and possibility can be found by stopping the dialogue with the internalised voices of other people's laws and expectations' (ibid.). Do therapists and their trainers, as well as clients, need sometimes to be reminded of this?

Of course therapy is painful, but good therapy should, on balance, nourish and illuminate:

> We are all meant to shine, as children do ... And as we let our light shine, we unconsciously give other people permission to do the same. As we are liberated from our own fear, our presence automatically liberates others. (Nelson Mandela's Inaugural Address)

Therapy needs to be liberated from fear – the fear around being 'too human', so that what we learn above all is how to be humane. There are many contradictions in the ways of psychotherapy. That those who spend years training to understand better the way we think and feel are then supposed to enable the client to discover her own unique truth for herself, without the intrusion of their own ideas, is only one of them.

Good therapy is a high-wire act, a balancing trick, and the trick is to get the balance right. The therapist must juggle between the two positions of respecting his client as she is and yet working to bring about change. It is a process which needs to be approached with love, optimism, humility and humour – concepts whose power lies in their ability to make us feel connected with each other, which remind us we are two of a kind, humankind. 'The greatest therapists . . . are comedians, advocates of a comic sense of life, who break open our serious efforts to arrange life as we think best' (Moore, 1997:183). Therapy needs laughter; it must do justice to joy as well as to pain.

There will be times when there are no words. The words that are used should embrace a broad vocabulary, a vocabulary of hope, a language of the heart, terms which expand and embellish. Other people's theories furnish us with labels, types, stages of development, explanations. When the problem has a name, it can seem more manageable. Familiar categories make us feel safe. But they also tie us down.

When it is tired and dry and soulless, then perhaps what therapy also needs is a touch of poetry, because poetry speaks most eloquently of the power of love and pain. The beauty of the poet is that he not only captures the sharpness and subtlety of our experience but, in writing his poem and allowing me to read it, he shares how he feels, and what it means to be alive. Although I am, in the end, alone, I do not feel alone.

There is a line in a song by Leonard Cohen: 'Dance me through the panic till I'm gathered safely in'. We will never be 'gathered safely in', but we can ask psychotherapists – when they offer to help us get the steps right – to do so not by standing on the sidelines but by being ready to join the dance.

Appendix

In a series of clinical seminars, in which we were looking at 'failed cases', the following interchange between a therapist and patient was reported. A female patient had been in twice-a-week therapy for three months with a male student therapist. Clinical material was presented from the penultimate session before the therapist was due to go away for his Easter holiday.

Patient: 'You will have to listen to me with extra care today because I have just been to the dentist. His drill slipped and he has hurt my tongue. It is difficult to talk.'

Therapist: (relating this immediately to the impending break) 'I think you are afraid I will be careless with you; that I may not exercise enough care with you with regard to my Easter holiday, so that my words could bore holes in you and leave you feeling hurt when I have gone.'

Patient: 'No, not at all.' (Silence)

Therapist: 'I think you are using the silence as a way of leaving me before I leave you.'

Patient: 'No. In fact I was thinking of leaving therapy anyway. I think things are better. My outside relationships are better.'

Therapist: (prompted by a recent seminar on ending therapy) 'Do you feel this improvement is due to work we have done together, or do you see this as your own achievement?'

Patient: 'I see it as my own achievement.'

The therapist was able to persuade the patient to allow some time to think over this sudden decision to leave therapy. In the next session the patient told her therapist she had decided that she could not afford her therapy any more. She could spend the money she would save on a course for learning to teach English to foreigners.

(Patrick Casement, *On Learning from the Patient*, 1996)

- What strikes me most forcibly about this exchange is its strangeness. The conversation borders on the absurd. If, for example, one of the therapist's colleagues had had a similar misfortune at the dentist's and had said the same thing to him at the beginning of a meeting, would he have spoken in this way? Why, because the patient has chosen to do psychotherapy with him, does she have this bizarre response inflicted on her?

- If I were the patient here, the feelings the therapist's remarks would generate in me would be shock, surprise, bewilderment, possibly amusement; I would also be offended. The therapist seems unconcerned about his patient's physical discomfort, her tongue having been hurt by the dentist's drill. The person listening to the therapist's responses – the patient – will, like me, do so with an 'untrained' ear.

- In his discussion of this interchange, Patrick Casement refers to the way in which the therapist imposes his 'therapy language' on the patient, but he does not draw attention to the lack of warmth in the exchange. He refers to the therapist *becoming* careless. Perhaps he has been 'care-less' in more than one sense.

- There is no acknowledgement of the patient's present reality – she has come to a therapy session in physical pain and finding it difficult to speak. Little attention is paid to what she actually says, only to why she might have said it. An alternative response might have been to offer to sit nearer to her, or to fetch her a glass of water, or to ask her if she felt well enough to cope with a full session.

- The therapist immediately thinks that what is uppermost in the patient's mind is her relationship with him. Could his comments be a projection about his own fears regarding his carelessness and his clumsy attempts to communicate with his patient? He is still a student and so is likely to be feeling anxious.

- The patient's silence is not surprising given the insensitive and unusual nature of the therapist's response. The therapist seems to assume that the patient is worried about the impending break. One could speculate that, in fact, she is only too glad to be free of him during the Easter holiday.

- When the therapist asks the patient how she sees the improvement in her outside relationships, he puts forward two possible causes as 'either/or', as mutually exclusive, pushing her to opt for one or the other. They might, in fact, both be true. The client says she sees it as her own achievement, but isn't this something that therapists encourage their clients to feel? Casement feels that, when the patient refers to finishing the therapy, she 'rubs [the therapist's] nose in this' by saying her outside relationships are going better. Is she, perhaps, simply explaining why she plans to finish? One could infer that her reference to improvements in her daily life is, in fact, something which she felt the therapist would like to hear.

- The patient later tells the therapist that she plans to leave therapy and use her money instead to train to teach English as a foreign language. Casement sees this parting comment as possibly containing 'the key to her feeling of injury'. He links her telling the therapist about her plan to train as a language teacher to the failure of the therapist to speak 'her' language.
  A failure of communication is likely to have been very important to the patient. But is this why she tells her therapist about her future plans? Couldn't the two be entirely separate? Her choice of career is unlikely to be connected to her dissatisfaction with her therapist. Giving him information about her future is something she would probably do in any case when she says goodbye to him.

- At least the patient feels able to disagree with the therapist here, and to leave what seems to be a soulless relationship. The therapist, we are told, persuades the patient to think over her decision to leave therapy, but she does not change her mind. Not all clients would have her strength of mind.

- Patrick Casement cites this example as part of a 'failed case'. He also mentions that the patient might have felt hurt by the therapist. This dialogue is the subject of a clinical seminar. Did the students considering this interchange feel, like me, concerned about how this person – this real, fellow human being – felt afterwards? Or did they simply analyse what she said? Given that the therapist had handled things poorly, was the client offered any kind of support or debriefing?

If people engage in these kinds of exchanges on a regular basis, how does it affect their perception of reality? What does it say about the importance attached in therapy to another person's pain? Although this is cited as an example of poor therapy, the fact that such an exchange took place at all begs questions about the sanity – and the humanity – of the approach that it exemplifies.

'Nobility and true innocence emerge as we live out
our comic natures in the face of the greater forces of fate and destiny.
Avoiding the embarrassment of failure, ignorance, and foolishness only keeps
us ignoble, humorless, and bound in our secularism, because deep humor
arises out of genuine piety, from a bighearted acknowledgement that life cannot
be circumscribed within the perimeters of our knowledge and intentions, no
matter how enlightened and well intentioned these may be.'

(Thomas Moore, *The Re-Enchantment of Everyday Life*)

References

Alexander, F. and French, T. M. *Psychoanalytic Therapy: Principles and Application*. Ronald Press, 1946: cited in Dryden, 1997.

Alexander, R. *Folie à Deux*. Free Association Books, 1995.

Austin, J. L. *How to Do Things with Words*. Oxford University Press, 1962.

Aveline, M. 'The Training and Supervision of Individual Therapists'. In Dryden, 1996.

Bannister, D. 'The Psychotic Disguise'. In Dryden, 1997.

Blanchard, K., Oncken, W. and Burrows, H. *The One Minute Manager Meets the Monkey*. Collins, 1990. Cited in Waters, A. 'Managing Monkeys in the ELT Classroom'. *English Language Teaching Journal*, vol. 52, no. 1, 1998, p. 11.

Brearley, M. 'Psychoanalysis: Emotions Brought to Heal'. *Guardian*, 3 April 1996.

Carvalho, R. 'Psychodynamic Therapy: The Jungian Approach'. In Dryden, 1990.

Casement, A. 'Psychodynamic Therapy: The Jungian Approach'. In Dryden, 1996.

Casement, P. '*On Learning from the Patient*'. Routledge, 1985.

Claxton, G. *Noises from the Darkroom*. Aquarian/HarperCollins, 1994.

Coelho, P. *By the River Piedra I Sat Down and Wept*. Thorsons/Harper-Collins, 1996.

Coltart, N. *How to Survive as a Psychotherapist*. Sheldon Press, 1993. Cited in Feasey, D. 'Will It or Won't It Work? A Discussion on the Topic of Suitability for Analytic Psychotherapy', *Changes*, vol. 16, no. 2, June 1998, p. 92.

Cooper, C. 'Psychodynamic Therapy: The Kleinian Approach'. In Dryden, 1996.

Dalai Lama. *The Dalai Lama's Book of Wisdom*, edited by M. E. Bunson. Rider Books, 1995.

David, J. Letters to the Editor. *The Psychotherapist* (UKCP), Issue No. 9, Autumn 1997.

Dorpat, T. 'On Neutrality'. *International Journal of Psychoanalytic Psychotherapy*, vol. 6, 1979. Cited in Smith, 1996.

Dryden, W. *Individual Therapy: A Handbook*. Sage Publications, 1990.

Dryden, W. *Handbook of Individual Therapy*. Sage Publications, 1996.

Dryden, W. *Therapists' Dilemmas*. Sage Publications, 1997.

Dryden, W. and Feltham, C. *Psychotherapy and Its Discontents*. Open University Press, 1992.

Ellis, A. 'Dilemmas in Giving Warmth or Love to Clients'. In Dryden, 1997.

Estés, C. Pinkola. *Women Who Run with the Wolves*. Rider, 1992.

Farrell, B. J. *The Standing of Psycho-analysis*. Oxford University Press, 1981. Cited in Cooper, 1996.

Foster, J. G. *Enquiry into the Practice and Effects of Scientology*. House of Commons Report 52. HMSO, December 1971. Cited in Mowbray, 1995.

France, A. *Consuming Therapy*. Free Association Books, 1988.

Freud, S. Observations on Transference-Love. Standard Edition, 12, 1915. Cited in Malcolm, 1980.

Fromm-Reichmann, F. *The Principles of Intensive Psychotherapy*. University of Chicago Press, 1950. Cited in France, 1988.

Gardner, F. 'In the Presence of Another'. *The Psychotherapist*, Issue No. 9, 1997.

Goldfried, M. 'In-vivo Intervention or Transference?' In Dryden, 1997.

Grof, S. and Grof, C. *Spiritual Emergency: When Personal Transformation Becomes a Crisis*. Jeremy P. Tarcher/Putnam, 1989.

Hall, N. *The Moon and the Virgin: A Voyage Towards Self-Discovery and Healing*. The Women's Press, 1980.

Hillman, J. *The Myth of Analysis*. HarperPerennial, 1992.

Hillman, J. *The Soul's Code*. Bantham Books, 1997.

Hillman, J. and Ventura, M. *We've Had a Hundred Years of Psychotherapy and the World is Getting Worse*. HarperCollins, 1993.

Holmes, J. Response to Masson, J. *The Tyranny of Psychotherapy*. In Dryden and Feltham, 1992.

Howard, A. *Challenges to Counselling and Psychotherapy*. Macmillan, 1996.

Howarth, I. 'Psychotherapy: who benefits?' *The Psychologist*, vol. 2, no. 4, 1989. Cited in Spinelli, 1995.

Jacobs, M. *Psychodynamic Counselling in Action*. Sage Publications, 1988.

Johnson, R. *Femininity Lost and Regained*. Harper Perennial, 1991.

Johnstone, L. '"I Hear What You're Saying": How to Avoid Jargon in Therapy'. *Changes*, vol. 16, no. 3, September 1998, p. 209.

Jung, C. *Principles of Practical Psychotherapy*, 1935. Cited in Masson, 1992.

Keenan, B. *An Evil Cradling*. Vintage, 1993.

Krishnamurti, J. *Beginnings of Learning*. Penguin Books, 1978.

Lee, L. 'The Firstborn', *I Can't Stay Long*. André Deutsch, 1975.

Levine, P. A. *Waking the Tiger: Healing Trauma*. North Atlantic Books, 1997.

Lomas, P. *True and False Experience*. Allen Lane, 1973. Cited in Jacobs, 1998: 98.

Mackay, D. 'Confrontation or Collusion? The Dilemma of a Lonely, Burdened Behaviour Therapist'. In Dryden, 1997.

Mair, K. 'The Myth of Therapist Expertise'. Cited in Spinelli, 1995.

Malcolm, J. *Psychoanalysis: The Impossible Profession*. Jason Aronson, 1980.

Masson, J. *Against Therapy*. Fontana, 1992.

Menninger, K. *Theory of Psychoanalytic Technique*. Basic Books, 1958. Cited in Aveline, 1996.

Moore, T. *The Re-Enchantment of Everyday Life*. Hodder & Stoughton Ltd, 1997.

Mowbray, R. *The Case against Psychotherapy Registration*. Trans Marginal Press, 1995.

Okri, B. *A Way of Being Free*. Phoenix House, 1997.

Okri, B. From a talk at *'Ways with Words'*, Dartington, July 1998.

Orbach, S. 'Can You Trust Trust?'. Guardian, 3 January 1998a.

Orbach, S. 'Therapy is a Two-way Process'. Guardian, 7 April 1998b.

Palmer-Barnes, F. *Complaints and Grievances in Psychotherapy: A Handbook of Ethical Practice*. Routledge, 1998.

Peck, M. S. *The Road Less Travelled*. Arrow Books, 1978.

Perrett, A. 'Sex, Lies and Psychotherapists'. *TCP News*, Sheffield, August 1993.

Pilgrim, D. 'British Psychotherapy in Context'. In Dryden, 1996.

Pinar, W. Source unknown.

Rosenberg, M. Source unknown.

Rowe, D. in Masson, 1992.

Russell, R. *Report on Effective Psychotherapy*. Cited in Russell, R., 1992.

Russell, R. with R. D. Laing. *R. D. Laing and Me: Lessons in Love*. Hillgarth Press, 1992.

Searle, J. *Speech Acts: An Essay in the Philosophy of Language*. Cambridge University Press, 1969.

Schafer, R. *The Analytic Attitude*. Hogarth, 1983. Cited in Smith, 1996.

Shainberg, D. 'Teaching Therapists How to Be With Their Clients'. In Welwood, 1983.

Shlien, J. M. 'A Countertheory of Transference'. In R. Levart and J. Shlien (eds), *Client Centred Therapy and the Person Centred Approach*. Praeger, 1984. Cited in Spinelli, 1995.

Smail, D. *Taking Care: an Alternative to Therapy*. Dent, 1987. Cited in Masson, 1992.

Smith, D. 'Psychodynamic Therapy: The Freudian Approach'. In Dryden, 1990.

Smith, D. 'Psychodynamic Therapy: The Freudian Approach'. In Dryden, 1996.

Spinelli, E. Afterword. In Alexander, 1995.

Stein, D. B. 'Eight Days to Change Your Life or How the Hoffman Quadrinity Process Transformed my Life'. Irish Association for Counselling and Therapy (Eisteach), Spring 1999.

Stewart, I. 'Juggling by Numbers'. *New Scientist*, 29 May 1995.

Strupp, H. H., Fox, R. and Lessler, K. *Patients View their Psychotherapy*. Johns Hopkins University Press, 1969.

Szasz T. *The Myth of Psychotherapy*. Anchor Press, Doubleday, 1979. Cited in Russell, R., 1992.

Tate, A. From 'Ode to the Confederate Dead'. Cited in *A Dictionary of Modern Quotations*. Penguin, 1971.

Tatham, P. 'Items and Motion'. In *The Meaning of Illness*. Routledge, 1988.

Trungpa, Chogyam. *Cutting Through Spiritual Materialism*. Shambala, 1987.

van Deurzen-Smith, E. 'Existential Therapy'. In Dryden, 1996.

Wachtel, P. 'The Non-Improving Patient'. In Dryden, 1997.

Wardhaugh, R. *An Introduction to Sociolinguistics*. Basil Blackwell, 1986.

Welwood, J. *Awakening the Heart: East/West Approaches to Psychotherapy and the Healing Relationship*. Shambala, 1985.

Wildemeersch, D. 'The Principal Meaning of Dialogue for the Construction and Transformation of Reality'. In S. W. Weil and I. McGill (eds), *Making Sense of Experiential Learning*. The Society for Research into Higher Education, 1989.

Williams, M. and Burden, B. *Psychology for Language Teachers: a Social Constructivist Approach*. Cambridge University Press, 1997.

Worthington, R. 'Theory and Practice in Holistic Healing'. *Kindred Spirit*, vol. 1, no. 12, Autumn 1990, p. 29.

Young, R. 'UKCP/BCP Split An Account'. *The Psychotherapist*, Issue No. 9, 1997.

Zeal, P. 'Love, Transference or True'. (A review of *R. D. Laing and Me: Lessons in Love* by Roberta Russell.) *Resurgence*, Issue 153, July/August 1992, p. 49.

Zeal, P. 'Psyche and the World'. (A review of *The Political Psyche* by Andrew Samuels.) *Resurgence*, Issue 164, May/June 1994, p. 53.